Political Philosophy
an introduction

political philosophy
an introduction

WILLIAM T. BLACKSTONE
University of Georgia

THOMAS Y. CROWELL COMPANY
New York   *Established 1834*

Library of Congress Cataloging in Publication Data

BLACKSTONE, WILLIAM T
Political Philosophy.

Includes bibliographies.
1. Political science.   I. Title
JA66.B5   301.5'92   72-13723
ISBN 0-690-64633-X

Manufactured in the United States of America

1 2 3 4 5 6 7 8 9 10

To my wife,
Jean

Resolver
of political conflicts

Preface

Much of the work passing as political philosophy or political theory today is far too one-sided and fragmentary. Political philosophy or theory is seen as *nothing but* the analysis and clarification of key political concepts. Or else it is seen as *nothing but* an empirical, behavioral account of the political life of man. Or it is seen as *nothing but* the formulation and defense of moral and political norms and goals. Whatever the motive behind these reductionistic theories—whether it is the effort to make political theory into a value-free science, to clarify the muddy, ambiguous concepts of politics, or to pass on divine illuminations about values—they provide us with impoverished theories and approaches to man's political life.

This book presents political philosophy or theory so that this one-sided reductionism is avoided. It defends the thesis that an adequate political philosophy must include all three of these dimensions—the analysis and clarification of key political concepts; an empirical, behavioral account of political life; and the formulation and rational defense of moral and political norms and goals. It shows that all of these dimensions are present in the work of classical political theorists, however inadequate those historical theories may be.

Part 1 of the volume focuses on the problem of the definition of political theory. The reductionistic approaches of the behaviorist, the positivist and the philosophical analyst are examined. Using the issue of civil disobedience as a point of reference for portraying the conceptual, empirical, and normative dimensions of political philosophy, a conception of political philosophy is developed within which the rest of the volume is cast. This conception, although it stresses the importance of the conceptual and empirical-behavioral dimensions, maintains that these concerns are subsidiary to the normative task, which is the justification of the general aims and purposes of political society and the provision of general guidelines for the rational resolution of political conflicts.

Part 2 deals with three models of political justification—that of the natural law theorist, that of the utilitarian, and that of the historicist. St. Thomas Aquinas, Thomas Hobbes and John Locke are treated as examples of natural law theory; Jeremy Bentham and John Stuart Mill as examples of utilitarian theory; and Friedrich Hegel, Friedrich Engels, and Karl Marx as examples of historicist political theory. The basic questions of political philosophy are presented to the student through the work of these theorists and in the perspective of these three models. This objective, and the need to restrict the contents of the volume to a one-term course, required that the views of many great political theorists be excluded. But the major issues and points of view are treated. Critical assessments of the views of these eight major theorists are offered, and the advantages and disadvantages of the three models of political justification—natural law theory, utilitarianism, and historicism—are presented.

Part 3 deals with general criteria of adequacy for any political theory. These criteria are explicated and formulated via a historical overview of the adequacies and inadequacies of classical political theories and through the analysis of normative concepts or principles—freedom, equality, and the public interest—which are central to any political philosophy. These criteria of adequacy, which include clarity, testability, consistency and coherence, normative completeness, and applicability, are then applied to the political theory of democracy (and indirectly to other political theories). The analysis of key normative concepts or principles central to democracy (in its various meanings) and to other political theories permits the student to see that alternative theories of government involve different interpretations of these norms or principles, or different priorities among these values, and different estimates of empirical states-of-affairs.

It is hoped that this volume's account of the multiple dimensions of political theory will provide the student with a more adequate introduction to this complex subject matter, and that it will assist in the development of greater critical understanding and evaluation of political issues.

I wish to express my deep appreciation to Professor William Frankena of the University of Michigan who kindly read an early version of Chapters 1–4. I have benefited from his comments, as I have over the years from his work in philosophy. I am indebted to Professor Henry West of Macalester College for his critical reading of my chapters on Bentham and Mill, and to several anonymous readers in both philosophy and political science provided by the publishers. Mr. Herb Addison, with whom it is a great pleasure to work, and Mr. James Bergin of Thomas Y. Crowell provided gentle encouragement and assistance; and Mrs. Carol Cleveland and Mrs. Lucile Smith expert secretarial help. My deepest debt of gratitude is to my wife who always understands and encourages.

William T. Blackstone
Athens, Georgia

Contents

part one: defining political philosophy 1

Chapter 1: What Is Political Philosophy? 3

The Problem of Definition 3
A Sample Issue: Civil Disobedience 5
Why Have Political Philosophy? 8
Political Philosophy as Normative 9
Political Philosophy as Analytic and Conceptual 10
The Relationship of Analysis and Norms 14
The Empirical Component of Political Philosophy 16
The Three Components of Political Philosophy 18
The Behaviorist Reduction 19
The Positivistic Reduction 21
The "Ordinary Use" Reduction 23
Summation 25
The Principal Questions of Political Philosophy 26
A Classificatory Scheme 28
  Recommended Readings 29

part two: three models of political justification 31

Model One: The Theory of Natural Law 33

Introduction 33

Chapter 2: St. Thomas Aquinas (1226–1274)   37

The Purposes and Aims of Society and Government   37
The Best Form of Government   39
Eternal and Natural Law   39
The Principles of Natural Law   40
Justice and Civil Disobedience   42
Critique   43
   Recommended Readings   45

Chapter 3: Thomas Hobbes (1588–1679)   46

Hobbes's Theory of Human Nature   46
The State of Nature   47
The Social Contract   49
The Laws of Nature   50
Absolute Sovereignty   51
Civil Disobedience   51
The Rights and Duties of Men   53
Duties to God and Sovereign   54
Critique   55
   Recommended Readings   57

Chapter 4: John Locke (1632–1704)   58

The State of Nature   58
The Social Contract   60
Natural Rights   60
Government by Consent   63
Civil Disobedience   64
Limited, Representative Government   65
Critique   66
   Recommended Readings   68

Model One: Conclusion   70

   Recommended Readings   73

Model Two: The Utilitarian Theory of the State   74

Introduction   74

Chapter 5: Jeremy Bentham (1748–1832)   76

Human Nature and Hedonism   76
Utility as the Grounds of Legislation   78
Justice and Utility   79
Bentham's Critique of Natural Law and Natural Rights   81
Bentham's Critique of the Social Contract Theory
   and Consent   83
The Role of Government   83
Freedom and Democracy   85
Civil Disobedience   86
Critique   87
   Recommended Readings   90

Chapter 6: John Stuart Mill (1806–1873)   92

Mill's Brand of Utilitarianism   92
Justice as the Basic Moral and Political Objective   95
The Meaning of Justice   97
Liberty as the Fundamental Right   100
Restrictions on Liberty   102
Mill's Defense of Freedom of Thought and Discussion   105
The Best Form of Government: Representative
   Democracy   107
Is Mill Really a Democrat?   110
   Recommended Readings   111

Model Two: Conclusion   113

   Recommended Readings   115

Model Three: The Historicist Theory of the State   117

Introduction   117

Chapter 7: Friedrich Hegel (1770–1831)   119

Hegel's Metaphysics   119
The Dialectic   122
Moral and Political Institutions   125
Abstract Right, Morality and Ethical Life   125

The Family, Civil Society, and the State   *128*
Freedom   *132*
Forms of Government and Constitutions   *133*
Divisions of Power in the State   *134*
Hegel on Democracy and Constitutional Monarchy   *136*
Public Opinion and Freedom of Speech   *138*
Justice and Power (Is and Ought)   *139*
War and International Relations   *141*
Critique   *142*
  Recommended Readings   144

Chapter 8: Karl Marx and Friedrich Engels (1818–1883 and 1820–1895)   146

The Hegelian Heritage   *147*
Dialectical Materialism and Economic Determinism   *148*
Classes and Class Struggles   *152*
Alienation and Freedom   *161*
The State   *165*
The Socialist Dictatorship   *168*
Mature Communism and Social Justice   *170*
Critique   *171*
  Recommended Readings   175

Model Three: Conclusion   176

  Recommended Readings   177

part three: criteria of adequacy for a political philosophy   179

Introduction   179

Chapter 9: Criteria of Adequacy   183

Adequacy and Openness   *190*
  Recommended Readings   192

Chapter 10: Freedom   194

Political Freedom: An Overview of the Concept   194
The Meaning and Justification of Political Freedom   200
The Application of the Norm of Political Freedom:
   Conflicting Values   204
   Recommended Readings   206

Chapter 11: Equality: Rights and Justice   208

The Norm of Equality: An Overview   208
Descriptive and Normative Equality   216
Criteria of Relevance for Differential Treatment   218
The Justification of Criteria of Relevance   221
The Application of the Equality Principle   222
   Recommended Readings   226

Chapter 12: The Public Interest   227

An Overview of the Concept   227
The Public Interest: An Interpretation   230
Private and Public Interests   233
   Recommended Readings   233

Chapter 13: Democracy and Its Alternatives   235

Introduction   235
The Definition of Democracy   236
The Justification of Democracy   242
Majoritarian and Totalitarian Democracy   246
The Extension of Social Justice   248
Democracy as an Adequate Political Theory   250
   Recommended Readings   254

Index   257

part 1
defining political philosophy

chapter 1
What Is Political Philosophy?

The Problem of Definition

To know what one is dealing with in any subject-matter area requires a definition of the subject matter. But acceptable definitions are notoriously difficult to come by. This is true not just of the humanities and social sciences but of the "hard" sciences as well. How are we to distinguish, for example, zoology and ecology? Or chemistry and biochemistry? There is controversy over where to draw the lines in these areas, just as in distinguishing political theory from economic or social theory. How does one distinguish a political issue from an economic one? Could not an economic issue also be a political one? And vice versa? What makes an issue *specifically* a political one? Where does one draw the line between a political issue and an issue of private morality? Between political issues and other areas of man's social existence such as the legal, religious, scientific and aesthetic aspects? The way in which these lines are drawn has tremendous implications, both for what constitutes political philosophy or theory and for the resolution or answer to issues *within* political theory.

Take this example. If "political" or "political institution" is narrowly defined, this has very important implications for the extent of citizen participation and control in a democracy. For if the participation of a citizen in a democracy is conceived as having to do

3

with the political only, and if the political is defined to include only key or central government decisions and policies, then the area of legitimate citizen participation is quite narrow. (Indeed, with this narrow definition of "political" one may arrive at complete scepticism on the very possibility of democracy, especially in a largely urban, technological society in which a small elite in fact makes all key government decisions.) On the other hand, if "political" is defined more broadly to include social systems and institutions such as economic corporations and educational institutions, then the norm of citizen participation or political equality (as a defining characteristic of a democracy) is given broader significance, and it thereby provides legitimacy for much wider participation in and control of institutions which, though not responsible directly for key government decisions and policies, are responsible for policies which dramatically affect the quality of our social life. However, the meaning of "political" can be extended so far that it includes the PTA, the local art association, and so on. If this is done, there is the obvious danger of restricting individual liberties of various types by political control of activities which we now regard as the private matters of individuals or groups.

Plainly, then, on both a theoretical and practical level, much depends on the definition of "political." Numerous questions are avoided or "begged" by too narrow a definition. Other problems are created by too broad a definition. What *is* the proper definition? It may be that this request itself is improper; that is, perhaps it is impossible to set forth necessary and sufficient conditions for this concept, that is, to arrive at one proper definition. Some philosophers do argue that certain concepts are necessarily "open" and cannot be closed. I am not suggesting that this is true of the term "political." But I am suggesting that although there is lexicographical consensus that a political issue is one which "pertains to public policy," or "pertains to civil government and its administration," such definitions do not take us very far. A case can even be made that nearly any issue fits this definition. There is disagreement about which issues pertain to public policy, and which issues *should* be matters of civil government and administration. The disagreement is not merely factual but normative or evaluative. Whether or not a given issue, act, or group is conceived as political, then, will depend on several factors: on the context of the issue, act, or group; on the particular objectives the classifier has in mind; and ultimately on his view of the purpose(s) of a political society.

There may be good reasons for defining "political" broadly for some purposes and narrowly for others. For certain purposes one may want to distinguish, for example, legal issues from political ones. We do distinguish between the functions of the judge and those of the legislator. This distinction reflects not only our usage of these concepts but also the social objectives in distinguishing these functions. We think it is *important* that judges not be direct instruments of political parties. For other purposes, however, we may want the political to include the legal, as perhaps when we discuss the overall social goals or ideals of a society.

Thus, the context of use, the particular objective of the user of the concept, and the general purpose(s) of political society as conceived by the user determine the definition—the breadth or narrowness—of the term "political." This means that the definition of "political issue" is itself an issue in political philosophy or theory. Certainly a book in political theory should not rule out in the very beginning any of these possible views of the nature and objective(s) of political society. Therefore we will not offer a strict definition. Rather, to avoid begging important questions, we will indicate the scope of political philosophy or political theory by taking a concrete problem acknowledged to be a political one and examining the sorts of issues involved. The problem chosen is whether acts of civil disobedience are justified. Not every problem in political theory necessarily involves all of the kinds of issues which are the concern of the political theorist. This problem appears to do so.

A Sample Issue: Civil Disobedience

Suppose that you have tried to be a law-abiding person all your life. You respect the law and recognize the value of a society ruled by law. Suppose further, however, that, as you grow older, you come to realize that there are many bad, unjust laws—laws, for instance, which discriminate on irrelevant grounds. Suppose that, as a result of these laws, you find that you cannot be admitted to your state university, that certain working opportunities afforded to others of your same abilities are not afforded to you, that the voting rights supposedly guaranteed for all are denied to you, that the legal protection afforded others is denied to you, and so on. You come to feel very strongly about these laws and unjust circumstances and decide that something must be done to alter them, for others as well as yourself. So you begin to try to change these conditions by calling the injustices to the attention of others. Then you protest to the authorities. You use every means within the legal order, but little or nothing happens. The power structure in society permits the same injustices to continue. Frustration or cynicism may set in and you may simply say to yourself: "Well, this is the way the world is. I'll adapt and get along by hook or by crook." If you feel as strongly as some, however, you may decide to resist and change these injustices in society, not merely by every legal means, but also by refusing to obey the unjust laws (or even by actively violating them), by demonstrating in organized protests against these conditions in order to bring pressure to bear on an otherwise unmoved power structure or society.

The above was (and in some cases, continues to be) the state of affairs and the reaction to that state of affairs of many black citizens in the United States. Similar unjust conditions and laws have existed in many countries over the years. The Jews certainly felt that many of the laws of Hitler's Third Reich were unjust. We in this country felt that way about some of the British laws prior to 1776. Today many South Africans feel the same way about some of the laws there. In each of these cases, there was protest against the unjust laws and an effort made to change them, but these met with little success. The problem of the dissenters is this: Is civil disobedience, even open rebellion, ever justified? If so, under what conditions?

At least some dissenters have sought to answer this question rationally, in the manner of a political philosopher. They have tried to think unemotionally and disinterestedly about it. They have not let the slogans or existing prejudices of the time determine their thinking. They have tried to get the facts clear. Most importantly, they have thought about the aims and purposes of political society and the rights and duties of men. They have offered reasoned arguments for such aims and principles, rights and duties, and then utilized them as normative premises from which they have deduced their conclusions on the problem of civil disobedience.

Suppose, in the face of the conditions described, you decide on civil disobedience. What would be your reasons? Would you argue that there is a standard of justice provided by "nature" or by God which constitutes a test of the justice of human laws and that only laws which conform to this standard are really laws and merit obedience? (This is the position of Martin Luther King, Jr.) [1] If so, what is this standard? How is it known? Suppose there is a disagreement

[1] See Martin Luther King, Jr., *Letters From Birmingham City Jail* (Philadelphia: American Friends Service Committee, 1963).

over the standard. Is there an independent test or method whereby this disagreement could be resolved?

Suppose it is argued that civil disobedience is never justified, on the grounds that it destroys the fabric of society and results in worse consequences than the unjust state of affairs. Would you disagree with the empirical or factual aspect of this claim? Suppose the bad consequences could be shown. Would you argue that justice must prevail, no matter what the cost? On the other hand, it could be argued that civil disobedience is never justified in a democracy, since channels for legal and peaceful change are always open. Would you agree that such channels are always open? Again, on the empirical level, suppose that a political scientist sets forth an explanatory hypothesis on the causes and conditions of acts of civil disobedience, such as, "Acts of civil disobedience occur when social dysfunctions of a moral, legal, and economic nature come into being." Does such a hypothesis explain anything? Can it serve a predictive function?

Consider the following suppositions about the meaning of justice: justice is simply the impartial application of rules, and discrimination on grounds of race or color, for example, are just as long as the rule is applied to all. What would be your response to this purely formal account of justice? That is, is justice more than the mere formal and uniform application of a rule or law? If so, what is it? Suppose even further that it is maintained that justice is relative to culture? Or that justice is simply the reflection of the ideas of those who have political power? Or that statements in which the concept of justice is used simply express the user's feelings? How would you respond to these questions and positions on the meaning of justice? How would you support your account of the meaning of justice?

I have mentioned all of these suppositions in order to indicate both the complexity and the multiplicity of issues involved in the attempt to answer rationally a single normative political issue, like the problem of civil disobedience. In the first place, and fundamentally, *normative* issues are involved. In our example justice is invoked as a normative principle underlying one's decision. Utility or the appeal to consequences is also invoked as a norm. Even a second-order kind of norm is invoked, namely, that justice as a norm should take precedence over the norm of utility (or vice versa) when these norms conflict (as indicated by the question, "Would you argue that justice must prevail, no matter what the cost?"). The appeal to basic norms and to priorities among those norms is fundamental to the resolution of this question.

Second, *empirical* issues are involved. Questions like "Would civil disobedience in fact result in disastrous consequences and destroy the fabric of society?" and "is it the case that some injustices cannot be overcome by legal means?" require estimates of empirical states of affairs for answers. Furthermore, questions like "What are the *causes* of acts of civil disobedience?" and "Is it possible to *predict* when acts of civil disobedience (or of revolution) are likely to occur?" call for explanatory hypotheses and empirical confirmation.

Third, semantical, conceptual, and epistemological issues are involved. That is, issues arise that bear on the meaning of political concepts or statements, on whether those statements constitute knowledge, and on the grounds by which they are verified or falsified. The questions, "Does justice *mean* simply the impartial application of a rule, no matter what the rule prescribes?," "Is justice simply a reflection of the ideas of those with political power?," and "How is the standard of justice *known* or discovered?" require an analysis of the meaning, use, or function of the concept of justice and the status of knowledge claims in which "justice" is used.

These three types of issues—normative, empirical, and conceptual —are invariably involved in the key questions of political philosophy. If one's decision or response to the question of civil disobedience and its justification is carefully and completely thought out, in the manner suggested by the political philosopher, it will involve all of these types of issues.

Why Have Political Philosophy?

Political philosophy operates on the assumption that political decisions (like refusing to obey the laws) and political institutions (forms of government) stand in need of justification, that both the general principles of such institutions and the policies and actions which reflect those principles must be rationally justified. Why this demand for rational justification? We can simply reply that humans are beings who make such demands. We require reasons for decisions and actions. But perhaps more to the point is the fact that the policies and actions of political institutions condition each of us, and, to a large extent, make us what we are. They have far-reaching consequences for human happiness and misery. Often those policies and actions conflict with what we as individuals *want* to do or think we *ought* to do. Political institutions sometimes embody incompatible principles and policies, and they often conflict with the political institutions of other countries. Such conflict situations force the evaluation of political principles and institutions.

The fact that the needs and purposes of men conflict, the philosopher David Hume argued in the eighteenth century, is the *raison d'être* for moral philosophy and the concern for justice.[2] Hume asked us to imagine a world in which there is no such conflict, one in which all desires and needs can be satisfied. In such a world there would be no demand for principles of justice or their justification. In Hume's imagined world, there are no moral problems or problems of justice, because there are no conflicts between persons.

Sir Isaiah Berlin recently argued the same point in regard to political philosophy.[3] He asked: In what kind of world is political philosophy possible? He answered: "Only in a world where ends collide," one in which there is conflict over political goals and purposes. In a world without such conflict, a world in which there is one agreed-upon goal, all conflict would fall in the area of the means to that goal. Such conflicts over means can be handled by the empirical sciences. Though Berlin admits that this oversimplifies the means-ends relationship, his point is plain. There would be no need and no demand for the moral evaluation or justification of political principles if we all agreed on political ends or goals. Our political world clearly is not of this conflict-free type. Nor is our moral world the type Hume asks us to imagine. Thus there is need for both moral and political philosophy.

Political Philosophy as Normative

Political conflict situations may arise on a variety of levels, ranging from the most general normative principles (Should life, liberty, and the pursuit of happiness constitute our political goals?) to the most specific (Should federal voter registrars be put in Mississippi?). Take a middle-range issue—the policy of the selective service system in the United States. Is it *fair* that college students be given the opportunity to defer military service and possibly avoid the draft entirely? In terms of the utilization of human resources, it may be better for the country if students complete their education. But the question here is the fairness or justice of the policy. The two norms operating

[2] David Hume, *A Treatise of Human Nature*, reprinted from the original edition, in three volumes, and edited by L. A. Selby-Bigge (Oxford: Clarendon Press, 1968, first edition; reprinted 1951); see especially Book 3.

[3] Sir Isaiah Berlin, "Does Political Theory Still Exist?", in *Philosophy, Politics and Society*, Second Series, ed. Peter Laslett and W. G. Runciman (Oxford: Basil Blackwell, 1962).

here seem to be: What is fair to the individual? and What is best for the country? Are they the true basis of military draft policy? Suppose the norms conflict. Which takes precedence?

The primary task of political philosophy is to seek rational answers to questions about political ends and means such as those above. Integral to this is the formulation and defense of a set of political norms, which are themselves used as the criteria for evaluating the use and abuse of political power. In this sense political philosophy is an extension or application of moral philosophy to the problems of political order. Political philosophers have set forth alternative normative principles and systems of justification. They have argued for these principles and systems in differing ways. The student of political philosophy must examine and evaluate these various principles and systems, not just to know what important and influential philosophers have said, but to be able to take a broader and more rational approach to political problems, conflicts and goals.

Political Philosophy as Analytic and Conceptual

In the effort to formulate a set of normative political principles, and to understand and explain the political order, human beings have developed and used concepts which are logically related to one another, such as justice, equality, freedom, law, and rights. Political philosophers have closely scrutinized these moral and political concepts, offering analyses of their meaning, logical functions, and relationships. Thus Plato tells us that "justice" refers to a "universal" and John Locke, the eighteenth-century British philosopher, remarks that "obligation" is a "mixed mode" and has no archetype in nature. Aristotle states that ethics and politics deal with "variables" and are to be considered sciences only "in some sense of that term" and Jeremy Bentham, the philosopher who initiated the doctrine of utilitarianism, argues that the notion of "natural rights" is "simple nonsense." These claims are not themselves moral or political statements, but statements *about* moral and political statements. They presumably inform us about the meaning, type, or status of the claim being made and the kind of evidence or method of verification appropriate to it. They thereby provide us with accounts of the nature and limits of moral and political justification, i.e., the role and limitation of reason in these enterprises.

This sort of analysis is going on when a contemporary philosopher like Margaret MacDonald claims that the term "natural rights" is a "hybrid concept," [4] when S. I. Benn and R. S. Peters remark that man has no essence,[5] or when H. L. A. Hart points out that the equal right of all men to be free is logically presupposed by all talk about "general" or "special" rights.[6] These are all efforts to become conceptually clear about the meaning and function of certain key concepts in political philosophy.

Take the example with which we began—civil disobedience.[7] Conceptual confusion abounds in discussions of this issue, due at least in part to the lack of a clear-cut definition of the phrase and those terms related to it. If we are to ask intelligibly, "Is civil disobedience ever justified, and if so, under what conditions?", we must have a definition of civil disobedience. Some persons maintain that there is no difference between an act of civil disobedience and ordinary law-breaking. But if we look at the history of this concept by examining the views of well-known exponents of civil disobedience —Thoreau, Gandhi, and Martin Luther King, Jr.—there are criteria which distinguish the two. First, the deliberate violation of the civil disobedient is not done for merely selfish or prudential motives but for moral reasons or reasons of conscience. The violation is for the express purpose of calling public attention to the unjust or iniquitous character of certain laws through the disturbance and arrests required to enforce those laws. Second, the civil disobedient generally publicly and openly violates the laws he thinks iniquitous. The violation is not clandestine in any sense; in fact the authorities are usually notified in advance of a planned infraction of the law. Third, he generally does not attempt to avoid apprehension by legal authorities; nor does he seek to avoid the punishment meted out by the authorities for his illegal act. He does not have to accept it happily, of course. All of these criteria distinguish civil disobedience from ordinary criminal activity.

A fourth condition associated with civil disobedience is that the violation of law must be of a nonviolent nature. When a person or

---

[4] Margaret MacDonald, "Natural Rights," *Proceedings of the Aristotelian Society*, Vol. 47 (1947–48).

[5] S. I. Benn and R. S. Peters, *The Principles of Political Thought* (New York: Collier Books, 1964); originally published as *Social Principles and the Democratic State* (London: Allen & Unwin, 1959), p. 125.

[6] H. L. A. Hart, "Are There Any Natural Rights?", *The Philosophical Review*, Vol. 64 (1955).

[7] For a detailed treatment of the question of the justification of civil disobedience, see my "Civil Disobedience: Is It Justified?", *Georgia Law Review*, Vol. 3, No. 4 (1969); reprinted in *The Southern Journal of Philosophy*, Vol. 8, No. 2-3 (1970).

group of persons deliberately inflicts injuries upon others, when they intentionally damage property, when they riot and commit various types of sabotage, they are not civilly disobeying. The civil disobedient acknowledges the value of law and its claim to his obedience and he respects the rights of others. In the case of certain laws, he decides to override this claim on the basis of what he considers to be a higher moral obligation. The civil disobedient is also distinguished from those who advocate rebellion or revolution in that he advocates neither the complete overthrow of existing authority nor the violation or subsequent change of all laws. The complete collapse of a government and of the basic structure of law in a given society or in general is not his objective, and this clearly distinguishes a civil disobedient from a revolutionary or a political anarchist, who seeks the complete overthrow of all constituted authority. When violence does occur with acts of civil disobedience (and violence *has* increasingly become involved with acts which began as acts of civil disobedience) it becomes difficult (but not impossible) to distinguish those acts from simple acts of rebellion. Also, when the civil disobedient begins to violate *any* law, not just the one he considers unjust and immoral, he makes it increasingly difficult (but not impossible) for others to distinguish him from those who advocate rebellion or revolution.

If the criteria discussed above define characteristics of acts of civil disobedience, it is essential to have them in mind when asking the question, "Is civil disobedience justified?" Otherwise, one does not know what he is asking, and one's response to the question will be poorly formulated and inadequate.

Sometimes, however, certain concepts are very difficult to define, and civil disobedience may well be one of them; for some of the very concepts used above in defining civil disobedience are themselves vague and in need of clarification. We used both the notion of "conscience" or "moral reason" and that of "violence" in defining civil disobedience, but are these terms themselves clear?

Two examples will illustrate the point. Suppose a doctor performs an act of mercy killing. Suppose that his reasons for this are clearly moral reasons or reasons of conscience; furthermore, suppose that he does this publicly and openly, does not make an attempt to avoid apprehension by legal authorities, and is willing to accept the punishment meted out for his illegal act. This act conforms to three of the criteria which have been specified as criteria normally associated with civil disobedience, but the act might be considered to be an act of a violent nature. After all, a person is now dead who was alive. On the other hand, one could question whether this is a violent act; if it were designated as a nonviolent act, then it would conform to the four criteria specified above. The point is that the very concept of violence is itself opaque and needs a great deal of analysis. There are many types of violence and not all of them are physical. Therefore, it is clear that an analysis of this concept is essential in clarifying the concept of civil disobedience.

Let us look at one more case. Suppose that members of the Ku Klux Klan engage in law violation on the basis of what they consider to be moral reasons or reasons of conscience. Suppose that they do this publicly and openly. They do it nonviolently. They do not seek to avoid apprehension by legal authorities, and they are willing to accept the punishment meted out. Would this act constitute an act of civil disobedience? Quite plainly the conscience of a Ku Klux Klan member will be quite different from the conscience of those who have different moral and political convictions. If one builds into the concept of conscience or the concept of a "moral rule" some particular set of moral convictions, then it may well be that on a different set of convictions one must conclude that this act by members of the Klan was not based upon conscience. Therefore, it was not a case of civil disobedience.

However, is not this view unacceptable? For if one builds into the concept of conscience only certain moral convictions, this arbitrarily restricts the concept of civil disobedience. Furthermore, it results in the fusing and confusing of two distinct and separable questions: First, does a given act constitute a case of civil disobedience? Second, is that act morally justified? To avoid this question-begging confusion, a morally neutral explication of the concept of "conscience" or "moral reason" is needed (which is itself no small task).

It must be recognized, of course, that language is fluid and that the use and meaning of concepts change. Perhaps things are not as fluid as Heraclitus, the ancient Greek philosopher, thought—that you cannot step in the same river twice, or use the same concept twice —for if the latter were true, communication would be impossible. But changes in the use and meaning of concepts must be taken into consideration. In the case of the notion of civil disobedience, it is now used in different ways, so not all of the criteria explicated above are always seen as essential to the proper use of the term. Thus, some speak of acts of civil disobedience where the actor does not violate the law openly and publicly; others, where the actor does seek to avoid punishment by legal authorities, as in the case of draft resisters going to Canada; and so on. Clarity in thought and argument requires that such uses be recognized and distinguished, perhaps by the use of terms like "classical civil disobedience," "recent civil disobedience," "ghetto civil disobedience," and so on. If the concept becomes so fluid that we cannot distinguish an act of civil disobedience from a revolutionary act, that is, if it is used so fluidly that we cannot talk about its proper use and cannot distinguish it from related concepts like "revolutionary act," then surely our language becomes impoverished and political distinctions which we want to make are obliterated. The question "Is revolution justified and if so, under what conditions?" is surely a different question from "Is civil disobedience justified, and if so, under what conditions?" Both questions are important ones in political philosophy but they are also distinct ones.

The Relationship of Analysis and Norms

The above examples make it clear that the analytic, conceptual activity of classical or contemporary philosophers is not mere ivory-tower conversation. It bears directly on the man on the street, for it is a response to puzzles about concepts, which have a direct relationship to conduct. A conceptual grasp of a concept like civil disobedience is essential for a rational evaluation of acts of civil disobedience.

Other examples of the essential relationship between the analysis and understanding of a concept, and the rational critique of norms and behavior come readily to mind. When Plato argues in the *Euthyphro* that justice does not mean "commanded by the Gods," this analysis occurs in a context where that appeal is utilized by Euthyphro to charge his father with murder. When Bentham claims that the notion of "natural rights" is nonsense, his assertion is grounded in the fear that this appeal will "excite and keep up a spirit of resistance to all laws." When Friedrich Engels, co-author with Karl Marx of *The Communist Manifesto*, denies that the idea of equality is an eternal truth, and asserts that any demand for equality which goes beyond the proletarian demand for the abolition of classes is absurd, he does this in a context where he is concerned to extend equality to the social and economic sphere. When Thomas Hobbes, the seventeenth-century British philosopher, uses the notion of a social contract, at least part of his concern is to voice a new conception of governmental authority, government by consent, and hence a way of asserting the demand for individual liberty.

The object in all of these cases is to get a conceptual grasp of man's moral and political life. Acceptance of a given concept or set of concepts amounts to a way of looking at moral and political life, hopefully an illuminating way. Different philosophers, focusing on diverse parts of our experience or on different data, have offered varying concepts and contrasting frameworks of explanation. However adequate or inadequate these frameworks may be, they were formulated for people who live and act; therefore, this conceptual activity invariably was, and continues to be, concerned with human activity and conduct.

The relationship between a philosopher's analysis of moral and political concepts and his normative moral and political theory is more complex than first appears. It is generally assumed that such analysis is normatively neutral, in the sense that no moral or political evaluations logically follow from theories *about* moral and political discourse. For example, the Platonist holds that "justice" refers to a universal or archetype in nature. Does it follow from this that we should keep our promises? The emotivist looks upon moral and political evaluations as expressions of emotion. Does it follow from this that we should not support nuclear disarmament or that we should exploit and take advantage of others? Evaluations of this kind do not seem to be implied by such theories.

However, such philosophical accounts of moral and political discourse invariably do involve other presuppositions—metaphysical, theological, epistemological, and so on. These presuppositions are integral to the various systems of justification offered by classical political philosophers. It is precisely here, within these presuppositions, that the distinction between logical analysis and normative suggestion can get fuzzy and perhaps collapse. Take, for example, the claim that certain rights are "natural rights," that certain moral or political principles are "natural laws," and that such rights and laws are grounded in the nature of the universe or in the nature of man. What kind of claims are these? Are they descriptive claims about certain rights or laws? Are they normative claims? They seem to be descriptive, that is, claims that certain laws and rights are independent of human legislation, that they are discoverable by reason, and in fact can be read right from human nature. But when these laws and rights are stated, one finds quite different ones being offered by different political theorists. This fact has led some philosophers to look carefully at the claims of the natural law theorist. They have asked how these moral and political principles can be discovered by reason? In what sense is the term "reason" being used? What is meant by "human nature"? Does human nature have an essence? Is the concept "human nature" normative, or descriptive? Some have argued that it is in fact normative and that political theorists simply build into that concept whatever norms they want or find desirable. The norms, principles, or human activities which they consider of paramount importance they characterize as "natural." If this is true, the claim that certain rights are "natural" or "human" is certainly more than a metalinguistic or conceptual point about the language of rights. It is the promulgation and advocacy of certain norms.

One can multiply examples. What about the claims that certain rights are God-given, that (Hegel) "the state is the actuality of the ethical idea," and that (Bentham) "the terms good, right, etc. have meaning in reference to the utility principle, otherwise they have none"? Are these statements "logical analyses" or are they normative and prescriptive? Only a detailed analysis of these respective political philosophies enables one to say anything enlightening here; and even then we may be led to say that elements of both are involved and possibly even to declare that the conceptual analysis of normative concepts and the advocacy of ethical and political norms are not always clear and distinct. However, if we keep these complications in mind, the distinction between analysis and normative argument is a useful one, and we may classify them as reasonably distinct types of activities.

The Empirical Component of Political Philosophy

A third type of activity carried on by the classical political philosopher has been directly empirical. He accumulated data (however unsystematic) and set forth empirical hypotheses which were used as premises in arguing for certain political norms or institutions. Accordingly, Hobbes cites empirical data for his thesis of psychological egoism—the view that the motivation of every man is self-interest. Then he uses this thesis as a key premise in arriving at some of his political norms. Sometimes it is difficult to tell whether a given claim is set forth as empirical or not. Thus, both Rousseau and Hobbes speak of the "state of nature," a condition prior to the social contract, and it seems at times that they are describing a historical state of affairs which actually existed. But perhaps they (at least Hobbes) are not setting this forth as an empirical, historical claim, but as a formulation of what would be the case if no social contract or political institutions existed. Marx and Engels set forth a theory of history which, at least on occasion, appears to be empirically grounded, and which functions as a basic premise in developing political standards. It is the task of the political philosopher as an analyst to introduce conceptual clarity by asking whether a given assertion by a political philosopher is empirical, normative, *a priori* and necessary (non-empirical), or metaphysical; for knowledge of the status or type of assertion made is necessary for understanding and evaluating that assertion.

Many apparently empirical theses turn out on examination not to be empirical at all, and those which are clearly empirical sometimes turn out to be false or at least inadequately substantiated. Some political theorists distort facts by paying exclusive attention to some details and not to others. Their normative concern to change what they take to be evil and to reorient the purposes of society leads them to give inaccurate pictures of existing societies and political institutions. That we obtain empirical truth about these matters is crucially important, for facts of this type are necessary in determining the rationality, the desirability, and the obligatory status of actions or policies of actions.

Suppose, for example, that all human beings were incorrigible egoists as Hobbes thought. Would it make sense to require of them what we call altruistic action or to have political institutions which assume that altruistic action is possible? Suppose with Marx that capitalism does result in the mass "alienation" of man (whatever this means). Would not this fact be relevant to the choice of an economic system? If an imbecile cannot distinguish his side from the other when in uniform, should he be drafted into military service? Functional political norms are always applied to existing states of affairs. If we are ignorant of those states of affairs, or misinformed about them, or if we choose to ignore them, then our normative policies will be irrational. In part at least, this careful attention to facts is what distinguishes the political philosopher from the Utopian dreamer or the ideologue.

Most of the empirical work formerly done inadequately by the classical political philosophers is now being done by the new sciences of man—psychology, sociology and political science—and the political philosopher or theorist must be aware of this empirical data and utilize it. Data from these sciences undoubtedly introduces greater rationality into political decisions or decisions of public policy. If, for example, those psychologists and sociologists who argue that capital punishment does not act as a deterrent to crime are correct, does not this affect the rationality of laws of capital punishment? Or suppose that data from these sciences show that certain men, though legally regarded as sane, cannot control their action. Would it be wise for society to treat them as criminals? Suppose that social scientists are able to isolate and specify the principal causes of conflict in labor-management relations or, say, between nations. Would not such data be crucial in the formulation of public policy on labor-management relations or on the policies of one government toward another? Clearly such data is very useful in arriving at rational public policy decisions, or rational rules of political institutions, and the advance of empirical knowledge in many areas frequently requires of us that we change or alter our normative judgments or policies. Thus if a philosophy is to be adequate the empirical work of the social and political scientist, the attempt to discover laws or regularities operative in social and political phenomena, must be used or incorporated into a political philosophy.

The Three Components of Political Philosophy

Although such empirical knowledge is necessary for an adequate political philosophy, it is by no means sufficient. In itself it provides us neither with political norms or directions for behavior nor with guidelines for resolving political conflicts. Some fundamental norms or ends of political institutions must be introduced which, in conjunction with these facts, enable us to arrive at normative conclusions.

Thus political philosophy cannot be purely empirical. Nor can it be purely analytical or conceptual. It must also be normative. Without its concern for norms, it cannot perform its principal and classical function—the rational justification of the aims and purposes of political society and the provision of guidelines for the rational resolution of political conflicts on all levels. The empirical and conceptual elements are necessary but, in the last analysis, they are subsidiary to this primary task. The example of civil disobedience in this chapter demonstrates the interrelationship of these three components in the treatment of one issue in political philosophy.

The above concept of political philosophy as a discipline is presented not merely as a persuasive definition but as an account of what traditionally has passed under this name and which is still exemplified in the work of many contemporary theorists. Perhaps, however, some persuasion is necessary, for some contemporary philosophers and political scientists alike have attempted to reduce political theory or philosophy to *one* of the three components which we have elucidated. Let us briefly examine three such reductive efforts, that of the behaviorist, that of the logical positivist, and that of the "ordinary use" or analytic philosopher.

The Behaviorist Reduction

The behaviorist has attempted to reduce political theory totally to the empirical component, that is, to empirical science. He has insisted that all issues in political science can be treated behaviorally, that the entire concern of the political scientist is the development of theories and laws which explain political behavior and which permit prediction, and that, committed to the methodological assumptions and techniques of empirical science, his theories must be value-free or value-neutral.[8]

There are good reasons why the behaviorist position has become so attractive. Contemporary scholars, under the impact of refined scientific methods, will no longer tolerate unfounded speculation and ungrounded generalization. They are tired of so-called political "theories" which explain nothing, which are based on no data, and which are simply surreptitious devices for hiding ideological commitments. They want to extend the ultra-successful methods of the natural sciences to the social sciences in order to establish laws of politics which accurately describe and explain, and hence further our knowledge of politics. Who can quarrel with the effort to introduce greater care and rigor in political science? And no one can doubt that great progress has been made in introducing this rigor, in the accumulation and use of social and political data, and in the extension of our political knowledge as a result of these methodological commitments. In this sense political science has become very successful. In many areas it has substituted accurate empirical data and explanatory theory for what in the past was speculation and unfounded generalization.

Clearly, more rigorous theory in political science is both possible

[8] For an account of the behaviorist approach, see Heinz Eulau, *The Behavioral Persuasion in Politics* (New York: Random House, 1963); David Easton, *A Framework for Political Analysis* (Englewood Cliffs, N.J.: Prentice-Hall, 1965) and James C. Charlesworth, ed., *The Limits of Behavioralism in Political Science* (Philadelphia: American Academy of Political and Social Science, 1962).

and desirable. The fundamental question, however, is whether it is possible to include all of the significant concerns of political science or theory under a set of empirically discoverable laws or regularities. Or are there significant elements of political science which simply cannot be treated by purely behavioral methods?

This question perhaps can best be reformulated in terms of two questions: (1) Can there be a value-free political science? (2) If value considerations are ruled out, what happens to the traditional normative function and rational critique which has been exercised in political science and political philosophy?

Concerning the first question, H. R. G. Greaves argues that a value-free political science is a myth and that "it has been insufficiently understood how far description in this field is dependent for significance upon analysis and explanation into which values enter." [9] Similarly Hans J. Morgenthau holds that empirical political studies—the accumulation of data—requires a philosophical framework and certain value perspectives within which those studies are cast. [10] Christian Bay argues that "much of the current work in political behavior generally fails to articulate its very real value biases, and that the political impact of this supposedly neutral literature is generally conservative and in a special sense anti-political." [11]

This is not the place to treat this question in detail or attempt to show the *locus* of value assumptions within explanatory frameworks invoked by political scientists. Nor is it the place to attempt to portray the *kind* of value biases which might lie there. [12] It is sufficient for our purpose here to raise the question and to suggest that knowledge and understanding in political theory require not only the discovery of general laws and regularities which make possible *causal* explanation and prediction; they also require the discovery of the *reasons* which persons or groups have for acting as they do. As K. W. Kim puts it, "measured in terms of the goal of understanding and not prediction, it is not warranted to say that one understands a certain action better because one has located its presumably determining conditions rather than the reasons behind the action in

[9] H. R. G. Greaves, "Political Theory Today," in *Apolitical Politics: A Critique of Behavioralism,* ed. Charles A. McCoy and John Playford (New York: Thomas Y. Crowell Co., 1967), p. 235.

[10] Hans Morgenthau, *Dilemmas of Politics* (Chicago: University of Chicago Press, 1958).

[11] Christian Bay, "Politics and Psuedopolitics: A Critical Evaluation," in McCoy and Playford, *Apolitical Politics: A Critique of Behavioralism,* p. 13.

[12] See Charles McCoy and John Playford, Ibid., for discussion of these issues.

question." [13] But an understanding of reasons for actions as opposed to causes necessarily involves norms and their evaluation.

This leads us to our second question: What happens to the traditional normative and appraisal functions of traditional political theory if those functions are ruled out of political theory? The answer is obvious. It impoverishes political theory. It strips it of a function which classically has been a central one, a function which is essential to human beings who are necessarily appraising beings and who are basically concerned with improving the human condition. This appraising function requires standards and an evaluation of standards, whereas a pure behaviorism substitutes mere description and explanation in its stead. It completely precludes the establishment of rational criteria for evaluating social and political institutions and the ends or goals which those institutions purport to serve.

There is certainly a point to David Easton's insistence that explanation and ethical evaluation be kept analytically distinct.[14] Indiscriminate fusing of these functions leads to great confusion. But analytic distinction of functions is one thing; the systematic preclusion of a function is quite another. A pure behaviorist who excludes the evaluative function takes from political theory the very function for which, presumably, the empirical data and regularities discovered by him have their significance. As Barrington Moore states, "if social science drops the mask of rational criticism from its program altogether, leaving it entirely to theology, journalism, and the Bohemian fringe of intellectual life, it can some day drown in a sea of verbiage, strewn with floating bits of meaningless data." [15] Excess verbiage is not the sole possession of dataless speculators or philosophers.

The Positivistic Reduction

The reductionism of philosophers has taken two somewhat different turns. The logical positivists exclude the normative component of political theory on the grounds that normative discourse is emotive or noncognitive. Normative statements are neither true nor false, they argue, for they are neither analytic nor tautological (that is, true simply because of the meaning of the terms used) statements

[13] K. W. Kim, "The Limits of Behavioural Explanation in Politics" in Charles McCoy and John Playford, Ibid., p. 51.
[14] David Easton, *A Framework for Political Analysis.*
[15] Barrington Moore, Jr., *Political Power and Social Theory: Six Studies* (Cambridge, Mass.: Harvard University Press, 1958), p. 110.

nor empirical statements. That is, they do not meet the verifiability criterion of meaning. Hence there can be no such thing as normative knowledge. The significance, even the possibility, of complete enterprises as they were classically conceived—ethics, aesthetics, theology, metaphysics, and political philosophy—are denied by the positivists on these grounds. The very possibility of meaningful value theory, in the sense of a systematic and rationally developed set of normative principles to be used as the basis for moral and political decisions, is denied. They then exclude the empirical component from political theory or philosophy on the grounds that this should be done by the social scientist. This of course does not exclude this activity from the political scientist. What is left for political philosophy to do? Nothing but logical or conceptual analysis. Thus, speaking of ethics, A. J. Ayer states that "a strictly philosophical treatise on ethics should . . . make no ethical pronouncements. But it should, by giving an analysis of ethical terms show what is the category to which all such pronouncements belong." [16] This applies *mutatis mutandis* to a strictly philosophical treatise on politics.

Since early logical positivism, there has been considerable change. The strict verifiability theory of meaning has been severely modified.[17] But the influence of this movement is still strong among social scientists and behaviorists. And, to some extent, it has had a salutary effect. Take, for example, a recent volume on the "public interest." Glendon Schubert writes that "a theory of the public interest in governmental decision-making ought to describe a relationship between concepts of the public interest and official behavior in such terms that it might be possible to attempt to validate empirically hypotheses concerning the relationship. If extant theory does not lend itself to such uses, it is difficult to comprehend the justification for teaching students of political science that subservience to the public interest is a relevant norm of official responsibility." [18] Schubert's concern here is that the concept, "public interest," be given some clear meaning. If it cannot be clarified, it can hardly serve as a guide for public policy decisions or as a basic principle in a political theory. Surely he is correct that some operational definition (an explication of the

[16] A. J. Ayer, *Language, Truth and Logic* (New York: Dover Publications, Inc., 1936), pp. 103–4.

[17] See, for example, Carl Hempel, "Problems and Changes in the Empiricist Criterion of Meaning," *Revue Internationale de Philosophie*, Vol. 2 (1950); reprinted in Leonard Linsky, ed., *Semantics and the Philosophy of Language* (Urbana: University of Illinois Press, 1952).

[18] Glendon Schubert, *The Public Interest* (Glencoe, Ill.: Free Press, 1961), p. 220.

operations by which one would identify an act which is in the public interest) is needed (though perhaps not an explication which reduced its meaning to such operations). But to go further, as some positivists have, and insist that all concepts which cannot be strictly operationally defined are meaningless is to go too far. Surely there are degrees of clarity of concepts. Some basic moral and political concepts seem incapable of being "closed" in this way—at least without vitiating their function and significance. And the basic thesis of the positivist concerning values, namely, that rational argument in value issues is possible only for the factual premises in those issues, value claims themselves being categorized as purely emotive and value argument as merely persuasive, appears to be a premature move to irrationality in value theory.

The "Ordinary Use" Reduction

The reduction of political theory to non-normative components takes a different turn with contemporary analytic or "ordinary use" philosophy. There is no wholesale use of the verification principle to rule out the cognitive significance of value judgments. The entire approach to meaning and knowledge is quite different, the principal thesis being that there are multiple uses and functions of discourse and that it is a mistake to try to reduce all significant uses of language to the analytic, empirical, or emotive categories. The simplistic model of meaning offered by the positivist does not account for the richness and multiple functions of our language, and so it leads to misconceptions of several types and areas of discourse, in particular the normative areas. With his preconceived set of linguistic categories, the positivist arbitrarily dumps all statements which do not immediately fit the analytic or empirical mold into the emotive, noncognitive bag.

"Ordinary use" philosophers avoid this kind of narrowness and insist that we should pay close attention to the actual uses and functions of areas of discourse. Rather than overgeneralize about our language and types of discourse, the ordinary use philosopher follows the paradigm case method, examining actual instances of language use. No simple model of empirical verification encompasses all of human knowledge, he argues, and normative discourse is seen as having a logic of its own. Gilbert Ryle, Stephen Toulmin, P. H. Nowell-Smith and others who philosophize in this way thus offer us a far more sophisticated and wider range of linguistic categories and a far more accurate account of both the uses of language and the kind of rationality characteristic of types of language uses (such as the moral and political areas).[19]

This approach is very critical of traditional philosophy. "Ordinary use" philosophers especially oppose the search for Platonic definitions, the search for the universal essence of this or that. They prefer to speak of "family resemblances." They are in fact very critical of the kind of questions raised by traditional philosophy, characterizing many of them as meaningless.

For example, in the area of political philosophy, Margaret Mac-Donald notes that it makes perfectly good sense to ask why one should oppose a given government and that we all know what criteria we use to decide this question. But she goes on to say that "although it looks harmless and even philosophical to generalize from these instances to 'Why should I obey any law or support any government?' the significance of the question evaporates. For the general question suggests an equally general answer and this is what every political philosopher has tried to give. But no general criterion applies to every instance. To ask why I should obey *any* law is to ask whether there might be a political society without political obligations, which is absurd. For we mean by political society, groups of people organized according to rules enforced by some of their number." [20]

T. D. Weldon, in his *The Vocabulary of Politics*, generalizes the MacDonald conclusion.[21] He claims that nearly all of the traditional questions of political philosophy are wrongly posed and further that the theoretical foundations of traditional political thinking—whether the appeal to natural law, dialectical materialism or what have you—are "all equally worthless." Why? Because all of them rest on various kinds of linguistic or conceptual confusion or, they violate the empirical verifiability criterion. (Weldon is at least as much of a positivist as he is a Wittgensteinian analyst, that is, one who is committed to the thesis that "meaning is use.") The political philosopher's task is to clear this deadwood away and restore both sensible questions and sensible answers. He aims at analysis and conceptual ground-clearing, not at answering substantive normative or empirical issues.

[19] See, for example, Patrick Nowell-Smith, *Ethics* (Harmondsworth, England: Penguin Books, 1954; and Stephen Toulmin, *An Examination of the Place of Reason in Ethics* (Cambridge: Cambridge University Press, 1950.)

[20] Margaret MacDonald, "The Language of Political Theory," in A. G. N. Flew, ed., *Logic and Language*, First Series (Oxford: Basil Blackwell, 1953), pp. 183–4.

[21] T. D. Weldon, *The Vocabulary of Politics* (Baltimore, Md.: Penguin Books, 1953).

The impact of this approach, characterized in some quarters as "the heyday of Weldonism," has been severe enough to lead some to ask, "Does political theory still exist?"[22]

Again, as in the case of the logical positivist, much of the work of "ordinary use" analysis is very helpful in political philosophy. For example, if someone claims that the basis of all law and of political institutions is and should be "natural law" and if one is unable to give an intelligible account of this concept, if the notion of natural law is so vacuous that it is used to justify even contradictory positions, then plainly something is badly wrong with this approach. Surely it is all to the good if "ordinary use" analysis permits us to see these problems. The question is not whether such analysis is helpful or whether it is an essential part of political theory. This seems undeniable. The question is whether this kind of analysis and clarification is the *total* purview of political theory, with all normative issues being abdicated. The question also is whether analysis of traditional political theories and their foundations necessarily results in Weldon's conclusion—that they are all equally worthless. Plainly there may be a middle ground, namely, that there are conceptual confusions in these traditional theories but also considerable truth in them when recast in the proper light. Indeed this is the position which will emerge in the subsequent chapters of this book. It seems to me that the proclaimed death of political philosophy (and of philosophy in general)[23] is simply premature. Political philosophy or theory not only *can* perform the classical functions elucidated above; it is in fact doing it. Even where the linguistic or "ordinary use" mode of philosophizing is strong, the traditional normative objectives of (political) philosophy are still pursued—but in a different manner.[24]

Summation

The primary concern of the political philosopher, then, is the justification of the aims and principles of political society. The conceptual and analytic concern and the empirical concern are subsidiary to this normative task. His task, however, is not political casuistry,

[22] Isaiah Berlin, "Does Political Theory Still Exist?"

[23] Lewis Fewer, "American Philosophy Is Dead," *New York Times Magazine,* April 24, 1966.

[24] For example, see Brian Barry, *Political Argument* (New York: Humanities Press, 1965); J. R. Lucas, *The Principles of Politics* (Oxford: Clarendon Press, 1966); and Carl Cohen, *Democracy* (Athens, Ga.: University of Georgia Press, 1971).

the detailed spelling out of specific conclusions to normative political issues. This sort of effort is as futile here as it is in ethics.[25] His task is, rather, that of developing very general normative political principles from which such highly specific conclusions could be deduced, given the required empirical data. This requires of him not only that he analyze and evaluate the principal theories of political justification historically advanced by philosophers, but also that he offer his own answers to the key normative questions, formulating his own theory with justificatory arguments. This in turn presupposes that rationality is possible in regard to normative issues and that political philosophy is more than mere Utopian dreaming and more than political ideology. Aristotle is as correct now as he was in the fourth century B.C.—too many theorists formulate heavenly cities and states unrelated to the facts of life and to man's needs and capacities, and too many are so immersed in their own existing political system and beliefs that they are unable to see anything good in another system. Their "arguments" serve only to reinforce the existing political order. In the face of this, is there any wonder that there has been and continues to be considerable scepticism about the very possibility of justification in the political area? It is admittedly difficult, if not impossible, to step completely outside of one's own national and political loyalties, but such disinterestedness is possible to some degree. To the extent to which this disinterestedness is present in a theory, we have political philosophy. When it is absent, when one seeks simply to justify national loyalties or a political institution which one happens to favor, we have rationalization, not reasoned arguments; political ideology, not political philosophy. The lack of complete impartiality may mean that pure political philosophy does not exist, but, in this sense, neither does pure science. It seems clear to me that the positions of the classical political theorists are for the most part properly classified as political philosophy, not political ideology.

The Principal Questions of Political Philosophy

What, then, are the principal questions which the political theorist must try to answer disinterestedly? There are several basic ones: Why should men live in society and have government at all? What should be the aims and purposes of political society? What form of government is the best instrument for realizing these aims and purposes?

[25] See R. M. Hare's *The Language of Morals* (Oxford: Oxford University Press, 1952), for a discussion of the futility of casuistry in ethics.

These general questions involve a number of subsidiary questions: Where should the locus of political power reside? Should there be limits to government authority? If so, what are they? Is civil disobedience or revolution ever justifiable? If so, under what conditions? What is meant by justice in society? How can it be realized? Can some laws be unjust? Are there any inalienable rights? What is the basis of moral obligation and of political obligation?

These questions are for the most part normative, and classical political theorists have offered different and opposing answers to them. Their answers were rooted in different moral beliefs, metaphysical beliefs, theological beliefs, epistemological beliefs, and scientific beliefs. Beliefs of these different types were combined by classical political philosophers as they offered both explanation and justification of political principles. To understand and to appraise the arguments and the models of justification of these philosophers requires that one understand and appraise what constitutes the essential parts of those models. Thus Aristotle's political philosophy cannot be understood or judged without understanding and appraising his moral theory, his metaphysics, epistemology, and his belief about facts in the world. The same holds for Aquinas, Hobbes, and the others. Thus, given Hobbes's beliefs about man, some of his political principles are understandable, and to appraise those principles one must appraise his theory of man. Locke and others challenged that theory and, consequently, much of Hobbes's political philosophy. In challenging Hobbes's theory of absolute sovereignty or his placing of the locus of political power in the hands of one man, Locke asks: "Are men so foolish that they take care to avoid what mischiefs can be done them by polecats and foxes, but are content, nay think it safety, to be devoured by lions." [26] Even if Hobbes's thesis of psychological egoism is correct, Locke claims, this does not justify placing complete political power in the hands of one man; it constitutes grounds for doing just the contrary.

Political philosophy is a complex and difficult task. New empirical data and new conceptual ways of looking at man and society are always appearing, and the conditions of human existence change constantly. Each of the classical political philosophers has had something significant to contribute to the normative questions of political philosophy and to our understanding of political reality. But each may be inadequate in various respects. It is the business of the political philoso-

[26] John Locke, *The Second Treatise on Civil Government*, originally published in 1690 (New York: Bobbs-Merrill, 1952).

pher and the student of political philosophy to sort out these inadequacies, whether they be empirical, conceptual, or normative, and to formulate reasoned answers to the key questions.

In the chapters that follow, this effort will be made. The political philosophies of a number of classical theorists will be examined. Within a volume of this scope, the examination of each must be brief, and some of the finer details of these theories must be omitted. But it is hoped that this does not result in distortion.

A Classificatory Scheme

We will use certain traditional classifications of political theories —natural law theory, utilitarianism, and historicism—as models, and each will be considered in Part 2.[27] Neither political scientists nor political philosophers spend much time attempting to prove that any one of these theories or accounts of political life is the correct one. This is undoubtedly a forward step, for there are overlappings and crisscrossings among the tenets of these theories, and what is embraced by any given one is often not clearly delineated. And some philosophers are difficult to categorize—Aristotle, for example—and cut across this classificatory scheme. Thus, if taken too strictly, this threefold classification can be misleading. It can cause one to overgeneralize and to ignore important differences between political philosophies classified under the same banner and important affinities with those classified under another. This, however, is a danger of any classification scheme, and we can guard against it.

Thus, although classifications of political theories other than natural law, utilitarian, and historist might be just as helpful, they too have their pitfalls. Furthermore, this scheme has a well-known history of use and there are common features of those philosophers in each category that make it fruitful to analyze them under these rubrics. The philosophers whom we will treat under each of these theories do subscribe to common and reasonably distinct *models* of justification, even if they differ widely on a normative level or in their assessment of empirical states of affairs.

Apologies must be made for the exclusion of some great classical and modern theorists—Plato and Aristotle, and Kant, Rousseau, Burke, and others. But in a volume of this length, many restrictions are

[27] These classificatory terms are common ones. Frederick Olafson uses them in his *Society, Law and Morality* (Englewood Cliffs, N.J.: Prentice-Hall, Inc., 1961).

necessary. It is felt that the philosophers chosen for examination—St. Thomas, Thomas Hobbes, and John Locke; Jeremy Bentham and John Stuart Mill; and Friedrich Hegel, Karl Marx and Friedrich Engels—constitute central figures in the history of political theory. They are theorists who have had great historical and contemporary impact, and they serve, perhaps better than others, to illustrate the three models of political justification which we are using. All of the major questions of political philosophy are brought up through the work of these theorists. They also serve as a very useful backdrop against which we can discuss the advantages and disadvantages of the various models of justification and the complex and difficult (but unavoidable) issue of criteria of adequacy for a political philosophy. This will be the task of Chapter 9, where criteria of adequacy embracing the three principal components of political philosophy elucidated above (the empirical, the analytic and conceptual, and the normative) will be treated.

Recommended Readings

Benn, S. I., and Peters, R. S. *The Principles of Political Thought.* New York, 1964; originally published as *Social Principles and the Democratic State,* London, 1959.

Berlin, Isaiah. "Does Political Theory Still Exist?" in Peter Laslett and W. G. Runciman, eds. *Philosophy, Politics and Society.* Second Series. Oxford, 1962.

Brecht, Arnold. *Political Theory.* Princeton, 1959.

Catlin, George. "Political Theory: What Is It?" *Political Science Quarterly,* Vol. 72, No. 1 (1957), 1–29.

Charlesworth, James G., ed. *The Limits of Behavioralism in Political Science.* Philadelphia, 1962.

Easton, David. *A Framework for Political Analysis.* Englewood Cliffs, N.J., 1965.

Easton, David. *The Political System.* New York, 1953.

Eulau, Heinz. *The Behavioral Persuasion in Politics.* New York, 1963.

Gewirth, Alan. *Political Philosophy,* Introduction. New York, 1965.

MacDonald, Margaret. "The Language of Political Theory" in A. G. N. Flew, ed., *Logic and Language.* First Series. Oxford, 1951.

McCoy, Charles A., and John Playford, eds. *Apolitical Politics. A Critique of Behavioralism.* New York, 1967.

Olafson, Frederick A., ed. *Society, Law and Morality*, Introduction. Englewood Cliffs, N.J., 1961.

Plamenatz, John. *Man and Society*, 2 Vols. New York, 1963. Introduction, Vol. I.

Sabine, George. *A History of Political Theory*. New York, 1961.

Shklar, Judith N., ed. *Political Theory and Ideology*. New York, 1966.

Weldon, T. D. *The Vocabulary of Politics*. Baltimore, 1953.

part 2
three
models
of political
justification

Model 1:
The Theory
of
Natural
Law

Introduction

What is (are) the thesis (theses) of the natural law theorist? A number of classical philosophers have traditionally been classified under this heading, including Cicero, Aristotle, St. Thomas Aquinas, Thomas Hobbes, John Locke, Immanuel Kant, and others. What do these theorists have in common? Their differences are many. They have different *empirical* estimates of facts in the world. They employ different sets of concepts or *categories* to explain the world and our experience of it. They offer different and often conflicting moral and political *norms*, and different forms of government. Kant denies, for example, that civil disobedience or resistance to the sovereign power is ever justified, whereas Locke maintains that it is justified under certain circumstances. Hobbes appeals to natural law, along with his contract theory, to justify absolute sovereignty; Rousseau and Locke use it to justify limited government. Natural law has been the justifying appeal for extreme liberalism and individualism as well as for conservatism and the status quo. On more specific issues, it has been cited as justifying grounds for slavery and for the abolition of it, for the practice of contraception and against it, and so on. These facts have led Professor Alf Ross to say that, "like a harlot, natural law is at the disposal of everyone. The ideology does not exist that cannot be defended by an appeal to the law of nature."[1] It certainly makes

[1] Alf Ross, "A Critique of the Philosophy of Natural Law," in *The Nature of Law*, Martin Golding, ed. (New York: Random House, 1966), p. 71.

one wonder about the status of the natural law theory and ask whether that theory is simply a useless device or what amounts to the same thing—a device that can be used to justify anything.

With this disagreement on empirical, conceptual, and normative issues, what could all of these theorists have in common? Perhaps they all simply use the same phrase, the same kind of language, which should not be taken as evidence that they hold similar positions. Language does frequently mislead. However, there are points of agreement among these theorists, points which not only justify the application of the term "natural law" to them all, but which also make clear the nature of the natural law thesis. All of them believe and assert that there are valid laws or rules prescribing or prohibiting conduct of a certain type which are antecedent to and independent of statute law or the prescriptions or prohibitions of the existing legal order. The rights and duties prescribed by natural law are valid simply because men are what they are—human—or more generally, because the world is the way it is. They are in no sense human contrivances or inventions—even though their specific application in concrete cases of action requires human judgment and knowledge. These natural laws, rights, and obligations are moral facts about man and his universe and are apprehended or known by man's natural capacities. Furthermore, these laws or rights which hold for all men simply because they are men constitute, the natural law theorists maintain, a valid, objective standard for the appraisal or evaluation of existing political institutions and laws, and for their correction. At the Nuremburg Trials at the end of World War II, this appeal to natural law was one of the basic grounds of those who criticized the laws and actions of the Nazis.

From what has been said we see that natural law theory involves both the assertion of moral and political norms and of epistemological and metaphysical theses which center around those norms (what some today call metaethics). Let us ask two questions: Are there any normative principles common to all natural law theorists? Is there a theory about the status of those norms common to them all?

There are certain general normative principles common to the natural law theorists—justice, equality, freedom, and "synderesis" (good is to be pursued, evil avoided). But these principles are to a great extent vacuous. When particularized to concrete cases, there is a wide variance on the meaning of just treatment, equal treatment, and on good and evil. In fact, these principles can be so interpreted that they support whatever one wants. Everything depends on how good and evil, justice and equality are defined. Until they are defined or filled in, these principles are purely formal, not substantive. Substantive norms held in common by these theorists are the wrongness of cruelty and of needless human suffering. But neither these formal principles nor the substantive ones are typical simply of natural law theorists. They are held also by the historicists and utilitarians.

Do all natural law theorists hold the same epistemological and metaphysical account of these norms? It seems not. All of them seem to hold to some form of cognitivism (moral judgments are truth-claims and are capable of being true or false) but they differ on the avenue of cognition and on what is cognized. For some the moral facts cognized are nonempirical, transcendental facts; for others, the facts are empirical ones about men. To the extent that cognized moral facts are natural facts about men, the natural law theorist has joined hands with the utilitarian, who similarly bases his ethic upon the nature of man, that is, upon empirical facts about man. What is at issue in this latter case is whether moral conclusions can be derived simply from descriptive, empirical premises. These have been and still are key issues in the contemporary metaethical debate. To the extent that a natural law theorist does go in this direction, he may not differ significantly from the utilitarian. However, even if he avoids ethical naturalism, holding that some moral facts are trans-empirical, transcendental, non-natural or the like; and further, even if he holds that there are moral and political obligations which are binding independent of their consequences (thereby rejecting utilitarianism as an adequate ethic), does this serve to distinguish him from the historicist? It appears not, for the historicist also believes that not all obligations are reducible to concern for consequences. Perhaps the label "natural law theorist" is simply not as useful as has been thought. To some extent this is true, as it is undoubtedly true of most labels. Hobbes and Locke in particular have a strong utilitarian emphasis in their theories. In spite of this, they, and to a much stronger extent, Cicero, Aristotle, Aquinas, and Kant emphasize deontological moral criteria in answering the normative problems of political society—criteria or principles like justice and equality, which are inherently obligatory (and not based merely on the calculation of their probable consequences, as the utilitarian holds) and which are known by rational insight or revelation into the nature of things. This rationalist-deontological thesis sets off the natural law theorist from the classical utilitarians. What sets him off from historicists, like Hegel or Engels, is that he affirms what they deny, namely, that there are unchanging, extra-legal norms or principles which serve as standards for praising or condemning the existing political norms or principles of one's own society and those of others.

Space does not permit an examination of all of the principal natural law theorists. I have therefore chosen St. Thomas, Hobbes, and Locke—Thomas because his version of natural law theory is heavily theological and still exerts a strong influence in contemporary moral and political theory; Hobbes, because, though he speaks the language of natural law, it is not clear that he really fits this tradition—and there has been considerable controversy over his position among contemporary scholars; Locke, because of his key role in the liberal, democratic tradition and his influence on the American Republic.

chapter 2
St. Thomas Aquinas
1225-1274

St. Thomas Aquinas, the son of the Count of Aquino, spent his boyhood years at the Benedictine monastery at Monte Cassino, Italy. Educated further in the University of Naples, he joined the Dominican Order in 1244. He studied at the University of Paris, and under Albertus Magnus at Cologne, returning to Paris in 1256 as Professor of Theology. He later taught at the Papal Curia in Rome and, a few years before his death, established a Dominican house of studies in Naples.

His basic works are the Summa Contra Gentiles, *and the* Summa Theologica *(incomplete). The former was intended to persuade nonbelievers of the truth of Christian doctrine; the latter, to be a synthesis of Christian doctrine. The philosophy espoused in these basic works was declared to be the authoritative teaching of the Catholic Church in 1879 by Pope Leo XIII. Thomas's political philosophy attempts to map out the proper roles of Church and State.*

The Purposes and Aims of Society and Government

How does St. Thomas answer the principal questions of political philosophy? Why should men live in society and have government? What should be the aims and purposes of political society? What form of government best realizes these aims? St. Thomas's answers to all of these questions are related, but let us begin with the first.

Primarily, man lives in society because he was created to live in a community and is naturally a social and political animal. Accepting Aristotle's teleological view of nature, the view that each creature has its own end, Thomas argues that societal living is an integral part of man's very nature. Man's nature, his potentialities, cannot be fulfilled independently of society. Men are biological (having appetites and desires) and rational beings. They seek to preserve themselves and their well-being. They are also rational and moral by nature and try to do that which is right and reasonable. Reason, Thomas maintains, can direct man's action to its proper end, but some political authority or government must exist if this is to be done; for ". . . if a great number of people were to live, each intent only upon his own interest, such a community would surely disintegrate unless there were one of its number to have a care for the common good. . . ." Human beings have diverse interests and goals which often conflict. In such conflict situations, they may act irrationally. And some men are governed for the most part by their instincts, not by reason, moral sense, or concern for justice. Government or political authority, with concentrated power, is necessary if chaos and irrationality are to be avoided and if the basic needs and goals of men, the good life for men, are to be achieved. It should be stressed, however, that for Thomas, government exists not merely to insure peace but also as a natural institution requisite for the fulfillment of man's nature.

This purely natural end, however, is not the only aim and purpose of the state. Thomas is not merely an Aristotelian; he is also a Christian. He is both a philosopher and a theologian. Political institutions on earth are simply part of the total divine plan. The end of man is more than the attainment of happiness via the virtuous life; it is also heavenly beatitude, the enjoyment of God. The work of the sovereign is an important component in the realization of that end.

St. Thomas does insist that the sphere of the sovereign is autonomous. It is the sovereign's task, not that of the Church, to preserve peace and order, and to assure the well-being of the state. On the other hand, the sovereign cannot take over the role of the Church. Salvation and beatitude he cannot insure, for they are beyond his power—indeed, all human power—and can be effected only through the Church and the grace of God. But, by instituting political principles and laws which are reflections of natural law, and hence of the divine or eternal law, the sovereign provides the necessary conditions not only for man's temporal good or well-being but also for the realization of God's purpose and man's enjoyment of God. The state is part of God's natural order of things, and the wise or genuine ruler governs by way of the natural law and the divine law. In this task, he is judged by God and rewarded or punished accordingly.

The Best Form of Government

What form of government is the best instrument to realize these ends? Again, Thomas follows Aristotle. The best government is monarchy, rule by one man with concentrated power, who looks after the common good. Fragmented political power, he holds, can easily lead to chaos, not peace and unity. However, few men possess the wisdom, virtue and justice requisite for the task. Most men would abuse such power, turning it to their own use rather than the common good. Absolute monarchy, then, can easily lead to tyranny, and in the absence of such rare individuals, some form of limited monarchy with diffusion of power is best. No particular form of government, however, is ordained by God—even though Thomas does speak of the creation of the world by God as a "convenient model" for the establishment of a political kingdom. The important point is that political authority, whatever form it takes, must fulfill its proper role.

Eternal and Natural Law

As with all natural law theorists, Thomas has a very broad concept of law, one that covers not only the existing legal framework but also the total governing scheme of God and nature. There are four kinds of law—eternal law, natural law, human law, and divine law. (1) "The very notion of the government of things in God, the ruler of the universe," Thomas asserts, "has the nature of law." This all-encompassing notion, "the government of things in God," is the eternal law. It is God's plan or direction for all things, via physical laws and other laws, to the realization of their ends. (2) Natural law is much narrower. It is the "rational creature's participation of the eternal law." Natural law is that part of eternal law which applies specifically to men as rational creatures and which can be rationally known by men who share in the "eternal reason." (3) Human law is the existing law or public policy of the state, the existing legal code. (4) Divine law is God's revealed law in the form of a table of commandments required for the direction of man's soul and for the preclusion of evils or sins not necessarily covered or forbidden by natural law or human law. The end of eternal happiness exceeds man's natural law and human law. Divine law is needed to direct man to this end. Also, by "curbing and directing interior acts," divine law forbids certain evils, which, if forbidden by human law, would make the state oppressive and "hinder the advance of the common good."

The predominant concern of the sovereign is with human law and natural law. He must care for the community by promulgating statutes directed at the common good. He must sanction conduct which insures the peace and stability of society. In doing this, his function is to discover the natural law by reason and apply it to existing states of affairs, putting into effect "particular determinations" of natural law. All human law should be derived from natural law; that is, it should not violate or be incompatible with natural law. In fact, only those human laws so derived are "truly" laws. Human laws that are oppressive or unjust do not bind in conscience. The sovereign is himself subject to the natural law, and he is never morally entitled to promulgate laws which pervert it.

The Principles of Natural Law

What are the principles of natural law and how are they discovered? They are discovered by man's reason, not by an insight into the eternal law, but by reflection on man's essence, his unchanging nature, and the conditions which are required if his nature or potentialities are to be fulfilled. Given Thomas's teleological or purposive view of nature and all creation, "good" is defined as the realization or fulfillment or the end or "telos" of a thing. Thus he sets forth as the most abstract and general principle of natural law, the principle of synderesis—". . . good is to be done and promoted, and evil is to be avoided." Thomas realizes that this general principle tells us very little. To find concrete suggestions for man and his action, we must discover what man's good is and how it can be realized. He goes on to say: "All of the other precepts of the natural law are based upon this [synderesis]; so that all the things which the practical reason naturally apprehends as man's good belong to the precepts of the natural law under the form of things to be done or avoided." [1] Practical reason, by reflecting on the fundamental tendencies and needs

---

[1] St. Thomas Aquinas, *Summa Theologica*, Dominican Translation; from the *Basic Works of St. Thomas Aquinas*, ed. Anton C. Pegis (New York: Random House, 1945), Question XCIV, Second Article.

of man, can discern the good for man and the precepts of natural law. The precepts or rules of action (which are of varying degrees of generality) requisite for the realization of man's good constitute the natural law.

Thomas gives us several examples of precepts which "flow from" or are "based on" the principles of synderesis. Man's nature is such that he tends toward self-preservation. Therefore those actions or precepts whereby man preserves himself and avoids death are natural laws. Man is also naturally inclined to propagate the species and rear his offspring. Therefore the precepts that the species is to be propagated and children cared for and educated are natural laws. Man is also a rational being and naturally desires to know. Therefore the precept that he should seek knowledge and avoid ignorance is a natural law. He also is naturally inclined to live in society, so the precept that he should live in society is a natural law. These principles themselves may yield more specific natural laws. For example, the precept of monogamy is based on the premise that children must be properly cared for and educated. Monogamy, Thomas argues, is necessary for this purpose.

Although the "first common principles" of natural law hold for everyone, "particular determinations" of those principles may vary according to time and circumstance. Thus, although it is a precept of the natural laws that goods held in trust should be restored, this precept would not hold if restoration results in injury or if the restored goods are used for the purpose of fighting against one's country. Such conflict between precepts of the natural law are apparently resolved by appealing to a more general precept. The certainty of any precept diminishes as "we descend further toward the particular." Again, Thomas is here setting forth an Aristotelian point, that ethics and politics deal with "variables" or changing states of affairs, not invariables, and so certainty is not possible.

Certain precepts Thomas characterizes as belonging to natural law, not in the primary sense that nature inclines one thereto or because they are requisite for the fulfillment of man's nature, but in the secondary sense that "nature did not bring with it the contrary." Thus, nakedness, common ownership, and universal freedom are natural in the secondary sense. This does not mean, however, that wearing clothes, the institution of private property, or slavery are violations of natural law in the primary sense. These practices are additions to the natural law and are compatible with it. Thus natural law can be neutral to certain practices and institutions, such as private property.

Justice and Civil Disobedience

St. Thomas recognizes that some human laws may violate natural law. They may be unjust. He offers four criteria for a just law: (1) It must be ordained to the common good. (2) It must not exceed the authorized power of the lawgiver. (3) It must lay burdens on subjects according to equality of proportion. (4) It must not be opposed to the divine good.

Suppose a given human law violates any of these criteria. Then it is unjust and does not "bind one in conscience." It is not "truly" a law. Is one justified in civil disobedience or even revolution in such cases? Thomas's answer to this question is not always clear. He does say straightforwardly that laws opposed to the divine good "must in no way be observed." Here he seems to advocate civil disobedience, perhaps even revolution if necessary, in regard to some unjust laws or states. But this applies only to violation of divine laws. He distinguishes between excessive and nonexcessive tyranny. Nonexcessive injustice should be tolerated rather than opposed by rebellion, for rebellion often brings greater peril by breeding strife and discord. What about excessive injustice or tyranny? Here it would seem that rebellion and violence are justified. But no—Thomas states that even in such cases, "it would be dangerous, both for the community and its rulers, if individuals were, upon private initiative to attempt the death of those who govern, albeit tyrannically. . . ." [2] The remedy for the evils of tyranny, he suggests, "lies rather in the hands of public authority than in the private judgment of individuals." But what if legal procedures such as impeachment are ineffective? Is rebellion and violence now justified? Thomas's answer again is No. We must turn to God for help and hope that he will depose the tyrant. We must stop sinning, for God allows tyrants to rule in punishment for our sins.

Aside from his inexplicit statement regarding a sovereign's violation of the divine good, Thomas does not support or encourage revolution or civil disobedience. He does hold that injustices should be corrected and that the ruler is responsible to a trust, but such correction or deposition must be through legitimate, authorized channels. Disobedience to constituted authority, revolution of any type, destroys the basic order and stability of civilization and justice. For Thomas,

---

[2] St. Thomas Aquinas, "On Princely Government," in *Aquinas, Selected Political Writings*, ed. A. P. D'Entreves, trans. J. G. Dawson (Oxford: Basil Blackwell, 1954), p. 31.

it is better to suffer injustice than to undermine the order and stability required for the common good.

Critique

It is plain from what has been said that Thomas's answers to the normative questions of political philosophy—Why do we have society and government? What should be the aims and principles of government? What is the best form of government? What are the rights and freedoms of citizens and the limits of government authority? Is civil disobedience or revolution justified? What does justice mean? What is the basis of moral and political obligation?—are all rooted in his acceptance of Aristotle's teleological view of nature and man and in his Christian theology. A critique of Thomas's political philosophy, then, must certainly begin here.

First of all, is there any good reason or evidence for accepting Thomas's view that man has an essential nature, a goal, direction or function uniquely his because he is a man? To be sure, men have purposes, desires, and goals, and these vary considerably from one person to the next. But does each of us have an "essential nature," a final end for which we were created? Many deny this, arguing that the facts appear to support the view that human nature has the potentiality for a wide spectrum of activities. Why, then, accept this Thomistic thesis? It is clear that Thomas's belief, that man's final end is the enjoyment of God or eternal beatitude, is a theological or metaphysical claim, not an empirical one. Consequently, one must ask if there is good reason for accepting this theological or metaphysical claim. If the basis for the claim is primarily Christian scripture or revelation, one must ask whether these are acceptable tests of knowledge.

An analysis of Thomas's natural law theory requires an analysis of his entire metaphysical, theological, and epistemological structure. His claim that man has a final end and that natural law exists goes beyond the claim that men are rational and purposive; it includes also a specific God.

Plainly the Pandora's box of natural and revealed theology must be opened and examined, if Thomas's natural law theory is to be understood. This would require a volume in itself. Much of contemporary philosophy calls into question not merely the truth of such theological-metaphysical claims but their very intelligibility or factual meaningfulness—at the minimum, their usefulness. Such an attack, if justified, would be devastating to the Thomistic form of natural law theory.

Several other critical points arise. What about the basic principle of natural law, the principle of synderesis? Is "good is to be done, evil avoided" a vacuous principle? Could it be made compatible with any ethic or political philosophy, depending on how one defines "good"? Thomas says that man's final end or the meaning of "good" is eternal beatitude or "possession of God." What does this mean? What would this state of affairs be like? If one cannot be any more specific, is the concept vacuous or useless?

The same point can be made in this way: The basic concept in Thomas's theory is "good." A right act is one that is conducive to man's good. This does not mean that the obligation to perform a given act is based merely on utilitarian grounds. If "good" meant only man's natural happiness (the supernatural excluded) and natural law included only those principles requisite for man's self-preservation and well-being, then Thomas's position would be a straightforward utilitarian one, and the metaphysical-theological underpinning would be unnecessary. But "good" means more than this. God's purpose for man is eternal happiness. Acts that lead to this end are right, but they are obligatory because they are made so by God, that is, because they are reflections of the eternal law. Thomas, then, includes both teleological and deontological elements in his theory. But if the terms "eternal happiness," "beatitude," or "possession of God" are not made clear, then we do not know the meaning of "good," Thomas's basic value term. And how can we recognize a right act unless the concept of good itself is clear?

Furthermore, if natural laws are general principles that may be applied variously in different contexts, yielding different subsidiary maxims of action, what happens to the absoluteness they presume to provide? Who can challenge a vacuous principle like "good is to be done, evil avoided"? But if particular specifications of what is good, which differ and perhaps oppose, are justifiable for a Thomist, are the moral and political norms he seeks absolute? Also, on the normative level Thomas subscribes to several moral principles, including "equality of proportion" and the "common good." Could these principles conflict? If so, how would he resolve such conflict?

Concerning Thomas's theory *about* moral and political discourse (his theory of normative knowledge) one must ask what he means by the phrases "flow from" or "based on" when he states that particular norms "flow from" or are "based on" the principle of synderesis? Does he mean logical deduction? If so, are we to view the normative disciplines of ethics and politics as "demonstrative sciences"? If not, what does he mean by "based on"? What is the status of knowledge claims in ethics and political philosophy? These and other questions must be answered in a detailed and careful scrutiny of Thomas's theory. This task is beyond our scope, but it should be clear what some of the problems confronting Thomistic natural law theory are. I now turn to Hobbes's type of natural law theory.

Recommended Readings

Aquinas, St. Thomas. *Aquinas, Selected Political Writings*. Edited by A. P. D'Entreves. Translated by A. G. Dawson. Oxford, 1954.

Aquinas, St. Thomas. *Basic Works of St. Thomas Aquinas*. Edited by Anton C. Regis. 2 vols. New York, 1945.

Copleston, F. C. *A History of Philosophy*. Westminster, Md., 1960.

Copleston, F. C. *Aquinas*. Harmondsworth, England, 1955.

Gilson, Etienne. *The Philosophy of St. Thomas Aquinas*. Freeport, New York, 1971.

McIlwain, C. H. *The Growth of Political Thought in the West from the Greeks to the End of the Middle Ages*. New York, 1932.

Meyer, Hans. *The Philosophy of St. Thomas Aquinas*. St. Louis, 1945.

Troeltsch, Ernst. *The Social Teaching of the Christian Churches*. Translated by Olive Wyon. New York, 1949.

chapter 3
Thomas Hobbes
1588-1679

The son of an Anglican clergyman, Thomas Hobbes was born in the year of the Spanish Armada. He entered Oxford at the age of fifteen, where he was unhappy with the Aristotelian thought in dominance. Subsequently he became a tutor to the powerful Cavendish family, with whom he remained most of his life. Travel on the continent brought him into contact with Galileo and Mersenne, and Hobbes developed a deep interest in philosophy. He decided to write treatises on physical nature, human nature, and society—in that sequence. But political concerns, the disagreement between Charles I and Parliament, prompted him to write on society first. The Citizen *was published in 1642 and* Leviathan *in 1651. Hobbes fled to France during the Civil War; he tutored the Prince of Wales, the future Charles II. His writings on nature,* De Corpore, *were published in 1655 and those on human nature,* De Homine, *in 1658. His views antagonized both religious and civil authorities. Hobbes's political philosophy, his theory of absolute sovereignty, was not an unnatural response to the political anarchy of his time.*

Hobbes's Theory of Human Nature

Hobbes's account of human nature, like that of St. Thomas, is fundamental to both his moral and political theory. He straightforwardly states that the goal of his political philosophy is "to understand

46

what the quality of human nature is, in what matters it is, in what not fit to make up a civil government, and how men must agree amongst themselves that intend to grow up into a well-grounded state." [1]

What is human nature like for Hobbes? Applying the new Galilean scientific outlook to human beings, Hobbes pictured man as a kind of machine which operates deterministically. This goes against the grain of Thomas's teleological view of man and nature. Man, for Hobbes, does not have a built-in final end or purpose. He has a multiplicity of purposes or goals, all of which are determined by the motions of the will, appetite and aversion. Appetite and aversion are components of man's "concupiscible" nature, which makes each of us seek his own goal, his own self-preservation, in whatever he does. One's appetite is toward that which enables him to survive or to have well-being; one's aversion is away from that which harms or threatens. Good and evil, for Hobbes, are not Platonic essences. They are names we apply to things and to actions according to our appetites and aversions: "Whatever is the object of any man's appetite or desire that is it which he for his part calleth good." [2]

All men, then, by nature are egoists and hedonists. "From their very birth, and naturally, [they] scramble for everything they covet, and would have all the world, if they could, to fear and obey them." In this quest for egoistic satisfaction, men perpetually seek power. "I put for a general inclination of all mankind, a perpetual and restless desire of power after power, that ceaseth only in death," Hobbes states, for men realize that such power is necessary for their individual security. Each man competes with all other men for the power to preserve himself and live well. But because not all men can have this power, they resort to contention, enmity, violence, and war.

But man has a side to his nature other than the concupiscible. He is also rational. His reason allows him to see himself as he is and to deduce ways of satisfying his needs and yet avoid the continual individual competition for power that leads to fear, conflict, and war.

The State of Nature

This is what men are like, Hobbes tells us. "The appearances, our pretensions to generosity or to disinterestedness, are," as Richard

---

[1] Thomas Hobbes, *De Cive* (*The Philosophical Rudiments Concerning Government and Society*), in *The English Works of Thomas Hobbes*, ed. Sir William Molesworth, 11 vols. (Aalen: Scientia, 1962), II, xiv.

[2] Thomas Hobbes, *Leviathan*, in Molesworth, *English Works of Hobbes*, III, 41.

Peters puts it, "but cloaks to hide the struggle betweeen pride and fear; the reality beneath is the thrust and recoil of a pleasure-pain calculating machine."[3] Man's reason does not of itself introduce impartiality or obviate his egoism. It does enable him to see how his interests and desires can best be attained and to concern himself with his long-range interests rather than short-term goals.

What is life like in the state of nature, the state in which there are no political institutions and no sovereign? It is almost utter chaos, a state of war in which autonomous egoistic individuals, dominated by the concupiscible element, struggle for power, glory, and security. This struggle, carried on without rules and without any common power to enforce such rules even if they existed, pits man against man. Furthermore, since all men are roughly equal in intelligence and physical strength, with even the weakest being able to out-scheme and kill the strongest, the result is a state of affairs in which there is continual suspicion, fear of violence, and death. Hobbes paints the picture graphically:

> In such condition, there is no place for industry; because the fruit thereof is uncertain: and consequently no culture of the earth, no navigation, nor use of the commodities that may be imported by sea; no commodious building; no instruments of moving, and removing, such things as require much force; no knowledge of the face of the earth; no account of time; no arts; no letters; no society; and which is worst of all, continual fear, and danger of violent death; and the life of man, solitary, poor, nasty, brutish, and short.[4]

Hobbes does not seem to take this state of affairs seriously as a historical occurrence, in spite of his reference to the "savages in America." Rather he is pointing out what *would* be the case if there were no social and political institutions and no powerful sovereign. Even with such institutions and rules, Hobbes asks, do you not lock your doors at night, evidencing your distrust of others? And the same holds true today; do you not check once or twice during a class period, to make sure your billfold is safely secured and buttoned in your pocket? Is it not perfectly plain what conditions would exist if there were no laws against theft and a power to enforce them? Each

[3] Richard Peters, *Hobbes* (Harmondsworth, England: Penguin Books, Ltd., 1956), p. 153.
[4] Thomas Hobbes, *Leviathan*, in Molesworth, *English Works of Hobbes*, III, 113.

of us, in our desire and drive for power and security and for general self-aggrandizement, Hobbes contends, would ravage other persons and their property, and in turn be ravaged.

In this state there are neither rights nor violations of rights. The only "right" is the fact that each man has the "liberty . . . to use his own power, as he will himself, for the preservation of his own nature. . . ." But there are no duties or responsibilities to act in a certain way or to accord one a certain mode of treatment. Nor is there justice or injustice. When there is no law, nothing *can* be unjust. Hobbes therefore declares that in the state of nature "the notions of right and wrong, justice and injustice, have there no place. Where there is no common power, there is no law; where no law, no injustice. Force and fraud are in war the two cardinal virtues." [5] In the state of nature each man has an equal right to everything, extending even to taking another's life if that person threatens his security or well-being. Thus there is not only continual conflict, but that conflict is also irresolvable in principle.

The Social Contract

Men are egoists, but, fortunately, most of them are rational egoists. When they reflect upon their predicament in the state of nature, they recognize that formalized and enforced restraint on their activities is necessary to avoid the state of war. They realize that survival itself requires giving up the total freedom of the state of nature and submitting to some authority. Such is the price of security—of a civilized society. This agreement is the social contract in which each man says: "I authorize and give up my right of governing myself, to this man, or this assembly of men, on this condition, that thou give up thy right to him, and authorize all actions in like manner." [6] The created entity is the commonwealth, the multitude united in one person, the great Leviathan, ". . . that mortal God, to which we owe under the immortal God, our peace and defense." With the contract and the powerful sovereign, justice and rights come into being. This is a conception of political authority quite different from that of the traditional "divine right of kings," for the sovereign receives his authority not from God but from the people through the social contract.

Again, as in the case of Hobbes's talk about the state of nature, we are not to take the social contract seriously as a historical event,

5 Ibid., p 115.
6 Ibid., chap. 17.

although some philosophers did believe that all states were based on a contract like the Mayflower Pact. Just as the state of nature enabled Hobbes to show us what life *would* be like without government, the device of a social contract enabled him to show the logical basis of any kind of government, and to show that the basic rules of political institutions could be deduced from the egoistic nature of man. The rules so deduced he called "laws of nature."

The Laws of Nature

The laws of nature, for Hobbes, are those precepts or rules "found out by Reason, by which a man is forbidden to do that, which is destructive of his life, or taketh away the means of preserving the same; and to omit that, by which he thinketh it may be best preserved." [7] He sometimes calls these precepts "maxims of prudence"; sometimes, "commands of God." They are not created by human governments. Rather they exist in the state of nature and constitute the basis of the social contract and civil law. They are discoverable by any rational man who reflects on the predicament of the state of nature. Although the laws of nature exist in the state of nature, they have little effect on man's conduct until the formation of the social contract. Why is this so? Because unless those rules are agreed upon and enforced by the power of government, it would be foolish for an individual to try to abide by them; for in doing so he would risk his well-being, even his life. Such risk is contrary to the "ground of all laws of nature," namely, the rule of self-preservation. Thus Hobbes insists that these laws in the state of nature oblige only *in foro interno*, not *in foro externo*. That is, they "bind to a desire that they should take place but . . . to the putting them in act, not always." [8]

What are these precepts or laws of nature? Hobbes cites about twenty of them, characterizing them as "eternal and immutable." They range from the very general precept that "man ought to endeavor peace" to the highly particular one that safe-conduct be allowed to peace emissaries. All of them are prescriptions, statements of what ought to be the case, if the state of nature or the state of war and chaos is to be avoided.

The first three laws of nature cited by Hobbes are: (1) "That every man ought to endeavor peace, as far as he has hope of attaining it; and when he cannot obtain it, that he may seek, and use, all

[7] Ibid., chap. 15.
[8] Ibid.

helps and advantages of war." (2) "That a man be willing, when others are so too, as far forth, as for peace, and defense of himself he shall think it necessary, to lay down his right to all things, and be contended with so much liberty against other men, as he would allow other men against himself." (3) "That men perform their covenants made." [9] (1) and (2) provide necessary conditions for the social contract, which itself is necessary if obedience to (3) and the other laws is to be rational. Without the contract such obedience would nearly always be irrational. The laws of nature are not the result of the contract. They are prior to it and are part of the awareness of any rational man; they are eternal and immutable in that such rules are always required for peace and self-preservation, even though the obligation to obey them in the state of nature is merely *in foro interno.*

Absolute Sovereignty

What form of government can best fulfill the intent of the social contract and create the conditions under which it is rational to obey the laws of nature? Hobbes's unqualified answer is an absolute sovereign, one with unlimited, indivisible power and authority. The sovereign, he states, "is the absolute representative of all the subjects, and therefore no other can be representative of any part of them, but so far forth as he shall give leave." [10] Even those who did not sign the contract are obliged to obey him if the majority contracted him as sovereign. If governmental authority is divided, Hobbes contends, the state will speak with a divided voice, and there is great danger of civil strife under those conditions. Democracy, or forms of government in which there is divided authority, are less effective in promoting peace and security or in preventing the return of the state of war.

Civil Disobedience

Is one ever justified in refusing to obey the sovereign? Hobbes replies that because no individual ever gives up his right to self-preservation (given Hobbes's psychological egoism, this would be impossible), one is justified in refusing to obey or in violating the sovereign's laws if they threaten his existence, for preservation of self is "the ground of all of the laws of nature." Of course, in virtue of

9 Ibid., chaps. 14, 15.
10 Ibid., chap. 30.

the contract, the sovereign at the same time is justified in ending your life if in his judgment your continued existence threatens the peace and security of society.

Are there any conditions under which one would be *morally* justified in civil disobedience (in a moral sense of "justified")? What if the instituted sovereign turns out to be a tyrant? Hobbes's answer is that the end for which the sovereign is given his power is the peace and security of the people. The citizen is justified in expecting him to fulfill his role and "the obligation of subjects to the sovereign is understood to last as long, and no longer, than the power lasts by which he is able to protect them." Hobbes here seems to say that a sovereign may be dismissed if he fails to provide protection from violence and death. Such "civil disobedience," however, may be a mere verbal point, for if protection from violence and death are not provided, then are we not back in the state of nature, where, by definition, each man has the right to do whatever he thinks will preserve himself and in which there is really no civil authority to disobey?

Suppose conditions under a tyrant do not degenerate this far. He provides security, but he is cruel, vicious, and inequitable, thereby transgressing the laws of nature. Is one justified in civil disobedience under these conditions? Hobbes does say of sovereigns that "it is their duty in all things, as much as possible they can, to yield obedience unto right reason, which is the Natural, Moral, and Divine Law." [11] Are there, then, certain moral or divine duties which, if violated or left unfulfilled by the sovereign, justify usurpation or revolution? Hobbes's answer, in agreement with Thomas, is no. Though obligated by natural law, the sovereign must "render an account thereof to God, the author of that Law, and to none but Him." To citizens he is accountable only for keeping the peace. "Must we resist princes, when we cannot obey them?" Hobbes asks—when submission is almost intolerable? He answers: "Truly, no: for this is contrary to our civil covenant. What must we do then? Go to Christ by martyrdom." [12] Hobbes's point here is that moral limitations on the authority of the sovereign, or the acceptance of the principle that individuals may disobey the sovereign if his laws transgress their individual moral standards, will simply return us to the state of nature. Sovereignty must be inviolate, even when tyrannical.

Furthermore, Hobbes adds, though the sovereign can be iniqui-

[11] Thomas Hobbes, *The Citizen,* ed. Sterling P. Lamprecht (New York: Appleton-Century-Crofts, 1949), p. 142.
[12] Ibid., p. 208.

tous, he *cannot* commit "injustice, or injury in the proper signification," for justice *means* whatever the sovereign's laws prescribe;
and further, whatever his laws are, they are duly authorized by the
social contract. For the social contract is not a contract between the
subjects and their sovereign but between the subjects themselves,
who irrevocably confer upon him the authority to do whatever, *in his
judgment*, will be conducive to peace and security. The sovereign,
not himself a party to the contract but created by it, commits himself
to nothing whatever—except the preservation of peace and security.

The Rights and Duties of Men

What are the rights and duties of men both before and after the
social contract? Hobbes's answer to this question is not clear. He
states that each of us has a natural right to "everything, even to another's body" in the state of nature. This "natural right" means that
in a world without laws and an enforcer of those laws, there are no
rights or obligations. A right to everything entails a duty to no one.
When the social contract is formed—when one's right or liberty to
everything (or, which comes to the same thing, the right to nothing),
is transferred to the sovereign—rights and duties come into existence;
and they are defined by the sovereign.

However, even in the state of nature there are rights and duties
which hold *in foro interno*. We should endeavor peace. We should
treat others as we would have them treat us. We should not harm
others unless it is required for self-preservation. These laws of nature
hold independently of the social contract and the establishment of a
sovereign. Sometimes characterized as commands of God, they are
not dependent upon the edicts of the sovereign. At least *in foro interno*
then, there are rights and obligations in the state of nature; hence,
in foro interno each of us does not have a right to everything. In this
state each man would *necessarily* be his own judge of what is or is
not a duty. Since there is no state or legal framework, man is here
responsible only to God for obeying or disobeying his commands
(laws of nature). He cannot be responsible to other men *in foro
externo* because the framework for attributing responsibility, the state,
is yet nonexistent. Furthermore, obedience to the laws of nature is
invariably unsafe, and hence irrational, in the state of nature.

Does Hobbes, then, believe in natural rights? If this is taken to
mean that there are obligations *in foro interno* in the state of nature,
then he does. There are rights and obligations not created by govern-

ment. But are rights and obligations *in foro interno* really rights and obligations in any genuine sense? They are merely obligations to desire that certain acts be done, not obligations to do those acts. Thus Hobbes does not hold a natural rights position in the sense of Locke, for example, who holds that even prior to government we are obliged to *do* certain actions, not just desire that they be done. For Hobbes we are obliged to do only one thing; that is, there is only one natural right—that of self-preservation; and since this is a right of each person to everything, it seems to amount to no right at all, in the usual sense in which this word is used.

What rights and duties do men have after the social contract? Always a man retains his right to preserve himself and to resist anyone who seeks to harm or imprison him, even if this be the sovereign. Aside from this "right" (which is psychologically impossible to give up but which need not be honored by the sovereign), the citizen has no rights other than the ones which the sovereign sees fit to give: "The liberty of a subject, lieth only in those things, which in regulating their actions, the sovereign hath pretermitted." [13] Here a man may do as he pleases. But man has no inherent or inalienable rights. To the sovereign belongs "the whole power of prescribing the rules, whereby every man may know what goals he may enjoy and what actions he may do without being molested by any of his fellow-subjects." The sovereign is even to be the "judge of what opinions and doctrines are averse, and what conducing to peace." Freedom of speech, assembly, of association, and of religion are rights only if the sovereign permits them. If, in the judgement of the sovereign, any given activity threatens the peace, it can justifiably be curtailed. This power and authority is granted by the contract.

Duties to God and Sovereign

What is the relationship between one's duties to God and to the sovereign? Does all obligation to the sovereign rest upon man's prior obligation to God?—so that the ultimate grounds of all rights and duties is God's will? Hobbes does say that the laws of nature are properly laws because they are commands of God, and this is what makes them obligatory (*in foro interno*). That men should keep their covenants is one of these laws in virtue of which the social contract, and hence the existence of the sovereign, is established. So one might say that for Hobbes the obligation to obey the sovereign rests on a

[13] Hobbes, *Leviathan*, in Molesworth, *English Works of Hobbes*, III, chap. 21.

prior obligation to God. But in fact Hobbes often speaks of the laws of nature simply as prudential rules, seemingly forgetting about them as commands of God. With God out of the picture, the obligation to obey the sovereign rests only on the social contract and upon the fact that the prudential interests of men are enhanced by legal enactment and enforcement of the law of nature.

One must add, however, that even with God in the picture, Hobbes's psychological egoism forces us to view one's obligation even to God as a prudential "ought." Men are so structured that they *must* do that which is in their own interest, so we must obey God's laws because of fear of punishment or hope of reward. Hobbes is frequently criticized for never distinguishing between moral and prudential "oughts" and for leaving out all genuine moral obligation, a sense of obligation which involves an *impartial* point of view. Theorists other than Hobbes have held that it is prudential to obey God's law, but they insist that this is not the total basis of the obligation. Independently of one's fears and hopes, such obedience is obligatory because the acts prescribed are right. This sense of "ought" is logically impossible in Hobbes's theory because of his thoroughgoing psychological egoism. Thus critique of its absence requires a critique of his account of man.

Critique

What are the problems confronting Hobbes's theory? In the first place, there is the problem of being clear about his position. Hobbes uses the language of natural law, but how well does he fit into this classification? He does speak of the laws of nature as being eternal and immutable, but with his emphasis upon them as rules of prudence discovered by reflecting upon man's predicament in the state of nature, they do not seem to have the status of *moral* facts discovered by reason (as in Cicero, St. Thomas, and Locke). They are merely prudential facts.

Whether there are moral facts for Hobbes is tied to his account of obligation, which is itself tied to his theory of man. All obligation *must* be prudential, for all men are psychological egoists. They always do that which is in their own interest, even if it be their long-range interests. This means that no man *could* ever act with *impartiality*, and if the principle of impartiality is essential to moral obligation, then there can be no genuine moral obligations in Hobbes's theory, and further, no genuine moral facts or rules. It must be said, however, that even if the laws of nature are commands of God to be followed for prudential reasons only, these laws still constitute a measure for evaluating the enacted laws of the sovereign. To this extent Hobbes is in agreement with Thomas.

This analysis and critique of Hobbes's account of obligation presupposes that his thesis of psychological egoism is false, for only then is impartiality possible. Are men totally selfish? Is everything they do a result of self-love? Certainly some actions are selfish, but we do speak of unselfish, altruistic action. Is this mere rationalization? Not so, if Bishop Butler and others are correct.[14] Men are benevolent, altruistic, and impartial on many occasions and our language must and does reflect this fact.

This point is also tied to Hobbes's account of man's rationality. Does not rationality itself imply more than the ability to apply names to things and to calculate? Does it not imply a kind of impartiality, an ability to evaluate evidence *disinterestedly?* This, if true, is also an argument against his psychological egoism.[15]

What about Hobbes's argument for absolute monarchy? If political authority is divided, he tells us, it will lead to chaos and back to the state of war. But are there not many examples of government in which authority is divided among different branches in which this is simply not true? Furthermore, are there not many cases of absolute monarchy which degenerated into absolute tyrannies? Locke warns us to learn from these historical experiences. Would not democracy, with divided authority and methods of impeaching rulers, be better, not only for avoiding tyranny but also violent revolution? Hobbes thinks not. He so fears the reemergence of the state of nature that he is willing to tolerate tyranny and the suppression of individual liberties. Is this threat as strong as Hobbes thinks? (Perhaps at his time it was.) Perhaps if he had not conceived of man as a psychological egoist he would not have thought it so severe. But even so, is it not better to run the risk of some chaos, even civil war, than exist under an arbitrary tyrant?

These are the kinds of questions which must be answered in evaluating Hobbes's political philosophy. To be sure the political situation at his time was near chaotic and his emphasis on stability and security is understandable in the light of those circumstances. Furthermore, if we accept his theory of man, his psychological egoism, his account

---

[14] Bishop Joseph Butler, *Fifteen Sermons Upon Human Nature* (London: Macmillan, 1726), Sermon XI, Section 7.

[15] Richard Peters, *Hobbes*, p. 175.

of obligation, his characterization of the state of nature and so on, then his political conclusions are reasonable. Here, of course, is the rub. Are these beliefs acceptable? An adequate evaluation of Hobbes requires a careful consideration of this entire package of beliefs.

Recommended Readings

Bowle, John. *Hobbes and His Critics: A Study in Seventeenth Century Constitutionalism*. London, 1969.

Brandt, F. *Thomas Hobbes' Mechanical Conception of Nature*. London, 1928).

Catlin, George. *Thomas Hobbes as Philosopher, Publicist and Man of Letters*. Oxford, 1922.

Laird, J. *Hobbes*. New York, 1968. Reprint of the 1934 edition.

Peters, Richard. *Hobbes*. Baltimore, 1956.

Strauss, Leo. *The Political Philosophy of Hobbes, Its Basis and Its Genesis*. Chicago, 1952.

Warrender, Howard. *The Political Philosophy of Hobbes; His Theory of Obligation*. Oxford, 1957.

chapter 4
John Locke
1632-1704

John Locke was born in Somerset, attended the Westminster School in London, and studied at Christ Church, Oxford, where he later became a tutor. He was interested in science and medicine as well as philosophy, and served as the personal physician of the Earl of Shaftesbury who became the Lord Chancellor of England. He became involved in Shaftesbury's political activities and assisted him in drawing up a constitution for the Carolinas, but, when Shaftesbury's opposition to the monarchy led to his dismissal, Locke was forced to flee to Holland. After six years (and the deposition of James II) Locke returned and was appointed to several high political offices, concluding his political career as Commissioner of Trade and Plantations.

Locke is best known for his Essay Concerning Human Under-standing, *written over a period of nearly two decades but not published until 1690, and* The Two Treatises of Civil Government *published in 1690 but written before his departure for Holland and generally seen as a justification for the rebellion against Charles II. Locke's political philosophy explicitly limited the power of government and defended a doctrine of inalienable rights. His impact on American political thought is well-known.*

The State of Nature

Locke, like Hobbes, begins his political philosophy by speaking of the state of nature:

58

To understand political power aright, and derive it from its original, we must consider what state all men are naturally in, and that is a state of perfect freedom to order their actions and dispose of their possessions and persons as they think fit, within the bounds of the law of nature, without asking leave or depending upon the will of any other man.[1]

Thus far he agrees with Hobbes. The state of nature is a state of "perfect freedom," a state in which there is no central power or jurisdiction. Locke insists, however, that it is "not a state of license." "The state of nature," he asserts, "has a law of nature to govern it, which obliges every one; and reason, which is that law, teaches all mankind who will but consult it, that being all equal and independent, no one ought to harm another in his life, health, liberty, or possessions." [2] Here Locke parts with Hobbes. In the state of nature, men are not pure egoists ready to butcher one another if need be. They are rational and moral beings who exist under the law of nature, a set of rights and obligations which are self-evident to all rational creatures. In general, men conform to these obligations even in the state of nature. Therefore, Locke does not speak of this state as a state of war, as one in which life is "solitary, poor, nasty, brutish, and short," as does Hobbes. He admits that it may become a state of war, because there is no common authority or objective judge. "The execution of the law of nature is in that state put into every man's hand whereby everyone has a right to punish the transgressors of that law. . . ." [3] In this state, "force without right, upon a man's person, makes a state of war." A common authority is necessary, he declares, because it is unreasonable for men to judge their own cases. When one's own interests are involved, it is difficult to be objective and impartial. If confusion and disorder, that is, the possibility of a state of war, are to be avoided, a "common superior on earth with authority to judge" is required. Thus, though all men even in the state of nature are bound by the law of nature, which prescribes equality of treatment for men, nonetheless, men must contract to submit to political authority to insure that order, security and equality prevail.

[1] John Locke, *Second Treatise of Civil Government*, chapter 2, para. 4 (1690). The edition used here is that of The Library of Liberal Arts (Indianapolis: Bobbs-Merrill, Inc.), Introduction by Thomas P. Peardon, 1952.

[2] Ibid., para. 6.

[3] Ibid., para. 7.

The Social Contract

Locke's description of the social contract is similar to Hobbes's. "Wherever therefore, any number of men so unite into one society, as to quit everyone his executive power of the Law of Nature, to resign it to the public, there, and there only, is a political, or civil society." [4] With the contract one authorizes others to make laws which one agrees to obey, laws which are designed to preserve one's life, liberty, and property. One gives up certain rights, in particular his personal "executive power," his right to punish others for what, in his judgment, constitutes a violation of the natural law. Henceforth, only the state can do this. But men do not give up all of their rights to the government when they contract, as they do with Hobbes (excepting self-preservation). Certain rights remain inviolate. Morally, they cannot be encroached upon by government. The device of the social contract enables Locke not only to explain and stress the fact that political authority rests on the consent of the governed, that one's obligation to obey political authority rests on one's own agreement, but also to stress that government is set up in order to insure the continued existence of certain natural rights—freedom, equality, and property.

Natural Rights

Unlike Hobbes who put no restrictions on political authority and who so feared the return of the state of nature that he was willing to restrict any and all human liberties, Locke insists that the instituted government protect man's natural rights. The very purpose of the contract is "an intention in everyone the better to preserve himself, his liberty and property," and "the power of the society or the legislative constituted by them, can never be supposed to extend further than the common good, but is obligated to secure everyone's property by providing against those defects" [5] of the state of nature. Natural rights, and in particular property rights, must become legal rights after the contract, and the state must see that they are secure. This is the duty of government.

What are these natural or moral rights which exist in the state of

[4] Ibid., para. 89.
[5] Ibid., para. 131.

nature and which become legal rights after political authority is established? And what is their order of importance? Locke states that "the great and chief end of men's uniting into commonwealths, and putting themselves under government, is the preservation of their property," [6] so the natural right to property appears to be fundamental. But he uses the term "property" in a very broad as well as a narrow sense. In the narrower sense, one's right to property is one's right to the exclusive use of certain objects and materials. In the broad sense it is roughly equivalent, it seems, to all of man's natural rights. "The mutual preservation of their lives, liberties, and estates . . . I call by the general name, property." [7] So we could read Locke here as saying that "the great and chief end" of government is the preservation of man's natural rights. Property in this broad sense is obviously fundamental, for it seems to embrace all the other natural rights.

On the other hand, Locke treats equality also as a fundamental natural right. "All men are by nature equal," Locke says, and "that equal right that every man hath to his natural freedom . . . was the equality I then spoke of." [8] "The sum of all we drive at," he declares, "is that every man enjoys the same rights that are granted to others." [9] Those natural rights that men share are life, liberty and property (narrow sense). Put negatively, the fundamental right—equality—means that there are no grounds for discriminating between human beings in regard to the possession of the rights to life, liberty, and property. All equally have them.

For Locke all of these natural rights are self-evident. They arise from man's nature and all rational men recognize them. These natural rights, however, are very general, indeed almost formal, and have little substantive content until particularized to some context. Just what specifically is entailed by the principle of equality in Locke's theory? Does Locke believe in political equality?—that all humans should have the franchise? No. He limits the franchise. Does he believe in social and economic equality? Not in the sense that all persons must be treated exactly alike, for he holds that there are certain characteristics or qualities which justify extending certain social and economic rights to some persons and denying them to others. Perhaps

[6] Ibid., para. 124.
[7] Ibid., para. 123.
[8] Ibid., para. 54.
[9] John Locke, *A Letter Concerning Toleration,* ed. J. W. Gough (Oxford: Basil Blackwell, 1948), p. 159.

such differential treatment can be shown to be consistent with the commitment to equality. But such questions must be answered before we can understand Locke's (or anyone else's) endorsement or subscription to equality.

What is entailed by the natural right to freedom? Though freedom is an absolute right, it is not unlimited (just as equality does not necessarily mean identical treatment of persons). The whole point of the social contract is to restrict freedom. Everything depends, however, on the criteria accepted as justifying grounds for the restriction of human actions. What is Locke's criterion? He offers "the common good." But surely this phrase is somewhat vague. For example, is compulsory education for children up to sixteen years of age, i.e., a restriction on the freedom of the child and parents, for "the common good"? Is the restriction on the sale of narcotics, the freedom to purchase dope of different types, for the common good? What are the limitations on freedom? In the case of Locke the notion of "the common good" as a criterion must be elucidated.

Similar problems arise in regard to the natural right to property, in the sense of one's right to the exclusive use of certain objects and materials. Locke states that originally God gave all property to mankind in common. But in order for this property to be of any use to man, it must be altered and turned into some sort of consumable commodity. By such alteration, does every man have an unlimited right to everything under the sun? Locke does say that "whatsoever, then, he removes out of the state that nature hath provided and left it in, he hath mixed his labor with, and joined to it something that is his own, and thereby makes it his property." [10] Suppose, then, you have mixed your labor with something. According to Locke, this gives you the property right to it. Now suppose someone else comes along and mixes his labor with it. Is the property now jointly owned? Or does the person who first mixed his labor with it retain the exclusive right to it? Locke seems to hold the latter (though those who later emphasized labor and the labor theory of value offered quite different conclusions from those of Locke). He also goes on to add the following qualification: "As much land as a man tills, plants, improves, cultivates, and can use the products of, so much is his property." [11] Locke is thinking of agricultural property here, but his restriction on property ownership is plain. Mixing your labor

[10] Locke, *Second Treatise of Civil Government*, para. 27.
[11] Ibid., para. 32.

with something gives you a right to it as property, but no matter how much you mix your labor with certain things in nature, you should own no more than you can use—"to any advantage of life." Ownership which involves waste or which is nonproductive or non-useful, which does not contribute "to any advantage of life," is to be prohibited. But again, everything depends upon how this criterion is interpreted. What is to be meant by "useful" or "any advantage of life"? This criterion is exceedingly general and becomes more so when Locke later adds that "a man may rightfully and without injury possess more than he himself can make use of by receiving gold and silver, which may continue long in a man's possession, without decaying for the overplus, and agreeing those metals should have a value." [12] The notions of "use," "advantage," or "waste" in a context of purely agricultural property are quite different than in a context of property with money. In the latter, "use" or "advantage" involves capital investment. This would appear to stretch Locke's criterion in such a way that property ownership is unlimited, perhaps making Locke's criterion itself useless; for one can accumulate and reinvest capital almost ad infinitum in a productive, non-wasteful way.

Natural rights, then, are general normative principles which hold for all men. What specific actions or policies of action they prescribe is not clear. This is true, of course, of any general principle. But even as broad, nonspecific principles, they are not entirely vacuous; they certainly emphasize the importance of man's freedom and the value of the individual, in a way not to be found in Hobbes. To be sure Hobbes leaves a wide range of activity completely without government restrictions, but he does not, as Locke does, maintain that there are certain inherent, natural rights which not only must not be encroached upon by political authority but also must be protected by that authority.

Government By Consent

What are the grounds of moral and political obligations for Locke? Moral obligations exist both in and outside of the state of nature and are grounded on man's natural rights (the inherent rightness of equality and freedom) and on general utilitarian considerations. What about political obligations? These rest on the overt or tacit consent of the individual citizen, his agreement to obey the laws of

12 Ibid., para. 50.

the political authority duly constituted by the social contract. Political authority without such consent is not legitimate authority.

What does Locke mean by consent? He uses this word in both a narrow and a wide sense. The former involves a deliberate choice. "Whatever engagements or promises any one made for himself, he is under the obligation of them, but cannot by any compact whatsoever bind his children or posterity." [13] Each person, to be politically obligated, must deliberately consent to authority. But Locke goes on to say that consent may be given simply by inheriting property or by being born under a given government and coming "to be of age." In the narrow sense, few of us ever consent to government, hence few of us would ever be under obligation to political authority. This is surely an unwelcome conclusion and perhaps it is the reason Locke extended the meaning of consent. But in the wider sense, does not everyone always consent to government? If so, this means that any and every government is legitimate, and consequently, that consent is useless as a criterion for distinguishing legitimate from illegitimate political authority.

Locke is concerned that government not be oppressive and that it function as a trust used in the interest of men. Obedience he wants to make conditional upon the proper use of that trust. If consent can be given a meaningful interpretation, Locke does give us a criterion of legitimacy; for he says that "the majority have a right to act and conclude the rest." [14] Government is legitimate if it has the consent of the majority. This criterion may be his way of emphasizing the fundamental natural right to equality—the equal right of each man to life, liberty, and property. If political authority does not have majority support, it is illegitimate. Locke assumes that a government which has majority support will not be "absolutely arbitrary over the lives and fortunes of the people." It will not rule by arbitrary degrees but will dispense justice by standing laws and authorized judges, and will act for the common good.

Civil Disobedience

Suppose a government is tyrannical and deprives men of their freedom. Do men have a right of civil disobedience or, indeed, of revolution? Neither St. Thomas nor Hobbes allowed this. Locke, however, states that "the community perpetually retains a supreme

[13] Ibid., para. 116.
[14] Ibid., para. 95.

power of saving themselves from the attempts and designs of anybody, even of their legislators whenever they should be so foolish or so wicked as to lay and carry on designs against the liberties and properties of the subject. . . ." [15] Citizens may certainly dismiss rulers who violate or do not protect their natural rights to liberty and property. If dismissal cannot be accomplished through legal channels with peaceful means, do citizens have the moral right to use force and violence? Locke answers: "And where the body of the people, or any single man, are deprived of their right, or are under the exercise of a power without right, having no appeal on earth, they have a liberty to appeal to Heaven whenever they judge the cause of sufficient moment." [16]

If this "appeal to Heaven" is not simply an appeal to prayer, as it seems to be in St. Thomas, but an appeal to force, then Locke does permit forceful revolution by either "the people" or individuals when the state deprives them of their rights. He does, however, insist that such action is justified only if the deprived citizen or people have "no appeal on earth." Prior to civil disobedience or revolution, the citizen must exhaust every avenue of orderly and peaceful change. Furthermore, such drastic action is justified only if the injustices and general societal conditions are so bad that it is clear that the best consequences for society require it.

Locke insists that no government has absolute authority, for "the law of nature stands an eternal rule to all men, legislators as well as others." [17] For Locke, that law appears under the guise of the natural rights of life, liberty and property. Unlike Hobbes, he believes that tyranny and suppression of those rights are always a worse evil than civil disobedience or, indeed, revolution.

Limited, Representative Government

For Locke, what form of government is best? What form of government best guarantees man's natural rights? He states that "if government is to be the remedy of those evils which necessarily follow from men's being judges in their own cases, and the state of nature is therefore not to be endured, I desire to know what kind of government that is, and how much better it is than the state

15 Ibid., para. 149.
16 Ibid., para. 168.
17 Ibid., para. 135.

of nature. . . ." [18] But Locke does not specify in any great detail what kind of government is most desirable. Government by consent it must be. But this leaves open a wide range of governments—monarchy, aristocracy, democracy. Locke does not explicitly argue for democracy, though it would seem that his commitment to the equality principle would push him in this direction. He seems to accept a limited franchise and an aristocracy, at least for his time. He does recommend that there be an elected legislature, though he does not make this a necessary condition of government by consent. He also recommends the separation of the executive and legislative branches of government, as a device for limiting governmental power.

Critique

There are a number of problems in Locke's theory. In contrast to Hobbes, he seems to take the social contract seriously as a historical event. He may have generalized from the example of the American colonies, but he admits that there is no evidence for the original contract. Is such a contract necessary to explain political obligation, as Locke thinks? It seems not. Furthermore, we have seen that Locke's notion of "consent" to the contract and to government is so broad that it includes simply existing under a government or receiving the smallest benefit from it. This leaves the notion of consent so general that it has little use.

What about the status of Locke's claim that men have natural rights? He sometimes speaks of these rights as descriptive properties which all men have. All men are equal in the state of nature—all have an equal right to life, liberty, and property. Is this an empirical thesis about men or is it a moral prescription? Locke clearly takes his natural law—natural right thesis to be a truth-claim, in fact a self-evident truth. Natural rights are moral facts and prescriptions for action which may be discovered by reflecting on the nature of man. As laws of God they are eternal. This kind of straightforward cognitivist meta-ethic and its theological basis requires defense. Furthermore, he does not seem to be consistent in this theory, for in Book II of his *Essay Concerning Human Understanding* he characterizes obligation as a "mixed mode." Mixed modes have no "archetypes in nature." They are human constructions, whereas natural law certainly has an archetype in nature, being God's eternal law.

18 Ibid., para. 13.

We have seen that the natural rights—equality, freedom, and property—are very general principles. What they entail for action depends upon interpretation and application in various contexts. The vagueness, perhaps uselessness, of Locke's criterion for limiting the natural right to property has been noted. A further problem is the possible conflict between the natural rights of some citizens and those of others. Locke knew that property and freedom, even life itself, were closely related. One cannot preserve his life without property, so without property this right is restricted. Neither can one plan his life and live it as he sees fit, i.e., have freedom, without property. How free are you to do what you want without the goods to do it with? Picture yourself without one item, a mode of transportation. Is your freedom restricted?

Suppose even further that conditions are such that you are unable to acquire property. The property rights of others have been so extended and your abilities and opportunities are such that you cannot exercise your natural right to property. One could say that you still have the natural right to property even though it is not possible for you to exercise it. But is not this a way of saying that you do not have this right? What do Locke's principles entail under such conditions? Is he committed to saying that ownership and control of property that results in denying others the possibility of fulfilling their natural right to property is unjust? If, even in the midst of such wealthy owners, there were yet more property available for expropriation—for "labor-mixing"—then this natural right would not be denied. But the point is that under certain circumstances the natural right to property of some persons may conflict with the same right in others. And since one's natural right to freedom is so intimately tied to one's property rights, this also means that under certain circumstances the natural right to freedom of some persons conflicts with the same right in others. And (carrying the causal and logical connections yet further) because the natural right of equality is the equal right to life, freedom and property, this means that one's natural right to equality may conflict under certain circumstances with the same right in others.

Locke's theory is that the principal role of government is to preserve man's natural rights and to create the conditions where these rights can be made secure. This means the natural rights of *all* men, not just some of them. But Locke, aware as he was of the unequal distribution of wealth, of the relationship between wealth and freedom and between wealth and equality of treatment, does not suggest that wealth be redistributed or that certain minimum conditions of living be assured for each person. In practice perhaps this would have been impossible in his day. He seems to assume that only a part of society can in fact fully exercise their natural rights. But he claims them for all men, and if the function of political authority is to insure the conditions for the exercise of these rights for *all*, then on Locke's premises, is not such redistribution justified? Is not the restriction of the property rights of some, and, consequently, of their freedom, justified if such restriction is required in order to allow other men the opportunity to exercise their natural rights? Though Locke himself does not suggest this, it seems to follow from his premises. Indeed, this is what the socialists have argued. Genuine equality and freedom can be assured only with such restrictions. Since the seventeenth century, these rights have been severely restricted—what with the income tax, inheritance tax, public schools, social security, and so on. It has been recognized that the uneducated and the propertyless cannot be free, that the unrestricted exercise of the rights to property by the wealthy can in effect deny these rights to others. Thus these rights have been extended in part by taking certain property rights out of the hands of individuals and vesting them in the public community.

Where is the line to be drawn? How far in the direction of a welfare state must government go? There is no easy or straightforward answer to this question. Decisions must be made on specific policies in specific contexts. But it is clear that strong government control, the vesting of property rights in the community as opposed to the individual, while extending some rights, may curtail others—in particular, the freedom of everyone. Locke, with his emphasis on individual freedom, would have us beware of this fact. Government must protect our rights, but it must be limited. His emphasis on these rights and liberties and on limited government makes him a key philosophical forerunner of liberalism and democracy, and his impact on the founders of the American republic is well known.

Recommended Readings

Gough, J. W. *John Locke's Political Philosophy*. Oxford, 1950.
Gough, J. W. *The Social Contract*. Oxford, 1957.

Lamprecht, S. P. *The Moral and Political Philosophy of John Locke.* New York, 1962.

Laski, Harold J. *Political Thought in England from Locke to Bentham.* London, 1920.

von Leyden, W., ed. *John Locke: Essays On The Law of Nature.* Oxford, 1954.

O'Connor, D. J. *Locke.* Baltimore, 1952.

Conclusion

Clearly there are problems with the natural law theories of St. Thomas, Hobbes and Locke. We will not recount those problems here. Nor will we attempt an evaluation of the entire spectrum of norms and policies advocated by these theorists. Such evaluation, at least of basic principles, must be a part of an adequate political philosophy, and, to some extent, it will be attempted in the last chapter of this volume. At this time we will concentrate on the conceptual, ontological or metaphysical, and epistemological issues confronting natural law theory.

A basic difficulty is the theory that human nature has an eternal essence, from which natural laws are presumably derived, and the accompanying theory that moral norms are embedded in reality. Does man have an essence, some unique, essential characteristics and functions or purposes which makes him what he is? And do moral judgments describe features of reality? The natural law theorist affirms both of these theses, and he generally points to reason as the essential component of human nature—as the faculty which enables man to discover moral truths about reality. But how far does this appeal to reason go in distinguishing man from other animals? Some philosophers argue that man has no such essence, that "if from human nature we abstract talents, dispositions, character, intelligence, and all the possible grounds of distinction, we are left with an undifferentiated potentiality." [1] On this analysis, human nature is not a specific quality which all men equally possess, but a potentiality for a certain range of qualities and experience.

[1] S. I. Benn and R. S. Peters, *The Principles of Political Thought* (New York: Collier Books, 1964), p. 125. Originally published in 1959 as *Social Principles and the Democratic State* (London: Allen and Unwin).

If this is so, how do we extract natural laws, that is, moral principles, from human nature? Even supposing there to be some quality(s) constitutive of human nature, the natural law theorist must show that those norms or principles can be validly inferred from the existence of those qualities. But, further, there is no consensus on the meaning of "human nature." Consequently, some argue that moral and political philosophers have simply built into that concept their own moral and political preferences, that the so-called deduction or derivation of norms for conduct from human nature actually is a circular process, and that there is no noncircular way of showing that certain functions and activities are essential to what it means to be a human being and that others are nonessential.[2] They argue that the attempt of the natural law theorist to provide an ontological foundation for certain moral and political norms by invoking an essentialistic theory of human nature is itself a surreptitious or disguised moral theory. The terms "man" and "human nature"—indeed, even "reason"—are not merely descriptive but evaluative; and when natural law theorists set forth their apparent "descriptions" of man and nature, they are also propounding norms for behavior.

When natural law theory is placed in a theological setting, additional problems arise. The questions of God's existence, his attributes, and his purposes are involved. To the extent that natural moral laws are made to rest on such religious beliefs, a rather large Pandora's box of theological perplexities must be opened and confronted.[3]

The great and persistent appeal of the theory of natural law has been that it provides objective support for certain fundamental moral and political norms. But, is it the case that if one rejects the epistemology of morals and the accompanying metaphysic of natural law theorists, one must also give up the belief in certain basic moral and political norms? Must these norms be seen as ontologically embedded to be justified? Put in another way, does the rejection of moral and political realism commit us to moral and political relativism and nihilism? Some theorists appear to think so.[4] But surely such conclusions are not logically entailed by this rejection. There are other

---

[2] Frederick Olafson, "Essence and Concept in Natural Law Theory," in Sidney Hook, ed., *Law and Philosophy* (New York: New York University Press, 1964). Also see my article, "On The Meaning and Justification of the Equality Principle," *Ethics*, Vol. 77, No. 4 (July, 1967).

[3] For a detailed treatment of this Pandora's box, see my *The Problem of Religious Knowledge* (Englewood Cliffs, N.J.: Prentice-Hall, Inc., 1963).

[4] For example, see John Hallowell's *The Moral Foundation of Democracy* (Chicago: University of Chicago Press, 1954).

grounds for subscribing to basic moral and political norms, as the utilitarian and the historicist make clear. Theorists can and do differ in their analyses of the epistemological status of moral and political norms—their status as knowledge-claims—without disagreeing on the norms themselves. None of these theories about the status of moral or political norms, including the emotive theory of value, entails moral nihilism and chaos, nor for that matter, moral utopia and order. As Richard Gale points out, we cannot blame the Nazi war crimes on the Vienna Circle, a group of philosophers who subscribed to the emotive theory of value.[5] Nor, we might add, can we attribute the civil rights movement to the metaethic of John Locke and other natural law theorists.

Even though there is no direct or necessary connection between one's normative moral and political theory or practice and one's theory about the epistemological status of moral and political norms, an adequate political philosophy must offer a theory about the status of these norms. We have suggested some problems confronting the account of the natural law theorist, but this is not to say that that theory is totally incorrect. Perhaps there is a sense in which moral facts do exist and in which moral and political normative judgments refer to those facts. Perhaps there is also a sense in which human nature is the basis for moral and political norms. If these senses can be articulated, some modified form of natural law may be correct. Such a form, containing what seems to be an important kernel of truth, will be treated in the final chapter of this book.

Thus, despite its difficulties, there may be much in natural law theory that is important for moral and political theory. This tradition, perhaps properly, maintains that some obligations are binding independently of consequences or, at least, binding not merely because of consequences. In this sense it differs radically from the utilitarian tradition (a difference which will be made clearer in the next chapter). The issue of whether all duties and obligations can be reduced to a utilitarian base is still a controversial one, but there are reasons and arguments for denying such a reductionism—as is made clear by a great deal of contemporary moral and political theory.

Furthermore, the natural law tradition, in emphasizing the right of self-preservation or the natural right to life and liberty, emphasizes factors and rules which must be fundamental to any ethical or political system. If men are to survive and live satisfactory and

[5] Richard Gale, "Natural Law and Human Rights," *Philosophy and Phenomenological Research*, Vol. 20 (1959–60), 528.

meaningful lives, certain rules must be observed. Many of the normative claims of the natural law theorists have this end in view. Social anthropologists point out that such rules are found in all known societies, and that without them society is not possible. This is the point of Locke's emphasis on property rights. Without such rights and obligations, society would crumble. Thus even if the ontological grounds offered by the natural law theorist do not help him justify his moral and political norms, the rights and norms which he stresses are fundamental in the sense that they express "the only set of reciprocally applicable priorities that most people are really prepared to live by . . . ," norms which can be rejected "only on pain of abandoning a whole sector of human activity and discourse, which in this case would be the enterprise of cooperative social living." There is much to be said, on pragmatic grounds alone, for some of the norms emphasized in the natural law tradition.

Finally, is not the natural law theorist obviously correct in emphasizing that not all of the laws of political society are acceptable? In the face of the Nazi system, few would deny this. The laws of society must surely be subject to continuous moral scrutiny, and St. Thomas and Locke would have us be acutely aware of that fact.

Recommended Readings

d'Entreves, A. P. *Natural Law*. London, 1951.
Hallowell, John. *The Moral Foundation of Democracy*. Chicago, 1954.
Lewis, E. *Medieval Political Ideas*. New York, 1954.
Ritchie, D. G. *Natural Rights*. London, 1903.
Sidney, Hook, ed. *Law and Philosophy*. New York, 1964.
Strauss, Leo. *Natural Right and History*. Chicago, 1953.

6 Olafson, "Essence and Concept in Natural Law Theory," 240.

Model 2:
The Utilitarianism
Theory
of the
State

Introduction

We saw in our discussion of Model One that natural law theory is sometimes compared to a harlot who is at the disposal of everyone. As Alf Ross states, "The ideology does not exist that cannot be defended by an appeal to the law of nature." The principle of utility is hardly less of a harlot. Nearly every form of government, from totalitarianism to democracy, and nearly every policy of action from revolution to maintaining the status quo has been justified under this banner. Thus there are many differences of opinion among the classical utilitarian theorists—Jeremy Bentham, John Stuart Mill, David Hume, Henry Sidgwick, John Austin, and others—on what the principle of utility justifies. All of them agree, however, that the norm of utility, the production of the greatest happiness for the greatest number, constitutes the fundamental norm for all moral and political decisions. They agree that all morally and politically relevant considerations are *ultimately reducible* to the principle of utility and that this principle provides an objective standard for moral and political evaluation. All reject the theory of natural law and that of the social contract as essential to understanding moral and political obligation.

I hasten to qualify these remarks. Utility for each theorist is fundamental, but Hume differs substantially from Mill and Bentham, and Mill differs considerabiy from Bentham. Justice, and the rules and institutions of justice, are ultimately grounded on their *usefulness* or their utility for Hume, because principles of cooperation are necessary if human beings are each to fulfill their interests and needs. For Hume justice itself is not merely an application of the principle of utility, as Bentham and Mill held. Hume, in general, prefers to speak of a right act as one which would be approved by an "impartial spectator." More than just a hedonistic calculus, that is, a method of calculating the pleasurable or painful consequences of an act, is required for correct evaluation of personal conduct or of social and political policies. In this regard Hume is closer to Mill than to Bentham; for Mill appealed to the judgment of a "wise and experienced man," not merely to a calculus or slide rule of consequences. In spite of these differences, these theorists are all properly characterized as utilitarians.

There are also differences among these classical theorists on the epistemological grounds of the norm of utility. Bentham and Mill are empiricists in approach. They reject metaphysical and theological appeals for justification, deny that the norm of utility can be proved, and then, perhaps inconsistently, attempt to justify it by reference to an account of human nature. Sidgwick argues that the principle of utility is true on the grounds that it is a rational intuition. Hume seems to vacillate between the view that moral judgments and principles are empirical truths (statements of what people approve at a given time), the view that they assert nothing at all (their function is emotive only, since they are neither "matters of fact" nor "relations of ideas") and the view that they state (when correct) what an "impartial spectator" would approve.

For our purposes we will concentrate on the views of Bentham and Mill. They are widely recognized as constituting the hard core of the utilitarian tradition. An examination of their theories will make clear both the advantages and disadvantages of the utilitarian approach to political philosophy.

chapter 5
Jeremy Bentham
1748-1832

*The son of a well-to-do London family, Jeremy Bentham was
educated at Westminster School in London and attended Oxford. Early
in his life he decided to concentrate on both the theoretical and practical reconstruction of the law of England. His work on the theory
of legislation, prison reform, and government efficiency became well
known during his life. He was the recognized intellectual leader of the
Radicals, a political group that heavily influenced social and political
events in nineteenth-century England. A prolific writer, Bentham's
most important works are* A Fragment on Government *(1776),*
Principles of Morals and Legislation *(1802), and* Principles of the
Constitutional Code *(1880). Famous for his effort to introduce scientific
precision into morality and politics, Bentham's political philosophy was
responsible for massive changes in both political theory and practice.*

Human Nature and Hedonism

Bentham, like the natural law theorists, attempts to base his moral
and political philosophy upon a theory of the nature of man. But that
theory is not metaphysical, he claims. Unlike St. Thomas and Locke,
he does not assume that man has a unique essence. On the contrary,
Bentham's theory is purely descriptive. What does he find when he
examines human nature? He finds that "Nature has placed mankind
under the governance of two sovereign masters, pain and pleasure. It
is for them alone to point out what we ought to do, as well as to

determine what we shall do. On the one hand the standard of right and wrong, on the other the chain of causes and effects, are fastened to their throne. . . . The principle of utility recognizes this subjection, and assumes it for the foundation of that system, the object of which is to rear the fabric of felicity by the hands of reason and law." [1]

Bentham here says that man is a psychological hedonist. Man's every action is dominated by his concern to seek pleasure and avoid pain. Furthermore, in some sense, the principle of utility is based on this psychological fact. The utility principle he defines as one "which approves or disapproves of every action whatsoever, according to the tendency which it appears to have to augment or diminish the happiness of the party whose interest is in question. . . . not only of every action of a private individual, but of every measure of government." [2] Utility itself he defines as the property of any object or act whereby it tends to produce pleasure or happiness or avoid pain or unhappiness. Utility is a property of things but the *principle* of utility is a norm for action. It is "the sole end which the legislator ought to have in view: the sole standard, in conformity to which each individual ought, as far as depends upon the legislator, to be made to fashion his behavior." [3]

It is plain from these remarks that Bentham not only argues for hedonism as a doctrine of motivation. He also argues for hedonistic utilitarianism as a norm for action, which somehow is to be seen as based on the former. But he never makes it clear how psychological hedonism justifies normative hedonism. Bentham is surely correct that it behooves the legislator to keep in mind psychological facts about the motivation of men. If men are hedonists, and if, as Bentham claims, "there are four distinguishable sources from which pleasure and pain are in use to flow" (the physical, political, moral, and religious), and if the pleasures or pains provided by these sources "are capable of giving a binding force to any law or rule of conduct," then obviously any legislator would defeat "his own designs and purposes" should he ignore these facts. But do these facts prove the principle of utility? They do support the thesis that any legislation which ignores these facts is apt to be ineffective. But Bentham goes

[1] Jeremy Bentham, *Introduction to the Principles of Morals and Legislation* in *The Works of Jeremy Bentham*, ed. John Bowring, 11 vols. (1838–1843; reprint ed., New York: Russell and Russell, 1962), Vol. I, p. 1.
[2] Ibid.
[3] Ibid., p. 14.

on to say that the principle of utility is not susceptible of any direct proof. It is the fundamental normative premise from which any "chain of proofs must have its commencement." As noted in our discussion of the natural law theorists, we cannot logically move from purely descriptive premises to normative conclusions. However, I will later offer an interpretation of Bentham's appeal to "human nature" as grounds for the principle of utility in which this leap is not involved.

Utility as the Grounds of Legislation

"It is the greatest happiness of the greatest number that is the measure of right and wrong," both on the moral and political level. A measure of government conforms to this principle when its tendency "to augment the happiness of the community is greater than any which it has to diminish it." Bentham views the social community as a fictitious body comprised of individual men, and the happiness of the community is simply the sum of the happiness of the members of the community. How do we test the rightness of an action or policy of action? Bentham, concerned to make ethical and political decisions as exact and scientific as possible, offers us his famous "hedonistic calculus." We can arrive at a purely quantitative answer by measuring seven circumstances of an act or policy of action: the intensity of the pleasure or pain produced, its duration, its certainty or uncertainty, its propinquity or remoteness, its fecundity, its purity, and finally, its extent—the number of persons affected by it. Bentham asks us to sum up the values of the pleasures on the one hand and the pains on the other for each person involved. Then we are asked to calculate the balance. The action or policy that produces the greatest possible amount of pleasure for the greatest number when contrasted with other possible acts or policies under the existing circumstances is the right one. Bentham does not expect us to use a slide rule every time we make a moral judgment or a political evaluation, but he does think this process should "be always kept in view" for "as near as the process actually pursued on these occasions approaches to it, so near will such process approach to the character of an exact one." [4] In enacting laws, legislators must be as scientific as possible.

There are, of course, difficulties in applying Bentham's calculus. Can pleasure or happiness be quantitatively measured? Do not the same things give quite different degrees or amounts of pleasure to

[4] Ibid., p. 16.

different persons? Let us take an example involving only two factors in the calculus—intensity and extent. Suppose that a given piece of legislation, the prohibition of interracial marriage, for example, intensely affects the happiness of some persons but not others. Suppose, of those affected by this rule (100 persons, for example), thirty received fifty units of pain by such legislation, while seventy received ten units of pleasure. Fifteen hundred units of pain versus seven hundred of pleasure is no contest; so presumably to legislate against interracial marriage would be characterized as wrong. The factor of intensity here means that the minority group dictates rightness. But Bentham stresses not merely the amount of happiness but the happiness *of the greatest number.* Stressing numbers, the legislation would be right, not wrong. This could lead to what has been called the "tyranny of the majority" while the former could lead to minority control and to a grossly inequitable distribution of goods. Inequitable distribution could be justified by showing that the total units of pleasure produced (when a minority is intensely affected and hence calculated at 50 units per person, for example, as opposed to one unit per person for the rest) are higher than under a policy of equitable distribution. Bentham, I think, would be opposed to such inequities, just as he would be opposed to the tyranny of the majority. However, to the extent that his utilitarian theory does not provide answers to these problems, it is inadequate.

Justice and Utility

Bentham seems to assume that justice and utility are not only compatible; but that justice is a necessary part of utility. The happiness of each person is morally on a par with all others and must be so considered in moral and political evaluations. In this sense he subscribes to the principles of equality and justice. He states: "The French have already discovered that the blackness of the skin is no reason why a human being should be abandoned without redress to the caprice of a tormentor. It may come one day to be recognized, that the number of the legs, the villosity of the skin, or the termination of the os sacrum, are reasons equally insufficient for abandoning a sensitive being to the same fate. What else is it that should trace the insuperable line? Is it the faculty of reason, or, perhaps, the faculty of discourse? But a full-grown horse or dog is beyond comparison a more rational, as well as a more conversable, animal than an infant of a day, or a week, or even a month old. But suppose the case were otherwise, what would it avail? The question is not, Can they *reason?* nor, Can they *talk?* but, Can they *suffer?"* [5]

Bentham argues, then, that in computing suffering or happiness, each person counts equally because every human has the capacity for pain or pleasure. But does not justice or equality require more than merely including the suffering or happiness of each person affected by a given act or policy of action in one's calculation of the total pain or pleasure involved? Suppose one does this and yet he discovers that a given policy which is unjust, which, say, inequitably distributes certain goods, produces the greatest happiness of society. Would not the principle of utility decree that we do the unjust act? If so, then justice or equality is not part of the very meaning of utility, even if the principle that each person's happiness must be considered is so included. In part, this is the objection of ethical deontologists like Ross and Pritchard to Bentham and the utilitarians.[6] Utility, they say, is not an adequate test of rightness. The appeal to consequences is a relevant consideration but there are other right-making considerations. Ross, for example, asks of two acts, both of which produce the *same* amount of pleasure but one of which involves breaking a promise or lying, which is right? The utilitarian must say that both are equally right, but our moral consciousness denies this, Ross claims. Furthermore, there are cases, like keeping a promise, where our moral consciousness indicates that an act is right even when it does not produce the best consequences. Does not this indicate the inadequacy of utility as a *sufficient* moral and political principle?, the deontologist asks.

The importance of these objections, if they are correct, for Bentham's political philosophy is obvious. If utility is to be the guiding principle for enacting legislation, we could end up not only with a society in which the laws violate what Ross calls our common moral consciousness, but also one in which certain fundamental, basic, (what some call "natural") rights are sacrificed to *general utility*. It could be argued that justice and concern for these so-called rights in fact *generally* are required for the public good. This may be true, but if there are clear cases where they conflict with the public good, then Bentham is committed to their restriction. This is made plain

[5] Ibid., p. 143.
[6] See W. P. Ross, *The Right and The Good* (1930; reprint ed., Oxford: Clarendon Press, 1961), and H. A. Pritchard, *Moral Obligation* (Oxford: Oxford University Press, 1949).

in the following account of Bentham's critique of the natural rights doctrine.

Bentham's Critique of Natural Law and Natural Rights

Bentham believed in an objective moral standard. The principle of utility provides that standard, he claims. Other theories which purport to provide an objective standard really leave us in the throes of subjectivism. The theological ethic, the appeal to a moral sense, the appeal to natural law, to natural rights, to rational intuition—all are reducible, he claims, to the "principle of sympathy and antipathy." They amount simply to statements of individual sentiments or feelings about what is right and wrong. None of them provide us with an objective test or method of testing the rightness or wrongness of acts. In fact, they are all "anarchical," committing us to the position that there are "as many different standards of right and wrong as there are men."

Bentham's critique of the appeal to natural law and natural rights deserves special attention. His critique is on two levels, the pragmatic or normative, and the conceptual. His objection on normative grounds is that the appeal to imprescriptible, natural rights, or to a law of nature which can in no way be contradicted by human laws, tends to impel a man "to rise up in arms against any law whatever that he happens not to like." Talk about natural rights and natural law, Bentham insists, is "terrorist language," for it excites and keeps up "a spirit of resistance to all laws—a spirit of resistance against all governments. . . ." [7] This leads to chaos and disorder.

On conceptual grounds, Bentham insists that the doctrines of natural law and natural rights, if taken literally, as they were apparently intended, are "simple nonsense." The only kind of law which exists is the specific, concrete rule of the constituted political authority. Such rules or laws are "whatever is given for law by the person or persons recognized as possessing the power of making laws. . . ." To speak of laws outside of this context is a conceptual error. The same holds for the appeal to natural rights. "There are no such things as natural rights—no such things as rights anterior to the establishment of government—no such things as natural rights opposed to, in contradistinction to, legal. . . ." [8] It is a conceptual error to

[7] Jeremy Bentham, *Anarchical Fallacies, Works,* vol. II, 501.
[8] Ibid., p. 500.

speak of rights prior to the establishment of government. But to speak of these so-called natural rights (liberty, property, security, and resistance to oppression) as "imprescriptible" compounds the nonsense. What could "imprescriptible" or "indefeasible" mean unless it means that the interference or denial of these rights by the laws or legal authorities is never justified?, Bentham asks. But, to take one so-called imprescriptible right—the right to liberty—it is plain, Bentham argues, that "all rights are made at the expense of liberty," and "no liberty can be given one man but in proportion as it is taken from another." [9]

Since all laws, then, that are creative of liberty are also abrogative of liberty, how can liberty be imprescriptible? It cannot, Bentham answers. The same holds for the other so-called imprescriptible rights. Taken literally, then, the doctrine of natural, imprescriptible rights is nonsense. Even taken figuratively, it is objectionable on the above normative grounds. The Declaration of Rights of the French National Assembly (1791), Bentham claims, which purported to be a penning of "a cluster of truths on which the fate of nations was to hang" was in fact written more like "an oriental tale or an allegory for a magazine. . . ." It contains "stale epigrams," "trite sentimental conceits," and "frippery ornaments" rather than "necessary distinctions" and "the majesty simplicity of good sound sense. . . ." [10]

Does this indictment of natural law and natural rights leave Bentham without any grounds for criticizing the existing legal framework? By no means. The grounds are moral: ". . . as there is no *right* (or law) which ought not to be maintained so long as it is upon the whole advantageous to the society that it should be maintained, so there is no right (or law) which, when the abolition of it is advantageous to society, should not be abolished." [11] The principle of utility constitutes the grounds for moral criticism.

Locke, we saw, insisted that natural rights, though inviolate, were not unlimited. With the contract, they become severely qualified— the limiting criterion being "the common good." To this extent he and Bentham agree, but Locke does not think that the phrase "natural rights" is nonsense. Furthermore, he gives those rights independent moral status. They are not simply deductions from the principle of the common good. Here Locke and Bentham diverge on a very fundamental issue.

[9] Ibid., p. 503.
[10] Ibid., p. 497.
[11] Ibid., p. 501.

Bentham's Critique of the Social Contract Theory and Consent

Locke and Hobbes both utilized the notions of a social contract and consent to show the basis of political obligation. Bentham rejects these notions as sheer fictions, unnecessary ones at that. "The origination of governments from a contract is a pure fiction, or in other words, a falsehood. It has never been known to be true in any instance. . . ." [12] On the contrary, all governments that we know of have been "gradually established by habit, after having been formed by force. . . ." Contracts derive their binding force from government, from the habit of enforcement, not government from contracts. Causally, then, and historically, the contract theory is wrong, Bentham claims. Furthermore, he insists, the contract theory, especially when combined with the notion of natural rights, leads us to the "unavoidable inference, that all governments . . . that have had any other origin . . . are illegal" and "resistance to them and subversion of them, lawful and commendable. . . ." [13] The dire consequences of this doctrine he regards as obvious.

Is the contract theory in any way necessary to explain political obligation? We do tend to regard contracts as binding. However, Bentham asks, "Suppose the constant and universal effect of an observance of promises were to produce mischief, would it then be men's duty to observe them?" His answer is no, and his thesis is that the basis of all political obligation, and of all moral obligation, for that matter, is the principle of utility, not contract and consent.

The Role of Government

"The business of government is to promote the happiness of the society, by punishing and rewarding." Bentham stresses punishment and the negative role of government, the removal of obstructions to man's welfare. Legislative interference must be limited. What is the limit? Bentham says that wherever punishment would be "groundless," "inefficacious," "unprofitable," or "needless" the state should stay out. "It is plain, that of individuals the legislator can know nothing: concerning those points of conduct which depend upon the particular circumstances of each individual, it is plain, therefore, that he can

[12] Ibid.
[13] Ibid., p. 500.

determine nothing to advantage. It is only with respect to those broad lines of conduct in which all persons, or very large and permanent descriptions of persons, may be in a way to engage, that he can have any pretense for interfering; and even here the propriety of his interference will, in most instances, lie very open to dispute." [14] Much must be left to private ethics or to sanctions other than legal ones. "Every act which promises to be beneficial upon the whole to the community (himself included), each individual ought to per- form of himself: but it is not every such act that the legislator ought to compel him to perform. Every act which promises to be pernicious upon the whole to the community (himself included), each individual ought to abstain from of himself; but it is not every such act that the legislator ought to compel him to abstain from." [15] Even when the legislator's motives are good, as with Louis XIV's concern to convert heretics, excessive interference can produce "all of the miseries which the most determined malevolence could have devised."

Bentham is as concerned with the freedom of the individual and with limitations on government activity as Locke—*but on differ- ent grounds.* He appeals only to utility, not to natural rights. Excessive narrowing of the liberties of individuals decreases the happiness of individuals and society. Restrictions are justified only when they "will make up for the expense." Even with drunkenness and fornica- tion, the legislator should not interfere, for any progress by legal means here also produces a "mass of evil . . . as would exceed, a thousand-fold, the utmost possible mischief of the offence." [16]

Although Bentham stresses the negative function of government, his principle of utility clearly leaves open a more positive approach to the functions of government. He in fact speaks of the "intro- duction of positive good" by the state. Suppose that it is highly probable that public education would greatly increase the happiness of society. Would not the utility principle decree public, government supported education? And this, of course, is what has happened with most governments, along with public housing, public health facilities, road systems, electric power systems, national parks—even nationalized industries. Where would the positive function of government end? Where *should* it end? Bentham would have us confront each issue,

[14] Jeremy Bentham, *An Introduction to the Principles of Morals and Legislation, Works,* Vol. 1, 146.
[15] Ibid., p. 144.
[16] Ibid., p. 146.

each possible government policy, with this question: Will this policy significantly increase the happiness of the citizens? If the answer is yes, then the policy should be instituted. If not, then it should be cast aside. If socialism is necessary to maximize human happiness, then socialism would be proper according to Bentham's principles.

In each case the facts of the matter must dictate the appropriateness of the policy, and the legislator must be aware of those facts if his decisions are to be rational. Bentham's legislator must be knowledgeable and rational. He must be scientific in his approach to policy-making, and not be governed simply by tradition or party concern. Bentham realizes that it is difficult, even for rational men, to sort out all the facts and to predict future states of affairs with accuracy. There will be disagreements. But as long as legislators are rational in their approach, the facts will sooner or later be seen for what they are, and the public interest consequently served.

Freedom and Democracy

Although the principle of utility is the overriding criterion of evaluation, we have seen that Bentham has great concern about any restrictions on man's freedom, for freedom is an important ingredient in the attainment of happiness. Despotism must be avoided, but how is this to be done? In fact, what is the difference between a free government and a despotic one?

Does the difference lie in the fact that the power of the rulers in the one case is less than that of the other? Bentham denies this. The difference lies in the approach of government to legislation and in the *distribution* of power within the state. If a legislator uses utility as his guideline for legislation and, if he employs the scientific method in collecting facts, then there is a built-in "corrective to his prejudices, and a check upon his passions . . . everything that is arbitrary in legislation vanishes." [17] So guided, the legislator will not exercise power which unnecessarily restricts human freedom and the common good.

However, the distinction between a free government and despotism also turns, Bentham claims, on

the manner in which that whole mass of power, which, taken together, is supreme, is, in a free state, *distributed* among the several ranks of persons that are sharers in it:—on the *source* from whence their titles to it are successively derived:—on the frequent

17 Ibid., p. 139.

and easy *changes* of condition between govern*ors* and govern*ed*; whereby the interests of the one class are more or less indistinguishably blended with those of the other:—on the *responsibility* of the governors; or the right which a subject has of having the reasons publicly assigned and canvassed of every act of power that is exerted over him:—on the *liberty of the press;* or the security with which every man, be he of the one class or the other, may make known his complaints and remonstrance to the whole community:—on the *liberty of public association;* or the security with which malcontents may communicate their sentiments, concert their plans, and practice every mode of opposition short of actual revolt before the executive power can be legally justified in disturbing them.[18]

Man's freedom, Bentham here argues, is assured by the distribution of power among a host of social and political institutions within the state, by a free press, the rotation of ruled and rulers and so on. Even without the appeal to natural rights, Bentham clearly fits into the liberal, democratic tradition, and he later came to hold that representative democracy best assures a government which acts in the public interest. Freedom, however, he never views as intrinsically good but only as a means to man's happiness. Though Bentham is in fact a liberal, this is not necessarily *entailed* by his utilitarian principle. If it could be shown that despotism and tyranny best maximize happiness, his theory would commit him to despotism and tyranny.

Civil Disobedience

Not all laws are habitually obeyed. Nor should they be, Bentham holds. It is the duty of government to legislate for the good of the public, and *legally* everyone under the jurisdiction of a given government must obey *whatever* laws are promulgated. But suppose those laws are bad. Do citizens have a moral right of resistance or of civil disobedience? Although Bentham does not encourage civil disobedience, he does appear to grant the moral right to disobey the law under certain conditions. Describing the view of some critics of laws, he states: "Some who speak of a law as being void . . . would persuade us to look upon the authors of it as having thereby forfeited, as the phrase is, their whole power: as well that of giving force to the particular law in question, as to any other. These are they who, had they arrived at the same practical conclusion through the prin-

[18] Jeremy Bentham, *A Fragment On Government, Works,* Vol. II, p. 288.

ciple of utility, would have spoken of the law as being to such a degree pernicious, as this, were the bulk of the community to see it in its true light, *the probable mischief of resisting it would be less than the probable mischief of submitting to it.*" [19]

Bentham expresses the hope that the distribution of power within the state and the self-correcting nature of the scientific method as applied to societal issues will preclude the need for such resistance. But if they do not, civil disobedience, *within the utilitarian restriction,* is justified; and presumably, the same moral criterion, under certain conditions, would justify total revolution.

Critique

Some of the *normative* problems confronting Bentham's political theory have already been discussed. We noted the claim of the deontologist that the principle of utility is inadequate as a total ethic, the possible conflict of utility and justice, and the possible restriction of the freedoms and rights of men in the name of happiness. It does bear repeating that although Bentham denies the doctrines of natural rights and natural law, he insists on the same rights and freedoms, the same assurance from oppression, as do Locke and others in the liberal, democratic tradition. His grounds are purely utilitarian. He is convinced that if we abide by the principle of utility, "everything that is arbitrary in legislation vanishes. An evil-intentioned or prejudiced legislator durst not look it (utility) in the face." [20] Why is this the case? Because the application of the utility principle requires the use of the scientific method in calculating the effects of various policies, and this method requires continuous checking and testing, what Bentham calls a "perpetual commentary of reasons." Bentham's insistence on a "perpetual commentary of reasons" for our moral and political decisions constitutes an essential bulwark against arbitrariness and totalitarianism in all phases of public and private life.

I turn now to conceptual and metaethical problems in Bentham's thought. In his utilitarian ethic, Bentham is frequently accused of committing the "naturalistic fallacy," that is, of reducing ethical claims to purely descriptive ones and of trying to deduce normative conclusions from purely descriptive premises. If "X is right" is translated as "X produces the greatest pleasure," is not the former emasculated

[19] Ibid., p. 289.
[20] Jeremy Bentham, *An Introduction to the Principles of Morals and Legislation,* in *Works,* Vol. I, p. 1939.

and robbed of its normative force? That is, does it not make sense to ask whether an act that produces the greatest pleasure is right? If this question is meaningful, then plainly "right" and "productive of the greatest pleasure" are not identical. The same problem confronts Bentham's definition of "good" in terms of pleasure. I do not want to enter here into a detailed analysis of the so-called "naturalistic fallacy" and of metaethical issues. I will discuss these issues to some extent in the final chapter of this book. However, it is clear that if the utilitarian analysis of "right" and "good" is inadequate, important repercussions follow for Bentham's political philosophy. For *it means that utilitarianism alone can give us neither a conceptual nor a normative grasp of political problems.*

However, I do want to return briefly to the issue discussed in the first section of this chapter, namely, Bentham's attempt to extract utility as a *norm* out of psychological hedonism as a *fact* about human nature. Earlier I indicated that this attempted move from "is" to "ought" is illegitimate, and Bentham often does view the *principle of utility as a norm*, that is, as a guideline for action. Sometimes, however, Bentham treats his utilitarian thesis as a thesis *about* moral discourse, i.e. as a metaethical theory.[21] "Of an action that is conformable to the principle of utility," he states, "one may always say either that it is one that ought to be done, or at least that it is one that ought not to be done. One may say also, that it is right it should be done; at least that it is not wrong it should be done; that it is a right action; at least that it is not a wrong action. When thus interpreted, the words ought, and right and wrong, and others of that stamp, have a meaning: when otherwise, they have none."[22]

If we are to have moral discourse at all, Bentham seems here to be saying, we must presuppose the utility principle. In fact, "by the natural constitution of the human frame, on most occasions of their lives, men in general embrace this principle without thinking of it; if not for the ordering of their own actions, yet for the trying of their own actions, as well as those of other men."[23] One could read Bentham here as saying that men, in virtue of their human nature, accept utility as an adequate test of the rightness of actions, even if they are often unwilling to abide by it. Such acceptance is almost part

[21] For discussion of this, see my article "Are Metaethical Theories Normatively Neutral?," *Australasian Journal of Philosophy*, Vol. 39 (1961); reprinted in *Readings in Contemporary Ethical Theory*, ed. Kenneth Pahel and Marion Schiller (Englewood Cliffs, N.J.: Prentice-Hall, 1970).

[22] Bentham, *Introduction to Morals and Legislation, Works*, Vol. I, p. 2.

[23] Ibid.

of what it means to be human. The principle of utility is not susceptible of proof, Bentham insists, but such proof is needless. Men, as
moral beings and as users of moral discourse, necessarily presuppose
it. Without it, we could not have moral discourse or even human
beings as we now know them.

In these passages Bentham's utilitarian thesis can be viewed, not
as normative, but as conceptual or metaethical. It is a thesis about
what it means to be human and about *what it means to have moral
discourse*. Even as a conceptual or metaethical thesis, it can surely
be questioned. Could not there be some moral discourse independent
of utility? Is acceptance of the principle of utility part of what it
means to be a human being? These are, at the very least, debatable
questions. But the significant point is that, interpreted as a metaethical
theory, the utilitarian thesis is not involved in the "is to ought"
leap, that is, the unjustified inference of normative utilitarianism from
psychological hedonism. This leap is not involved because the principle of utility *here* functions not as a normative guide for action
but as a supposedly correct analysis of the meaning of ethical terms.
As a conceptual or metaethical thesis, utilitarianism must be evaluated
on grounds different from those of a normative thesis.[24]

Another way of looking at Bentham's appeal to man's psychological nature, or to his hedonism, so that no "is to ought" leap is involved is this: because all men are motivated in all they do by their
concern for their own pleasure and avoidance of pain, any ethical
principle incompatible with this fact about men will be ineffective
and hence unacceptable. Men simply would not be motivated to abide
by it. Herein lies the advantage of the utility principle and a sense
in which it can be "proven." The principle of utility is realistic. It
fits the facts about human beings; although it requires the impartial
consideration of the consequences of any act in assessing its rightness (the happiness of each person counts), men will in fact abide
by this because they realize that the adoption and application of that
principle is generally in their interest. It squares with their selfish,
hedonistic nature. Thus, Bentham's egoistic hedonism and his utilitarianism are hardly contradictory doctrines or mutually exclusive
ones (as some have argued). On the contrary, they complement each
other; as soon as a man realizes that adoption of the greatest happiness
principle is generally in his own interest, he necessarily accepts it.

[24] Of course, the relationship between normative ethics and metaethics is a
controversial issue. Some purported neutral metaethical analyses may be disguised
normative ethical theories. See my article, "Are Metaethical Theories Normatively
Neutral?," in *Australasian Journal of Philosophy*.

The principle "has been combated by argument," Bentham states, but only by those who have not properly understood it. When man fully understands what he is, a creature governed by pleasure and pain, and when he understands that the utility principle is necessary for the fulfillment of that pursuit, he will adopt that principle. To do anything else would be contrary to his nature and to rationality.

Seen in this way Bentham's thesis includes several causal relationships. (1) Given man's nature, utility is efficacious. It is a principle which will move men to act. Principles that do not recognize the essential facts of human nature are ineffective as norms to guide conduct. (2) Furthermore, adoption of the utility principle in fact results in the fulfillment of man's interests and happiness. (3) When a man fully understands his nature, he *must* accept the utility principle.

A full evaluation of Bentham's utilitarianism, then, requires not only an evaluation of it on a *normative* level—whether it is an adequate theory for the resolution of moral and political issues. It must also be evaluated as an *empirical* thesis, a thesis about man's nature, his motivations, and the causal relationships just discussed. Is man a pure hedonist? Are moral principles (Kant's categorical imperative, for example) that involve a denial of the doctrine of hedonism both incorrect and inefficacious in moving men to act? And finally, Bentham's utilitarianism must be evaluated as a *conceptual, metaethical* thesis. Must moral concepts, in order to be meaningful, be interpreted along utilitarian lines, as Bentham claims?

Perhaps Bentham's theory can be defended against these objections. But whatever problems confront his theory, there is much to be said for his empiricist, nonmetaphysical approach to ethics and political philosophy. Similarly, despite the problems with his hedonistic calculus, if we are able to devise quantitative, or at least objective, criteria for testing the rightness of an act or policy of action, then we have a means whereby moral and political conflicts can *in principle* be rationally resolved.

We turn now to the political theory of John Stuart Mill, Bentham's successor as the leading exponent of utilitarianism.

Recommended Readings

Baumgardt, David. *Bentham and the Ethics of Today*. Princeton, 1952.
Bentham, Jeremy, *The Works of Jeremy Bentham*. Edited by John Bowring. 11 vols. 1838–1843. Reprint, New York, 1962.

Davidson, William. *Political Thought in England: The Utilitarians from Bentham to Mill.* New York, 1916.

Keeton, G. W. and Schwurzenberger, George, eds. *Jeremy Bentham and the Law.* London, 1948.

Mack, Mary Peter. *Jeremy Bentham: An Odyssey of Ideas.* London, 1963.

Plamenatz, John. *The English Utilitarians.* Oxford, 1958.

Stephen, Leslie. *The English Utilitarians.* Reprints of Economic Classics. New York, 1968.

chapter 6
John Stuart Mill
1806-1873

John Stuart Mill was the son of James Mill, a philosopher and close friend of Jeremy Bentham. His father put him through a rigorous early education and exposed him to the utilitarian circle of thinkers whose influence is evident in his work. Although he held an important administrative position with the East India Company, Mill had time to play an active role in the Radical political party. He served in the House of Commons for three years. Mill's principal works are The System of Logic *(1843),* Principles of Political Economy *(1848),* On Liberty *(1859), and* Utilitarianism *(1863). His political philosophy extends the basic ideas of utilitarianism, but there are a number of innovations in his theory. His views on political equality and human freedom won him the reputation of being England's most outstanding political theorist of his day, and his views continue to have great influence in political theory and practice.*

Mill's Brand of Utilitarianism

John Stuart Mill was born in 1806, some twenty-six years before Bentham's death. Bentham was the dominant philosophical influence on him (Mill's father was a close friend of Bentham); and Mill, with some important exceptions and innovations, carried on the utilitarian tradition. The rightness or wrongness of actions were to be judged by their probable effects upon the lives and characters of the persons affected. Mill not only embraced Bentham's hedonistic utilitarianism; he also endorsed strongly Bentham's position that "those habits of thought and modes of investigation which are essential to the idea of science" must be introduced into morals and politics. We must have a scientific morality, one which rests upon an empirical science of human nature and in which the rightness or wrongness of actions is established by inductive reasoning.

To this extent Mill is a Benthamite. But he differs significantly from Bentham in his recognition that pleasures vary qualitatively. Qualitative differences in pleasures, he insisted, must be weighed in assessing the rightness and wrongness of an action. "It is quite compatible with the principle of utility to recognize the fact, that some kinds of pleasure are more desirable and more valuable than others. It would be absurd that while, in estimating all other things, quality is considered as well as quantity, the estimation of pleasures should be supposed to depend on quantity alone." [1]

But how are we to assess quality? Mill recognized that a purely quantitative hedonistic calculus would not do and again he departs from Bentham: "On a question which is the best worth having of two pleasures, or which of two modes of existence is the most grateful to the feelings, apart from its moral attributes and its consequences, the judgment of those who are qualified by knowledge of both, or, if they differ, that of the majority among them, must be admitted as final." [2] The appeal here is not to a mathematical slide rule but to a wise, experienced judge. On the question of the rightness of an action, the criterion again is the opinion of the wise, impartial, experienced person; for "as between his own happiness and that of others, utilitarianism requires him to be as strictly impartial as a disinterested and benevolent spectator. In the golden rule of Jesus of Nazareth, we read the complete spirit of the ethics of utility. To do as you would be done by and to love your neighbor as yourself, constitute the ideal perfection of utilitarian morality." [3]

It is important to keep two points firmly in mind if one is to understand Mill's ethic. Though he subscribes to a kind of hedonism, it is not the egoistic variety. In fact, Mill explicitly states that in the present condition of the world, "paradoxical as the assertion may be, the conscious ability to do without happiness gives the best prospect of realizing such happiness as is attainable." [4] Combined with this rejec-

[1] John Stuart Mill, *Utilitarianism* (London: Everyman Edition, 1910; reprinted, 1948), p. 7.
[2] Ibid., p. 10.
[3] Ibid., p. 16.
[4] Ibid., p. 15.

tion of egoism is the positive affirmation that in judging the rightness of an act, namely, whether an act probably produces the greatest happiness of the greatest number, each person is to count for one and nobody for more than one. A right act is one which maximizes the amount of happiness but such maximization requires the proper distribution of happiness among those affected by an act. As with Bentham, the principle of utility necessarily entails the principle of justice, or the proper distribution of happiness.

We noted, however, in our discussion of Bentham that the thesis that justice is entailed by utility may be false, for it appears possible for an act to be unjust and produce the best consequences for the majority affected by the act. It may even be that it is an empirical fact that most utilitarian acts are also just ones and that justice and just institutions are invariably utilitarian instruments. But if it is theoretically possible for utility and justice to conflict, then substantial alterations of utilitarianism may be required if it is to be an adequate guide for the construction of political institutions and for enacting legislation. We are speaking here in terms of the adequacy of Mill's (and Bentham's) *theory*. In actual practice, convinced as he was that utility entails justice, Mill (and Bentham) worked hard for legislation which embodied justice and not merely for legislation which would produce the greatest amount of happiness.

Political optimism—if all men would but be intelligent utilitarians! —abounds in Mill's work. "Poverty, in any sense implying suffering, may be completely extinguished by the wisdom of society, combined with the good sense and providence of individuals," he declares, and "all the grand sources, in short, of human suffering are in a great degree, many of them almost entirely, conquerable by human care and effort. . . ." [5] Still he agrees with Bentham (again with qualifications) that the norm of utility whose application would justify that optimism, cannot be rationally proven. Acceptance of the utility principle, however, does not depend "on blind impulse, or arbitrary choice. . . ," for ". . . considerations may be presented capable of determining the intellect either to give or withhold its assent to the doctrine; and this is equivalent to proof." [6] Mill offers this consideration: ". . . if human nature is so constituted as to desire nothing which is not either a part of happiness or a means of happiness, we can have no other proof, and we require no other, that these are the only things desirable. If so, happiness is the sole end of human action, and

[5] Ibid., p. 14.
[6] Ibid., p. 4.

the promotion of it the test by which to judge of all human conduct; from whence it necessarily follows that it must be the criterion
of morality, since a part is included in the whole." [7]

Some philosophers have been determined not to accept this argument. It rests, they claim, on a move from the fact that something is
desired to the conclusion that it is *desirable,* surely not a logical inference (a jump from "is" to "ought"). Second, it is frequently
argued that Mill commits the fallacy of composition by moving from
the fact that each person desires his own happiness to the conclusion
that the happiness of everyone is desired by the aggregate of all. Mill
perhaps would have been on safer grounds if he had stayed with his
first position—that the principle of utility cannot be proven. On the
other hand, an interpretation of Mill's position in which this fallacy is
not involved may be possible (one in which he argues from the fact
that each person's happiness is desirable to the conclusion that the
happiness of everyone is desirable). [8]

Justice as the Basic Moral and Political Objective

We have seen that justice is a part of utility for Mill. He straightforwardly states that justice "is involved in the very meaning of
utility, or the Greatest Happiness Principle. That principle is a mere
form of words without rational signification, unless one person's
happiness, supposed equal in degree (with the proper allowance made
for kind), is counted for exactly as much as another's. Those conditions being supplied, Bentham's dictum, 'everybody to count for one,
nobody for more than one,' might be written under the principle of
utility as an explanatory commentary." [9]

But it must be kept in mind that, for Mill, justice ranks at the top
of all social utilities. Justice is "a name for certain moral requirements
which, regarded collectively, stand higher in the scale of social utility, and are therefore of more paramount obligation than any
others. . . ." [10] It follows, therefore, that for both the moralist and the
legislator "the equal claim of everybody to happiness," which "involves an equal claim to all the means of happiness," must be
their primary objective. [11] There are limitations to the primacy of

7 Ibid., p. 36.
8 I am indebted to Professor Henry West of Macalester College for valuable
discussion of this issue.
9 Ibid., p. 58.
10 Ibid., p. 59.
11 Ibid., p. 58.

social justice—when "the inevitable conditions of human life, and the general interest, in which that of every individual is included, sets limit to the maxim. . . ." [12] But for Mill "all persons are deemed to have a right to equality of treatment, except when some recognized social expediency requires the reverse." [13] These he thinks will be rare occasions. They may occur. For example, "to save a life, it may not only be allowable but a duty to steal or take by force the necessary food or medicine, or to kidnap or compel to officiate the only qualified medical practitioner." [14] Such actions are unjust, for they violate the rights of individuals, but they are nonetheless morally right acts.

Thus Mill recognizes, implicitly at least, that justice and utility may conflict. He agrees that linguistically we ordinarily "do not call anything justice which is not a virtue" and that "by this useful accommodation of language, the character of indefeasibility attributed to justice is kept up, and we are saved from the necessity of maintaining that there can be laudable injustice." [15] But this is merely a "useful accommodation" of language. There may be "laudable injustice," namely, whenever the greater social good requires overriding the rights of individuals. Although Mill insists that this overriding of rights is sometimes morally justified, it "ought to be strictly construed," [16] and he is aware that there is as much difference of opinion on what is useful to society as there is about what is just.

Mill recognizes the possible conflict between justice and utility, but he still insists that justice is part of the very meaning of utility. This appears to be an inconsistency. Perhaps he can be extricated from this appearance if we distinguish two senses of justice—that in which the happiness of each person is counted as equal to that of any other person, and that which is based on a system of rights—and read Mill as maintaining that the former but not the latter is part of the meaning of utility. On this reading, justice in the sense of individual rights in a system of rights may be seen as having a status not reducible to utilitarian considerations, but a status which might be overridden by utilitarian considerations. Much of what Mill says does not support the nonreducible status of justice. He does object strongly to those who would merge all morality in justice: "Whenever there is a right, the case is one of justice, and not of the virtue of beneficence; and

[12] Ibid., p. 59.
[13] Ibid.
[14] Ibid.
[15] Ibid.
[16] Ibid.

whoever does not place the distinction between justice and morality in general, where we have now placed it, will be found to make no distinction between them at all, but to merge all morality in justice." [17] However, what Mill seems to do is merge all morality into utility. It may be that both positions are equally wrong. That is, a theory which emphasized merely justice or the rights of the individual as the basic norm or principle for morals and legislation might result in the ruling out of other relevant considerations in the making of moral decisions and in enacting legislation. On the other hand, a theory which considered only utility or which places utility above all other considerations might have equally undesirable results. This issue is a complex and difficult one, involving not merely the problem of the proper interpretation of Mill but that of specifying criteria for an adequate moral and political philosophy. We will turn to this question again in our final chapter. I have belabored it here because of its central role.

The Meaning of Justice

Whether or not it is reducible to utility, justice as a norm plays a key role in Mill's political philosophy. But what does he mean by justice? He recognizes that there are "many diverse applications of the term 'justice' and that it is a matter of some difficulty to seize the mental link which holds them together. . . ." [18] We speak of justice in contexts involving legal rights and conformity to law, in contexts of moral rights, in contexts involving living up to promises or contracts, in contexts where we emphasize what a person *deserves*, and in contexts in which equality and impartiality are emphasized. But contracts can be justly broken, laws can be unjust (as Mill put it, the legal rights of which a person is deprived "may be rights which *ought* not to have belonged to him; in other words, the law which confers on him these rights, may be a bad law"),[19] some inequalities and partialities may be just ones, and so on. These elements, for Mill, do not capture the essence of justice, which is "that of a right residing in an individual. . . ." [20] He puts it this way: "Justice implies something which is not only right to do, and wrong not to do, but which some individual person can claim from us as his moral right." [21] It involves

17 Ibid., p. 47.
18 Ibid., p. 43.
19 Ibid., p. 40.
20 Ibid., p. 55.
21 Ibid., p. 46.

giving "equal protection to the rights of all." [22] Basically, then, justice involves giving or according to individuals their moral rights. When a person has a right, "he has a valid claim on society to protect him in the possession of it, either by force of law, or by that of education and opinion." [23] It is the moral, not the legal, right which is the essence of justice. It is also not the result of a social contract "whereby at some unknown period all the members of society engaged to obey the laws." [24] Such a contract Mill characterizes as a fiction. In fact Mill stresses that we should not apply the term "injustice" to all violations of law "but only to violations of such laws as *ought* to exist, including such that ought to exist but do not; and to laws themselves, if supposed to be contrary to what ought to be law." [25]

The question of the meaning of justice in its most fundamental sense, then, boils down to the question of what *are* the moral rights of individuals. What should be their rights? Mill gives us no clear answer to this question. The rights of individuals do and should vary, depending on circumstances, abilities, and needs. This is not viewed as inconsistent with equality of rights, for equality does not necessarily require identical treatment of persons. But what, for Mill, are the relevant criteria for differential treatment in according rights? He recognizes the multiplicity of criteria to which appeal is made by individuals and groups. For example, "some communists consider it unjust that the produce of the labor of the community should be shared on any other principle than exact equality; others think it just that those should receive most whose wants are greatest; while others hold that those who work harder, or who produce more, or whose services are more valuable to the community may justly claim a larger quota in the division of the produce. And the sense of natural justice may be appealed to in behalf of every one of these opinions." [26] Thus, Mill clearly recognizes that there are conflicting criteria and insists that in such conflicts, "each, from his own point of view, is unanswerable; . . . social utility alone can decide the preference." [27]

Mill himself obviously thinks that rights based on "desert" are central. He states: "The principle, therefore, of giving to each what they deserve, that is, good for good as well as evil for evil, is not only

[22] Ibid., p. 42.
[23] Ibid., p. 49.
[24] Ibid., p. 52.
[25] Ibid., p. 44.
[26] Ibid.
[27] Ibid., p. 54.

included within the idea of justice as we have defined it, but is a proper object of that intensity of sentiment which places the just, in human estimation, above the simply expedient." [28] He goes on to say that "if it is a duty to do to each according to his deserts, . . . it necessarily follows that we should treat all equally well (where no higher duty forbids) who have deserved equally well of us, and that society should treat equally well who have deserved equally well of it, that is, who have deserved equally well absolutely. This is the highest abstract standard of social and distributive justice; towards which all institutions, and the efforts of all virtuous citizens, should be made in the utmost possible degree to converge." [29]

Although these central passages emphasize merit-criteria and desert, Mill clearly appeals to a host of criteria, for he argues that "the entire history of social improvement has been a series of transitions, by which one custom or institution after another, from being a supposed primary necessity of social existence, has passed into the rank of a universally stigmatized injustice and tyranny. So it has been with the distinctions of slaves and freemen, nobles and serfs, patricians and plebians; and so it will be, and in part already is, with the aristocracies of color, race, and sex." [30] Implicit in this remark are a cluster of criteria—at least criteria of what should *not* count in according equal rights. But what constitutes Mill's own positive merit-criteria are not clearly spelled out.

I have focused in some detail upon Mill's account of justice and his treatment of the connection between justice and utility for several reasons. First, it is still one of the most perceptive essays ever written on this topic. Second, it is important to see the high priority placed on justice in Mill's hierarchy of values, and hence its central role in his political philosophy. Third, Mill's ambivalent account of justice as, on occasion, "part of the meaning of utility," and, on other occasions, as a separate, independent norm which may conflict with utility (though he seems to subscribe most consistently to the former) makes us attend to an issue which is still controversial and of great concern to contemporary moral and political theorists, namely, whether a purely utilitarian theory of rights is adequate or whether some norms or values other than utility (the Kantian emphasis, for example, upon the intrinsic worth and dignity of each person as opposed to mere maximization of pleasure) are required for an adequate theory of

[28] Ibid., p. 57.
[29] Ibid., p. 57–8.
[30] Ibid., p. 59.

rights and of justice—and hence required for an adequate political philosophy. This is indeed one of the most fundamental issues in political philosophy and we will return to it in our concluding chapter.

Liberty as the Fundamental Right

That Mill emphasizes more than the mere maximization of happiness, that there is at least a glimmer of an account of political obligation (and moral) which is not entirely utilitarian in nature comes out (to some extent) in his treatment of the right to freedom. Perhaps it is no more than a glimmer, for Mill always returns to the utilitarian base; but to properly understand Mill's political philosophy, it is important to see the complete moral base of his defense of liberty or personal freedom, which includes several norms and lines of argument.

For Mill our most basic moral and political concern must be criteria for the "wrongful interference with each other's freedom." Why? Because rules which embody restrictions on freedoms "are more vital to human well-being than any maxims. . . ." [31] Freedom from the unjustified interference or intrusion of others is absolutely essential if one is to attain happiness. Whether the unjustified interference is by another individual, the majority of the population, or the state (Mill's concern is not so much with "the tyranny of the magistrate" but with "the tyranny of the majority" with its "collective opinion"), the result is equally bad. Mill agrees that there certainly must be restrictions on individuals; otherwise there could be no viable society. But those restrictions must be properly limited. To find that limit is the purpose of his essay "On Liberty."

Briefly stated, Mill's thesis is "that the sole end for which mankind are warranted, individually or collectively, in interfering with the liberty of action of any of their number, is self-protection. That the only purpose of which power can be rightfully exercised over any member of a civilized community, against his will, is to prevent harm to others. His own good, either physical or moral, is not a sufficient warrant." [32] Mill's emphasis upon the prevention of harm and of self-protection is perfectly consistent with his treatment of "utility as the ultimate appeal on all ethical questions." [33] But, as he stresses, "it must be utility in the largest sense, grounded on the

[31] Ibid., p. 55.

[32] John Stuart Mill, *On Liberty* (London: Everyman Edition, 1910; reprinted, 1948), p. 73.

[33] Ibid., p. 74.

permanent interests of a man as a progressive being." The problem now is to delineate this larger sense of utility which invokes a theory of man "as a progressive being" and the notion of "permanent interests." These norms involve more than merely maximizing happiness. What more do they involve? What are the permanent interests of man as a progressive being?

To answer this question requires an explication of Mill's concept of a human being. That concept, it seems to me, involves a theory of human or moral rights. It does not involve a doctrine of natural rights, for Mill explicitly states that "I forego any advantage which could be derived to my argument from the idea of abstract right, as a thing independent of utility." [34] That is, Mill rejects a defense of liberty as an inalienable, absolute right provided either by Nature or by God. But one can hold a theory of moral rights or human rights without necessarily embracing a doctrine of natural rights and this is what Mill appears to do.

First, he offers an account of what it means to be human which, briefly stated, conceives of man as a rational being with freedom of choice and with a wide range of capacities for development. Human well-being depends upon the exercise of freedom and spontaneity within the strictures of rationality, and Mill makes it perfectly clear that the right to liberty as he conceives it is meant to apply only to rational beings (not to children or barbarians and so on). He then stresses that "it is the privilege and proper condition of a human being, arrived at the maturity of his faculties, to use and interpret experience in his own way. . . ." [35] and "the evil is, that individual spontaneity is hardly recognized by the common modes of thinking as having any intrinsic worth, or deserving any regard on its own account." [36] For Mill, freedom or spontaneity has both intrinsic worth and extrinsic worth. He states:

> It is not by wearing down into uniformity all that is individual in themselves, but by cultivating it, and calling it forth, within the limits imposed by the rights and interests of others, that human beings become a noble and beautiful object of contemplation; and as the works partake the character of those who do them, by the same process human life also becomes rich, diversified, and animating, furnishing more abundant aliment to high thoughts and elevated feelings, and strengthening the tie which binds every in-

[34] Ibid.
[35] Ibid., p. 116.
[36] Ibid., p. 115.

dividual to the race, by making the race infinitely better worth belonging to. In proportion to the development of his individuality, each person becomes more valuable to himself, and is therefore capable of being more valuable to others.[37]

Note that liberty must be "within the limits imposed by the rights of others." We must give "fair play to the nature" of each individual.[38] That is, the right to liberty requires the equal right to freedom for all persons. The mere existence as a person justifies, or is the ground for the possession of, the right to freedom. And the condition of equal freedom results in the best society—the richest and most diverse society.

Both a doctrine of moral rights and concern for maximizing the happiness of mankind, then, underlie the larger sense of utility "grounded in the permanent interests of a man as a progressive being." And the doctrine of moral rights rests upon Mill's commitment to the intrinsic value of freedom and his account of what it means to be human. He sounds almost like Aristotle and "self-realization" theorists when he asks: ". . . for what more or better can be said of any condition of human affairs than that it brings human beings themselves nearer to the best thing they can be? or what worse can be said of any obstruction to good than that it prevents this?" [39]

Restrictions on Liberty

Up to this point we have discussed the moral base of Mill's defense of liberty—which is also the moral base of his political philosophy. We have not discussed what Mill's principle entails. Nor have we attempted to evaluate that principle.

To do this it is necessary to examine further Mill's principle of self-protection. One of the criticisms sometimes offered of the principle is that it is vague. How can we distinguish human actions which affect only the individual and not society? Does not every action of a human being either directly or indirectly affect other members of society? And hence, should not all human actions be open to state or societal control? Mill is aware of these objections and he attempts to refine and delineate his principle in several ways. "No person is an entirely isolated being" and one must "fully admit that the mischief which a person does to himself

37 Ibid., p. 120–1.
38 Ibid., p. 120.
39 Ibid., p. 121.

may seriously affect, both through their sympathies and their interests, those nearly connected with him, and in a minor degree, society at large. When, by conduct of this sort, a person is led to violate a distinct and assignable obligation to any other person or persons, the case is taken out of the self-regarding class, and becomes amenable to moral disapprobation in the proper sense of the term. If, for example, a man, through intemperance or extravagance, becomes unable to pay his debts, or having undertaken the moral responsibility of a family, becomes from the same cause incapable of supporting or educating them, he is deservedly reprobated and might be justly punished, but it is for the breach of duty to his family or creditors, not for the extravagance." [40]

Note that Mill's basic emphasis is on the violation of "a distinct and assignable obligation to any other person." Elsewhere he states that his principle rules out "injuring the interests of one another; or rather certain interests, which, either by express legal provision or by tacit understanding, ought to be considered as rights. . . ." [41] The key notions here are rights and obligations—both moral and legal. The application of the self-protection principle, the protection of others' "interests," or the preclusion of "harm" is restricted basically to actions which violate the rights of others. He in fact goes on to insist that "with regard to the merely contingent, or, as it may be called, constructive injury which a person causes to society, by conduct which neither violates any specific duty to the public, nor occasions perceptible hurt to any assignable individual except himself, the inconvenience is one which society can afford to bear, for the sake of the greater good of human freedom." [42] Mill also recognizes that "the acts of an individual may be hurtful to others, or wanting in due consideration of their welfare, without going to the length of violating any of their constitutional rights." [43] In such cases the offender may then be justly punished by opinion, though not by law." [44] However, in cases in which one's conduct affects basically only oneself and not the rights or interests of others, Mill insists that "there should be perfect freedom, legal and social, to do the action and stand the consequences." [45]

[40] Ibid., p. 137–8.
[41] Ibid., p. 132.
[42] Ibid., p. 138.
[43] Ibid., p. 132.
[44] Ibid.
[45] Ibid.

With Mill's qualifications, it is still difficult to draw the line. He does not adequately clarify the notion of the "interests of others." Even if "interests" is seen essentially in terms of "the rights of others" we have problems. For Mill recognizes rights which *ought* to exist but do not, rights which exist but should not (slavery), and rights which exist and should exist. What should be the rights of persons? This question must be answered if we are to apply Mill's criterion. Mill would revert at this stage to the principle of utility. But in his kind of utilitarianism, he cannot support a theory of rights which merely maximizes happiness. That theory and set of rights must be grounded in the "permanent interests of a man as a progressive being." Mill, so far as I can discover, does not provide such a theory.

Whether or not one can articulate a clear theory of rights in Mill's works, the application of his principle of self-protection or any similar principle will always be controversial, for it necessarily involves a value-decision in the light of one's interpretation of facts. Frequently, we simply disagree on our value commitments *and* on our interpretation of facts. Mill recognizes this, but he himself specifies some of the restrictions and freedoms which he believes are entailed by his principle. There is no need to specify these in detail but samples are instructive.

The principle entails, Mill believes, complete freedom of thought and discussion. Censorship in any form, for adults, is a violation of the public interest. His principle also rules out such practices as legislative support of the Sabbath, compulsory vaccination, and restrictions on the sale of drugs and alcohol. On the other hand it justifies compulsory education, marriage laws, and the abolition of public gambling houses. The presumption for Mill, however, is always in favor of a laissez-faire state. The burden of proof is placed on the person or groups who would introduce restrictions, for Mill is ever wary of the fact "that to extend the bounds of what may be called moral police, until it encroaches on the most unquestionably legitimate liberty of the individual, is one of the most universal of all human propensities." [46]

Nonetheless, it should be noted that Mill's basic principle, "No state interference unless there is harm to society," embraces a wide sense of utility grounded upon the "permanent interests of man as a progressive being" which in turn embraces a theory of moral rights. Although he did not spell out that theory of moral rights in detail, the

[46] Ibid., p. 141.

protection of those rights theoretically could make legitimate a large number of state interferences with individual freedoms—in the same way in which Locke's commitment to equality of rights, though grounded on a different moral base, would appear to justify a wide variety of state restrictions on the actions of individuals or groups.

Mill's Defense of Freedom of Thought and Discussion

Mill's defense of freedom of thought and discussion is forceful and has had great impact in political theory. Basically his defense is utilitarian, though he also argues that restrictions on freedom of speech violate "the moral nature of man." [47] Freedom of speech is required to guard against "corrupt or tyrannical government." Whether the government be good or bad, whether the people and the government hold the same opinions or not, restrictions on freedom of speech and opinion are unjustified. In fact,

> if all mankind minus one were of one opinion, mankind would be no more justified in silencing that one person, than he, if he had the power, would be justified in silencing mankind. . . . The peculiar evil of silencing the expression of an opinion is, that it is robbing the human race; posterity as well as the existing generation; those who dissent from the opinion, still more than those who hold it. If the opinion is right, they are deprived of the opportunity of exchanging error for truth: if wrong, they lose, what is almost as great a benefit, the clearer perception and livelier impression of truth, produced by its collision with error.[48]

Mill argues further that

> we can never be sure that the opinion we are endeavouring to stifle is a false opinion; and if we were sure, stifling it would be an evil still. . . . The opinion which it is attempted to suppress by authority may possibly be true. Those who desire to suppress it, of course deny its truth; but they are not infallible. They have no authority to decide the question for all mankind, and exclude every other person from the means of judging. To refuse a hearing to an opinion, because they are sure that it is false, is to assume that *their* certainty is the same thing as *absolute* certainty. All silencing of discussion is an assumption of infallibility.[49]

These are powerful arguments, and they are surely as applicable today as when Mill wrote them. It is essential to the nature of man as

[47] Ibid., p. 114.
[48] Ibid., p. 79.
[49] Ibid.

a rational being—the "moral nature of man" as Mill puts it—to have freedom of speech, to be able to criticize his society and to convince others of the correctness of his criticisms. This freedom is of great value both to the individual (for his self-realization) and to society. And yet most societies still try hard to curtail and restrict such criticism.

Some restrictions are necessary, Mill agrees. He insists that "even opinions lose their immunity when the circumstances in which they are expressed are such as to constitute their expression a positive justification to some mischievous act. An opinion that corn-dealers are starvers of the poor, or that private property is robbery, ought to be unmolested when simply circulated through the press, but may justly incur punishment when delivered orally to an excited mob assembled before the house of a corn-dealer, or when handed about among the same mob in the form of a placard." [50] However, such instances of justified restrictions on speech are rare. To those who look upon the speech of some radicals (or conservatives) as injurious to society and its values and institutions, Mill's response is that such speech should be met by yet more speech, not by silencing it. We need what Bentham called a "perpetual commentary of reasons." Such open and free discussion is in the long-term interest of society.

Mill admonishes us to be wary indeed of ideologists and defenders of myths—of whatever persuasion. The quest for truth and open discussion is essential to the welfare of society. Societies which live by myths alone and which ignore the facts about the world and themselves run very high risks, for awareness of facts is required if we are to adjust to and cope with the world and if we are to devise political institutions which assist us to do this. Long before the development of mass media, Mill was fearful of the effects of myth-makers and propagandists, and not merely of the political variety of propagandists. He states: "When society is itself the tyrant—society collectively over the separate individuals who comprise it—its means of tyrannizing are not restricted to the acts which it may do by the hands of its political functionaries." [51] The insipid, all-pervasive never-ending social influences penetrate "much more deeply into the details of life, and enslaving the soul itself." [52] Uniqueness, autonomy, individuality, and originality are crushed by these forces. Mill clearly anticipates the problem so well formulated in our own time by David Riesman in

[50] Ibid., p. 114.
[51] Ibid., p. 49.
[52] Ibid.

his *The Lonely Crowd*, that of how to prevent the pressures of large urbanized societies from destroying the autonomy and inner life of the individual.

The fear of mass conformity, uniformity, and ideological subservience was also at the base of Mill's scepticism about the communistic organization of society. He acknowledged that for the generality of laborers "the restraints of Communism would be freedom in comparison with the present condition of the majority of the human race." [53] But Mill insists that "it is not by comparison with the present bad state of society that the claims of Communism can be estimated; nor is it sufficient that it should promise greater personal and mental freedom than is now enjoyed by those who have not enough of either to deserve the name. The question is, whether public opinion would not be a tyrannical yoke; whether the absolute dependence of each on all, and surveillance of each by all, would not grind all down into a tame uniformity of thoughts, feelings, and actions." [54]

Any social system which required men "to exchange the control of their own actions for any amount of comfort or affluence, or to renounce liberty for the sake of equality, would deprive them of one of the most elevated characteristics of human nature." [55] For Mill both equality and liberty are to be highly prized. Neither must be sacrificed, and that system of government which best implements both of these values is the most desirable form.

The Best Form of Government: Representative Democracy

What is the best form of government? Mill's answer to this question is highly qualified. First, he insists that "the capability of any given people for fulfilling the conditions of a given form of government cannot be pronounced on by any sweeping rule. Knowledge of the particular people, and general practical judgment and sagacity, must be the guides." [56] Some peoples "may be unprepared for good institutions" and "institutions need to be radically different,

[53] John Stuart Mill, *Principles of Political Economy*, 7th ed., in Peter Radcliff, *Limits of Liberty* (Belmont, California, 1966), p. 65.
[54] Ibid.
[55] Ibid., p. 64.
[56] John Stuart Mill, *Representative Government* (London: Everyman Edition, 1910; reprinted, 1948), p. 181.

according to the stage of advancement already reached." [57] The "ideally best form of government is that in which the sovereignty, or supreme controlling power in the last resort, is vested in the entire aggregate of the community; every citizen not only having a voice in the exercise of that ultimate sovereignty, but being, at least occasionally, called on to take an actual part in the government. . . ." [58] Of course, in large communities, everyone cannot directly participate. Therefore "the ideal type of a perfect government must be representative." [59] However, for savages, despotism (even slavery) may be the best form of government.[60] A people must have reached a certain stage of order, intelligence, and civilization for representative democracy to work.

Why is representative democracy the best form (when these conditions have been met)? Mill cites two basic reasons:

> The first is, that the rights and interests of every or any person are only secure from being disregarded when the person interested is himself able, and habitually disposed, to stand up for them. . . . We need not suppose that when power resides in an exclusive class, that class will knowingly and deliberately sacrifice the other classes to themselves: it suffices that, in the absence of its natural defenders, the interests of the excluded is always in danger of being overlooked; and, when looked at, is seen with very different eyes from those of the persons whom it directly concerns.[61]

His second reason is that "the general prosperity attains a greater height, and is more widely diffused, in proportion to the amount and variety of the personal energies enlisted in promoting it." [62] Mill emphasizes that "the most important point of excellence which any form of government can possess is to promote the virtue and intelligence of the people themselves. . . ." [63] Representative democracy best accomplishes this.

However, Mill straightforwardly rejects a "one man-one vote" type of democracy. He fears the danger which results from "representation which does not secure an adequate amount of intelli-

[57] Ibid., p. 197.
[58] Ibid., p. 207.
[59] Ibid., p. 218.
[60] Ibid., p. 198.
[61] Ibid., p. 208–9.
[62] Ibid., p. 208.
[63] Ibid., p. 193.

gence and knowledge in the representative assembly." [64] He also fears the danger of the assembly coming "under the influence of interests not identical with the general welfare of the community." [65] How are we to avoid these evils—the evils of class legislation or "of government intended for . . . the immediate benefit of the dominant class" and the evil of ignorance in government?

Mill offers several recommendations. First, he insists that although "it is essential to representative government that the practical supremacy in the state should reside in the representatives of the people, it is an open question what actual functions, what precise part in the machinery of the government, shall be directly and personally discharged by the representative body." [66] We can combine representative government with intelligent legislation by utilizing a small group of intelligentsia, a "Cabinet, who should act as a Commission of legislation having for its appointed office to make the laws." [67] The representative assembly is "radically unfit" to govern; it should "watch and control the government: to throw the light of publicity on its acts: to compel a full exposition and justification of all of them which any one considers questionable. . . ." [68] But it should not draft legislation.

Second, we must avoid the evil of class legislation and the tyranny of the majority (whoever the majority might be—white, black, Catholic, or Protestant) and effect "equal justice" for all. How is this to be done? Mill suggests that the two basic classes in society, laborers and employers of labor, "should be, in the arrangement of the representative system, equally balanced, each influencing about an equal number of votes. . . ." [69] A minority of each of these classes will subordinate their class interests "to reason, justice, and the good of the whole; and this minority of either, joining with the whole of the other, would turn the scale against any demands of their own majority which were not such as ought to prevail." [70] Furthermore, democracy must *not* be conceived as "the government of the whole people by a mere majority of the people, exclusively represented." [71] This is "false" democracy. True democracy requires the representation of all

[64] Ibid., p. 248.
[65] Ibid., p. 243.
[66] Ibid., p. 229.
[67] Ibid., p. 237.
[68] Ibid., p. 239.
[69] Ibid., p. 255.
[70] Ibid.
[71] Ibid., p. 256.

—not the disfranchisement of minorities. The majority should prevail but the minority must be heard and be properly represented.

Mill greatly feared the power of a monolithic majority, which democracy tends to encourage. He especially feared mass, class movements based on économic interests. Partiality, injustice and despotism are bred by such movements. He notes that "in the United States where the numerical majority have long been in full possession of collective despotism, they would probably be as unwilling to part with it as a single despot or an aristocracy." [72] Both majority rule and political equality as found in America, he rejects. The representative assembly should not initiate or draft legislation; it should simply ratify or refuse to ratify the legislation proposed by the elitist Cabinet. Furthermore, the vote must be restricted, if not by property *qualifications*, then by the criteria of taxpaying and of literacy. "Universal teaching must precede universal enfranchisement" and the state owes this education to everyone.[73] The educated must not themselves be permitted "to practice class legislation on their own account," [74] but Mill does maintain that the elections should be weighted in favor of educated persons by the practice of plural voting (some persons would have two or more votes).

Through the use of these devices—a restricted franchise, an elitist Cabinet which proposes all legislation and which is free from political influence, and a representative assembly which truly represents all interests in society, including minorities—Mill believes that the evils of democracy can be overcome, and legislation which embodies the long-term interests of each person and of the nation will ensue.

Is Mill Really a Democrat?

Is Mill really a disguised elitist with only a verbal commitment to democracy? One commentator straightforwardly claims that Mill's *Representative Democracy* "is mainly an appeal to British liberals to stand firm in opposing those democratic reforms which would allow the 'untutored masses' to participate in exercising governmental authority." [75] There is *some* truth in this remark. Mill did ex-

[72] Ibid., p. 269–70.
[73] Ibid., p. 280.
[74] Ibid., p. 286.
[75] Currin Shields, "Introduction" to Mill's *Considerations On Representative Government* (Indianapolis: Bobbs-Merrill, 1958), xxv.

press considerable fear about the "leveling" effect of democracy on the quality of civilization. He clearly felt that "the natural tendency of representative government, as of modern civilization, is toward collective mediocrity. . . ." [76] However, he stresses the intrinsic value of each person and the freedom and rights of all. "Every one is degraded, whether aware of it or not, when other people, without consulting him, take upon themselves unlimited power to regulate his destiny." [77] These are surely democratic, not elitist sentiments. Mill does endorse an educational elitism, which is rooted in his assessment of the educational level of the average man and his concern for intelligent decisions in government. But a completely educated populace with full political participation is his ideal, and he leaves open this possibility for a future state of civilization. Thus, in theory, if not in practice, Mill is a democrat.

It may be argued that Mill too much feared the tyranny of the majority and too little feared the tyranny of the educated elite (though he does warn us about the latter). They too are capable of acting contrary to the general interest. Although Mill rejects aristocratic elitism, his political theory in effect substitutes middle-class control—a middle-class elitism—for the older aristocratic variety. Many would argue that complete political equality (one-man, one-vote) is required if the rights and freedoms of everyone are to be protected, and if we are to have a genuine democracy. Mill himself suggests this when he states that "the rights and interests of every or any person are only secure from being disregarded when the person interested is himself able, and habitually disposed, to stand up for them." [78] But he does reject political equality for his time. What is required for a "genuine" democracy—whether "one-man, one-vote" is essential—will be discussed in our concluding chapter.

Recommended Readings

Anschutz, R. P. *The Philosophy of J. S. Mill.* Oxford, 1953.
Brinton, Crane. *English Political Thought in the Nineteenth Century.* London, 1933.

[76] Mill, *Representative Government*, p. 265.
[77] Ibid., p. 279.
[78] Ibid., p. 208.

Britton, Karl. *John Stuart Mill*. Baltimore, 1953.

Davidson, William L. *Political Thought in England: The Utilitarians From Bentham To J. S. Mill*. New York, 1916.

Halevy, Elie. *The Growth of Philosophic Radicalism*. London, 1928.

Mill, John Stuart. *Utilitarianism, Liberty, and Representative Government*. London, 1948.

Morlan, G. *America's Heritage from John Stuart Mill*. New York, 1936.

Conclusion

The fundamental problem confronting the utilitarian approach to political norms and organization is whether or not the underlying utilitarian ethic is adequate. The utilitarian rejects both the theory of natural law and that of the social contract. For him, neither the metaphysical appeal to moral and political norms seen as part of the furniture of the universe nor the historical appeal to some social contract formulated at some time in man's existence are necessary to explain political obligation or to justify political norms. Political norms—rights, justice, and forms of government—are to be seen simply as utilitarian devices, devices which permit the maximization of the pleasure of all and which provide the maximum harmony between the interests of each basically egoistically motivated member of society and that of every other member. Political norms are artificial conventions which fundamentally selfish but also rational beings recognize as essential principles of cooperation and reciprocity. Everything from the form of government for a given society to a theory of legal punishment within a society to the issue of whether civil disobedience is ever proper, is justified on these grounds for the utilitarian. No metaphysics, only a calculus, or a sound judgment by an *experienced* and wise man, is required.

The challenge to this position can be put in several ways: Is the utilitarian ethic adequate to account for both moral and political obligation and norms? This question entails the following ones: Is the utilitarian account of justice as a necessary and constitutive aspect of utility a correct or adequate account? And this question in turn entails asking whether or not a utilitarian theory of rights (human, moral, legal, or political) is an adequate theory.

113

These challenges involve two interrelated levels—normative and conceptual. On the normative level, we have seen in our treatment of both Bentham and Mill that utility as a norm, understood in the sense of maximizing the greatest happiness, might justify what we intuitively believe to be immoral conduct. For example, we argued that the appeal to utility could be used to justify the systematic exclusion of an entire class or groups of people from consideration at all, *if it could be shown that this exclusion results in maximizing the greatest happiness.* If this is correct, then an act could conform to the norm of utility but at the same time violate the norm of justice. This possible normative result of the application of the utilitarian ethic raises the conceptual issue of the relationship between utility and justice. Are these not separate and independent norms, both of which must be weighed in political decisions—even if it is empirically true that rules of justice *generally* maximize happiness? Indeed, this question forces one to consider the relationship between utility and the entire enterprise of morality. Is the maximization of happiness the only morally relevant consideration? If the correct answer to this is negative, then the adequacy of utilitarianism as an ethic is seriously challenged. And since a moral theory provides the basic framework for political decisions, the adequacy of the utilitarian political philosophy is also challenged.

It should be added that the basic problem for Bentham and Mill themselves is *conceptual*, not normative. Both placed justice at the top of the list as a political and moral objective, and we saw that Mill on occasion comes close to acknowledging justice as a norm which is quite independent of utility. Indeed, on occasion he embraces a theory of rights which is rooted in a theory of man as a moral and progressive being. Such a theory, when fully developed, would appear to go well beyond a purely utilitarian ethic. Also, both Bentham and Mill, although they reject the doctrines of natural law and natural rights, affirm the same rights and freedoms espoused by Locke and other natural rights theorists of the liberal, democratic tradition. Arbitrariness and totalitarianism in any phase of public or private life they reject. Equality and liberty are basic moral and political values for both Mill and Bentham, and representative democracy is seen as the best form of government because it best brings these values to fruition.

Recommended Readings

Brandt, Richard. *Ethical Theory*. Englewood Cliffs, N.J., 1963.

Frankena, William. *Ethics*. Englewood Cliffs, N.J., 1963.

Lyons, David. *The Forms and Limits of Utilitarianism*. Oxford, 1965.

Narvson, Jan. *Morality and Utility*. Baltimore, 1967.

Olafson, Frederick, ed. *Society, Law and Morality*. Englewood Cliffs, N.J., 1961.

Smart, J. J. C. *An Outline of a System of Utilitarian Ethics*. Melbourne, 1961.

Model 3:
The Historicist
Theory
of the
State

Introduction

The historicist theory of the state is in part a reaction against both natural law theory and utilitarianism. The view that there are eternal, unchanging moral and political principles which are part of the furniture of the universe, principles which can be discovered and applied by man and which provide a completely objective point of reference for the evaluation of man's social and political activities—this natural law thesis is flatly rejected by the historicist political theorists. There is no God's-eye perspective. All moral and political norms and institutions are historically conditioned and there is no *locus standi* outside of the historical process. Men are not essences outside of history. They are born into specific historical societies and conditions. Those conditions largely shape their capacities and perspectives, and their moral and political lives and institutions cannot be properly understood apart from those historical conditions.

Nor is a social contract or consent seen by the historicists as essential to the existence of, or to the understanding of, political obligation. Society is not a mere agglomerate of individuals bound together by an agreement. It is an organic unity which, for Hegel, has a kind of life of its own in terms of a historically evolving national spirit or Volkgeist, and which, for Marx and Engels, is manifested in terms of class consciousness and proletarian unity.

The historicists furthermore reject the utilitarian thesis that the greatest happiness of the greatest number is the basic norm for all moral and political evaluations. The world is not "the theatre of happiness," Hegel declares, and Marx and Engels insist that much of what men think is required for their happiness are items which fulfill artificial or manufactured needs, not *real* human needs. These artificial needs, born of a "fetishism of commodities" which itself is the result of economic class conflict, make men inhuman and exploitative animals. But in a purely utilitarian calculus, such fetishism is incorporated into the calculus of consequences. This is not to say that Hegel, Marx, and Engels are unconcerned with human welfare, for their ethical theories are certainly man-centered, particularly so with Marx and Engels. It is to say that that concern is differently conceived than with the utilitarians, and that, for these historicists, there are grounds for moral and political obligation other than mere utility or a hedonistic calculus.

Although the historicists agree in their rejection of natural law theory and of utilitarianism, and in the affirmation that all norms and institutions are historically conditioned, they differ in their theories of the causally efficacious factors which make man and his social and political institutions what they are. Hegel's idealistic metaphysic and his analysis of social change contrasts sharply with Marx's and Engel's economic determinism. On the normative level, also, there are very significant differences between Hegel, and Marx and Engels, especially in their views of what constitutes a free and just society and their advocacy of forms of government. These differences—and the affinities—between these historicist political philosophers will be spelled out in the following chapters, as will the advantages and disadvantages of the historicist approach to social and political phenomena and institutions.

chapter 7
Friedrich Hegel
1770-1831

Friedrich Hegel was born in Stuttgart, Germany. He studied theology and philosophy at the University of Tübingen, taught as a private tutor in Bern and Frankfurt, and served as principal of a Gymnasium in Nuremberg. He was appointed to a chair at the Uni- versity of Berlin in 1818 *where he taught until his death. His* Phenomenology of the Mind *was published in 1807; the* Science of Logic *in 1812–16; and the* Encyclopedia of the Social Sciences *in 1817 (while he taught at Heidelberg). Hegel's basic work in political philosophy,* The Philosophy of Right, *appeared in 1821 and his* Philosophy of History *was published posthumously in 1838. His early thought was heavily influenced by Immanuel Kant, but his later political thought was decidedly conservative in tone and highly collectivistic in perspective. Individuals he conceived as having subordinate status to groups and to the ontological forces which act through groups or nations. Hegel's political theory strongly emphasizes national power and he was accepted as the political ideologue of the Prussian regime of his time. His influence on the thought of Marx and Engels is well known.*

Hegel's Metaphysics

Unlike the utilitarians, who for the most part avoided metaphysics, Hegel's social and political theory is steeped in metaphysics, indeed in a metaphysical system of great complexity and obscurity.

119

One simply cannot understand Hegel's social and political philosophy without understanding to some extent his metaphysical system. It may be that some of his social and political ideas have validity quite independent of the metaphysical trappings in which he places them, in the same way, for example, that Locke's doctrine of rights might have validity independent of the theory of natural law. But Hegel's formulation of those ideas must be seen within his system of idealistic metaphysics. For example, he calls the State "Objective Spirit." To understand what he means by this we must know what "spirit" means for him. Indeed we must know what he means by an entire cluster of related concepts like "spirit," "nature," "the Absolute," "subjective spirit," "objective spirit," and "absolute spirit." Let us turn first, then, to a sketch of these concepts, which amounts to a sketch of Hegel's metaphysical system.

All of reality is essentially spiritual for Hegel. Reality is of the nature of thought or idea, but this thought is not simply a property of an individual knower. It is objective, and Hegel's position is often called "objective idealism" as opposed to subjective idealism or solipsism, the view that reality is nothing but the person and his consciousness. He speaks of Absolute Spirit as the world-process which includes the totality of all that exists. That process involves the development or making explicit of a plan or a goal which is inherent in it. This plan Hegel calls the Absolute Idea. Absolute Spirit is a process of evolving self-consciousness, in which the Idea or plan immanent therein becomes conscious of itself, and in which it comes to know the world as its own product. That is, things come into being and changes occur through the thought of the Absolute. Its thought is the world and the process of its thinking is the world process.

Hegel obviously fuses a distinction which we ordinarily make, namely, the distinction between thought or knowledge and the object of thought or knowledge. These are seen as two sides of the same thing for Hegel. So spirit, in developing for itself a knowledge of the world, at the same time creates the world which is the object of its knowledge. Also spirit comes to know and hence create or develop itself in the process of knowing or creating the world.

Hegel does distinguish spirit and nature, but it is really a distinction without a difference. Nature is characterized as the "experience" of the Spirit or The Absolute. Nature is spatial, temporal and material. It is what Hegel calls the "outwardness" and "otherness" of the Idea. But Hegel insists that from a larger perspective there is no difference between spirit and nature. For although it appears, from a temporal and human perspective, that thought and consciousness evolved from inorganic and organic life, this is in reality not the case. Actually nature is produced by spirit and is the experience of Spirit or the Absolute. Spirit does not know, at a certain stage in its evolving self-consciousness, that it has produced nature. It assumes at that time that nature is independent of and external to it. But as Spirit evolves it comes to know that nature is its own creation. "Man is the creature within which Spirit works," Hegel states. In human beings, spirit and nature unite, producing the conditions required for the self-conscious development of Absolute Spirit.

For Hegel the laws of thought or of logic and the laws of reality or of events are the same. Both are equally necessary and rational. He calls these laws "Reason" and states that "all that is real is rational and all that is rational is real." These are the central premises of his type of metaphysical idealism. A passage in Hegel's *Philosophy of History* summarizes some of the points we have made:

> If the clear idea of Reason is not already developed in our minds, in beginning the study of Universal History, we should at least have the firm, unconquerable faith that Reason does exist there; and that the world of intelligence and conscious volition is not abandoned to chance, but must show itself in the light of the self-cognizant Idea. . . . It is only an inference from the history of the world, that its development has been a rational process; that the history in question has constituted the rational necessary course of the World Spirit—that Spirit whose nature is always one and the same, but which unfolds this its one nature in the phe-nomena of the World's existence. This must . . . present itself as the ultimate result of history." [1]

That the idea exists—that Spirit exists with a plan or purpose—is a fact discernible by a study of history, Hegel argues. Without knowl-edge of that plan or Idea we can understand nothing. This certainly includes political beliefs and institutions. Only by grasping the overall purposeful pattern of history can the moral and political ideas and institutions (keep in mind that ideas and institutions are the same) of man be understood. And only with this understanding can man act properly or rationally or freely.

The purpose of Hegel's philosophy of history was to show or demonstrate the necessary order of development of the Absolute Idea in the moral, social, and political institutions of man. But the point

[1] G. W. F. Hegel, *Philosophy of History*, trans. J. Sibree (New York: John Wiley & Sons, 1944), p. 10.

in showing and understanding this necessary order of development was to discover the objective principles of evaluation which are immanent in the world process. Those principles or standards—moral, political, and scientific—enable one both to understand the particular stages of world-history and man's (spirit's) evolution and, for the discerning one, to grasp the direction and laws of that evolution. Thus, the study of the flux of history can provide us with historically objective norms of evaluation.

What are these norms? The purpose of writing *The Philosophy of Right* was to portray those norms. Hegel writes: "This book, then, containing as it does the science of the state, is to be nothing other than the endeavor to apprehend and portray the state as something inherently rational." [2] Historical analysis, for Hegel, enables us to perceive not only the progressive evolution of forms of government (descriptive truths) but also the necessity and rationality—indeed the "oughtness" of certain forms. (Whether there is a genuine difference between what *is* and what *ought* to be, for Hegel, is a much debated point, and one to which we will return.) National cultures and states do progressively evolve and succeed one another. There is, he argues, a logic and a pattern to this evolution. Indeed the pattern is necessary and rational (after all, *all* that is real is rational and vice-versa). Before examining that progressive evolution and formulating what for Hegel are the historically objective norms and institutions, we must first examine the logical (and ontological) device which, for Hegel, is essential in understanding the evolutionary growth and development of all phenomena, whether they be the organic processes of nature or social and political phenomena, namely, the dialectic.

The Dialectic

The Greeks understood dialectic to be a mode of argument and discussion, one in which a statement or thesis was countered or contradicted by an opposing statement or point of view. Out of the conflict a third statement or thesis emerged which attempted to reconcile the opposing views or which led to a new thesis. The new thesis was then challenged and the process of rational dialogue continued. For Hegel, however, the process of dialectic is not only one of logic or of thought but an ontological process or a process which occurs in the world as well.

[2] G. W. F. Hegel, *Hegel's Philosophy of Right*, trans. with notes by T. M. Knox (New York: Oxford University Press, 1967; first published by The Clarendon Press, 1952), p. 11.

Everything, for Hegel, develops dialectically, but at whatever level the dialectic operates, there are three stages—a thesis, antithesis, and synthesis. The "thesis" is the established pattern of thought and existence at a given time. But "theses" sooner or later grow and develop internal elements which oppose or contradict the existing pattern of thought and existence. Though in a state of tension, these internally developed contradictory elements—the "antithesis"—may exist for a time simultaneously with the thesis. But at some time (no matter whether the dialectic process is at the level of the development of organic life or at the level of evolving political institutions) the tension becomes too much. The "thesis" gives way to the "antithesis" resulting in a "synthesis." The new synthesis embraces the surviving and hence the "necessary" elements of both the thesis and antithesis. It then becomes the prevailing pattern of thought and existence, that is, the new thesis. It is in turn challenged by an antithesis, and the process goes on and on. The dialectic process should not be viewed as one in which two separate and opposing forces are engaged in struggle but one in which the thesis in the dialectic process gradually negates and changes itself. Change is a kind of internal necessity of Spirit or the Absolute.

The dialectical struggle is unending (at least until World-History is complete), but it is a creative process. Man and history advance "from the imperfect to the perfect." Put in terms of Hegel's metaphysic, all of history is the progressive self-determination and self-realization of the Spirit or Absolute. The goal of history is the self-knowledge and (since what is rational is real) the self-fulfilling development of the Absolute. All of the stages of history are necessary and lead up to this goal, which, in some sense, includes all of the early stages of history and of the evolution of spirit.

A three-part distinction which Hegel makes will perhaps make this clearer. He distinguishes between subjective, objective, and absolute spirit as three different stages in the self-realization of Spirit. Under subjective spirit Hegel includes the preconscious activities of organisms, sensation, and perception. Included also is the development of a state of self-consciousness in which there is recognition of other selves (and objects) with different and conflicting interests. This results in the evolution of social consciousness and the recognition of the need for social organization.

At this stage subjective spirit has negated itself and undergoes the transition to objective spirit. Objective spirit is a different level in the development of Spirit. It includes new kinds of reflection and hence of action. Spirit (through individual men, of course) begins to think about morality, law and the principles underlying the organization of society. Man, at this stage, has become a rational being. Indeed, for Hegel, it is only in and through morality and social institutions that man can become fully rational; for rationality requires that individuals identify themselves with the social and political institutions which exemplify universal spirit.

Absolute Spirit is the final level of development of Spirit. All of the conflicts, contradictions, and differences manifest in the early stages of the history and evolution of Spirit are here reconciled. The tensions of the world-process are overcome in the unified and harmonious self-consciousness of the Absolute. This ultimate height of self-awareness and self-knowledge of Spirit is made possible through philosophy, art, and religion. Absolute Spirit, as fully rational and consistent, is said to contain, in some sense, all of the concepts and lower stages of the evolution of Spirit. Presumably, Absolute Spirit, being the culminating stage of world-history, could not be fully explained until the process of world-history is a *fait accompli*.

Hegel's philosophy of history was an attempt to show, with special reference to western civilization, that this dialectic process exists. The Greek city-state represented an early stage in the dialectical development of social institutions; Christianity and its beliefs and values, a later stage; the Germanic nations at the time of Protestantism and the Reformation yet another stage. Each is a progressive, creative leap or development of social values and institutions, and hence a development of Spirit. Each stage also is necessary for the progressive move to better or to ideal social institutions, which is the goal of the spirit in world-history. Therefore, those societies and social institutions which appear to be evil and tyrannical are not to be completely condemned; for even inadequate and outmoded social institutions and conventions are the result of the efforts of generations of men who found those institutions, perhaps only for a short time, useful in achieving social harmony. The elements of their own negation are internally present—their antitheses—and both thesis and antithesis are necessary for the progressive development of higher forms of social institutions. Each institution lives its life but necessarily dies—at least until the end of world-history when there is a complete self-realization of Absolute Spirit. In fact Hegel declares that "those who can imagine that institutions, constitutions, and laws can persist after they have ceased to be in accord with the morals, the needs, and the purposes of mankind, and after the meaning has gone out of them" are blind.

They can neither see nor understand history. Thus the birth and death of multiple social arrangements and institutions are seen as necessary steps in the development of more rational, coherent, and inclusive political systems.

Moral and Political Institutions

We have stated that for Hegel the State is Absolute Spirit, and we have recognized that Hegel's political philosophy can be understood only as a part of his idealistic metaphysic, in which the world-process and all it contains is seen as the dialectical evolution of Spirit. All moral and political concepts (right, good, conscience, political obligation, society, freedom, the State, and so on), the institutions which embody those concepts, and the concrete actions which arise from them can be properly understood only within this framework. Hegel deals with these concepts most systematically in his *Philosophy of Right* where he discusses the relationship between the individual and the institutions—social and economic—within which he exists, and the relationship between these institutions and the State as the most unique institution and embodiment of Spirit. It will be fruitful to briefly examine the principal distinctions and arguments of the *Philosophy of Right*.

Abstract Right, Morality, and Ethical Life

Hegel pictures the State as the end of an evolutionary process comprised of two dialectical triads: (1) abstract right, morality, and ethical life; and (2) the family, civil society, and the State. Let us briefly examine each of these triads.

The "thesis" of the first triad, "abstract right," affirms that each man, in virtue of the fact that he is a man, has certain rights. "Personality essentially involves the capacity for rights and constitutes the concept and the basis (itself abstract) of the system of abstract and therefore formal right. Hence the imperative of right is: 'Be a person and respect others as persons.' " [3] Claims of rights men have as rational, free and purposeful creatures, and Hegel includes among these rights the right to possess property, to have contracts respected, and so on. At this level ethics centers around the keeping of contracts and the "warrants" or "permissions" for making them; it excludes questions "of particular interests, of my advantage or my welfare. . . .

[3] Ibid., p. 37.

and intention." [4] Slavery is necessarily incompatible with the thesis of abstract right. Hegel states: "This false, comparatively primitive phenomenon of slavery is one which befalls mind when mind is only at the level of consciousness." [5] At the level of self-consciousness which instantiates the idea of freedom, that is, the State, slavery cannot possibly occur.

The "antithesis" of abstract right Hegel calls "morality." Two basic concepts are subsumed under morality—the good and conscience. "The good," Hegel states, is "freedom realized, the absolute end and aim of the world." [6] (We will see what freedom means later.) It has priority over abstract right: "Since the good must of necessity be actualized through the particular will and is at the same time its substance, it has absolute right in contrast with the abstract right of property and the particular aims of welfare." [7] Conscience, on the other hand, "is the expression of the absolute title of subjective self-consciousness to know in itself and from within itself what is right and obligatory, to give recognition only to what it thus knows as good, and at the same time, to maintain that whatever in this way it knows and wills is in truth right and obligatory." [8] Thus the moral consciousness and feelings of a man (his right and duty to act on the basis of the principles or rules which he believes to be correct) are conscience, for Hegel.

Though a man has a right and duty to act on the basis of conscience, this does not mean that his conscience is correct. As Hegel states, "whether the conscience of a specific individual corresponds with this Idea of conscience, or whether what it takes or declares to be good is actually so, is ascertainable only from the content of the good it seeks to realize." [9] Thus Hegel distinguishes between "formal conscience" and "true conscience." The latter necessarily accords with the Idea or universal laws and principles; the former may not. He insists that "what is right and obligatory is the absolutely rational element in the will's volitions and therefore it is not in essence the particular property of an individual, and its form is not that of feeling or any other private (i.e. sensuous) type of knowing, but essentially that of universals determined by thought, i.e. the form of laws and prin-

---

4 Ibid., p. 38.
5 Ibid., p. 48.
6 Ibid., p. 86.
7 Ibid., p. 87.
8 Ibid., p. 91.
9 Ibid.

ciples." [10] Thus though the exercise of conscience is essential if one is to be a complete moral agent or being, and though the use of conscience is required in (and takes priority over) the evaluation of abstract rights, still Hegel insists that conscience is "subject to the judgment of its truth or falsity, and when it appeals only to itself for a decision, it is directly at variance with what it wishes to be, namely the rule for a mode of conduct which is rational, absolutely valid, and universal. For this reason, the state cannot give recognition to conscience in its private form as subjective knowing, any more than science can grant validity to subjective opinion, dogmatism, and the appeal to a subjective opinion." [11]

In sum, Hegel seems to be saying that the first stage of ethics involves a recognition of universal rights (though not necessarily identical rights). Ethics here involves basically the respecting of rights and the keeping of contracts. The second stage, which is to be seen as evolving out of the first, involves new concepts—the good and conscience—and a challenge to existing systems of rights on the basis of these concepts. For example, the right to own other persons or the "right to the first night" which were established and legal rights within certain systems of rights were challenged on the basis of conscience and emerging concepts of the good life. This dialectical tension resulted in a higher order of ethics, hence of rationality and freedom. Thus there evolve distinctions between (1) rightness as conformity to contract, (2) goodness as conformity to the Idea or Freedom, (3) conscience (formal) as conformity to what one *thinks* is morally right, and (4) conscience (true) as conformity to the rational, absolutely valid, and universal standards. Goodness and true conscience apparently turn out to be the same thing, for Hegel states that "true conscience is the disposition to will what is absolutely valid." [12]

The dialectical tension, then, between abstract right and morality (the thesis and antithesis) involves the recognition that acts may be morally right in the sense of conforming to contract or to a right in some system of rights and yet violate one's sense of conscience. That is, an act could be formally or legally good but morally bad, or it could be morally good (conforming to formal conscience) and yet illegal or in violation of rights.

Obviously an act could conform to abstract right and meet the demands of formal conscience and yet not conform to the good or to

[10] Ibid.
[11] Ibid.
[12] Ibid., p. 90.

rational, objective and universal standards (the dictates of "true" conscience). Awareness of the latter, that is, of "absolutely valid laws and institutions" and of an "objective ethical order" occurs when the synthesis of abstract right and morality occurs. This synthesis, the necessary result of the necessary conflict between abstract right and morality, Hegel calls "ethical life." In this synthesis Hegel claims that there is "identity of the universal will with the particular will, right and duty coalesce, and by being in the ethical order a man has rights insofar as he has duties, and duties insofar as he has rights. In the sphere of abstract right, I have the right and another has the corresponding duty. In the moral sphere, the right of my private judgment and will, as of my happiness, has not, but only ought to have, coalesced with duties and become objective." [13] But in ethical life welfare, duty, right and conscience agree. Only in ethical life are men "actually in possession of their own essence or their own inner universality," [14] for "ethical life is the concept of freedom developed into the existing world and the nature of self-consciousness" [15] and it is only "in duty [that] the individual acquires his substantive freedom." [16] (We will explicate this concept of freedom momentarily.) Let us now turn to the second dialectical triad which is basic to Hegel's theory.

The Family, Civil Society, and the State

In the evolution of the State, Hegel pictures the "family" as the thesis, "civil society" as the antithesis and the "State" as the synthesis. The family, the smallest organizational unit, is "specifically characterized by love," and is completed through marriage, family property, the education of children, and, finally, dissolution of itself. The family and marriage has its natural basis in physical life and sexual union, but Hegel also insists that "marriage, and especially monogomy, is one of the absolute principles on which the ethical life of a community depends." [17] Though it may seem that union in marriage is a self-restriction (for each partner agrees to restrictions of liberties), Hegel states that "in fact it is their liberation because in it they attain their substantive self-consciousness." [18] They are conscious of a "unity as their substantive aim, and so in their love, trust, and common

[13] Ibid., pp. 109–110.
[14] Ibid., p. 109.
[15] Ibid., p. 105.
[16] Ibid., p. 107.
[17] Ibid., p. 115.
[18] Ibid., p. 111.

sharing, of their entire existence as individuals." [19] The family, then, is based on love and moral unity, not so much on rights or justice. For example, "the right of the parents over the wishes of their children is determined by the object in view—discipline and education. The punishment of children does not aim at justice as such; the aim is more subjective and moral in character, i.e. to deter them from exercising a freedom still in the toils of nature and to lift the universal into their consciousness and will." [20]

The family—and the basic emphasis on love and moral unity—is necessarily superseded by a more complex social relationship. As men strive to fulfill their wants and needs, "there is formed a system of complete interdependence, wherein the livelihood, happiness, and legal status of one man is interwoven with the livelihood, happiness, and rights of all. On this system, individual happiness, etc. depend, and only in this connected system are they actualized and secured." [21] Hegel calls this connected system the "external state" or "civil society." It is comprised of three "moments"—the development of a "system of needs" in which the interests and needs of all are mediated, the development and administration of a system of justice, and the formulation of the police and of corporations. The system of need fulfillment, in which there is both competition and cooperation, results in the development of three social classes—the agricultural class, the business class, and the class of civil servants (which Hegel calls the "universal" class). The task of the latter is the maintainance of order and the administration of justice, which Hegel calls "the universal interests of the community."

Abstract right or equality is essential to justice for Hegel. He states: "It is part of education, of thinking as the consciousness of the single in the form of universality, that the ego comes to be apprehended as a universal person in which all are identical. A man counts as a man in virtue of his manhood alone, not because he is a Jew, Catholic, Protestant, German, Italian, etc. This is an assertion which thinking ratifies and to be conscious of it is of infinite importance. It is defective only when it is crystallized, e.g. as a cosmopolitanism in opposition to the concrete life of the state." [22]

Hegel's reservation that equality may be carried so far that it is "in opposition to the concrete life of the state" and hence may vitiate

19 Ibid., p. 112.
20 Ibid., p. 117.
21 Ibid., p. 123.
22 Ibid., p. 134.

justice calls for clarification. We can know what he means by justice and a just society only when this has been clarified, and since this is central to his entire political philosophy we will return to this issue in some detail later. The issue is that of the relationship of the individual (and his rights) to the state (and its goals).

Hegel distinguishes between "the principle of rightness" and "the law" or the content of law. Abstract right becomes determinate when "posited as positive law" and in positive law, Hegel states, "it is the legal which is the source of our knowledge of what is right, or more exactly, of our legal rights. . . . Thus the science of positive law is to that extent an historical science with authority as its guiding principle." [23] But Hegel insists that "there may enter the contingency of self-will and other particular circumstances and hence there may be a discrepancy between the content of the law and the principle of rightness." [24] Thus justice in the sense of abstract right may not coincide with justice in the sense of legal rights; in order for them to coincide the latter apparently must embody rationality and universality. In fact, "a fruitful source of complexity in legislation is the gradual intrusion of reason, of what is inherently and actually right, into primitive institutions which have something wrong at their roots and so are purely historical survivals." [25] The problem for Hegel is the specification of criteria for what is "inherently and actually right" or for rationality and universality. To this question we will return. For now let us recognize Hegel's principal point concerning civil society as the antithesis to family life: When the principle of rightness is embodied in law, "my individual right, whose embodiment has hitherto been immediate and abstract, now similarly becomes embodied in the existent will and knowledge of everyone, in the sense that it becomes recognized. Hence property acquisitions and transfers must now be undertaken and concluded only in the form which that embodiment gives to them. In civil society, property rests on contract and on the formalities which make ownership capable of proof and valid in law." [26] Courts of justice and legal systems evolve in different ways and forms but, whatever the origin, "legal and political institutions are rational in principle and therefore absolutely necessary, and the question of the form in which they arose or were introduced is entirely irrelevant to a consideration of their rational basis." [27] Fur-

[23] Ibid., p. 136.
[24] Ibid.
[25] Ibid., p. 138.
[26] Ibid., p. 139.
[27] Ibid., p. 141.

thermore, the administration of justice is not a suppression of freedom ("as it was in the days when might was right"); on the contrary it is essential for the very existence of freedom.

Police or public authority in civil society is required to control conflict-of-interest situations between producers and consumers and parents and children, and to look after the poor. Also, the formation of corporations in civil society is necessary for the business class. But corporations, police, courts of justice, and positive laws—these organs of civil society—are insufficient. Just as family life contains the seeds of civil society and cannot remain self-contained, so also civil society cannot be a self-contained system and necessarily evolves into the State, which is the synthesis of family life and civil society.

What is the State for Hegel? We saw that the "external state" is comprised of the organs of civil society. But the internal state, the real state, is more than the social, political, and legal organs of civil society. It includes these but its essence is "the actuality of the ethical idea. It is ethical mind qua that substantial will manifest and revealed to it, knowing and thinking itself, accomplishing what it knows and insofar as it knows it. The state exists immediately in custom, immediately in individual self-consciousness, knowledge and activity, while self-consciousness in virtue of its sentiment toward the state finds in the state, as its essence and the end and product of its activity, its substantive freedom." [28] This substantial freedom and self-consciousness of spirit "is an absolute unmoved end in itself." [29] The state must not be confused with civil society, for

> if its specific end is laid down as the security and protection of property and personal freedom, then the interests of the individuals as such becomes the ultimate end of their association, and it follows that membership in the state is something optional. But the state's relation to the individual is quite different from this. Since the state is mind objectified, it is only as one of its members that the individual has objectivity, genuine individuality, and an ethical life. Unification pure and simple is the true content and aim of the individual, and the individual's destiny is the living of a universal life.[30]

Hegel's metaphysic comes through loud and clear in this passage. The central theme is "universal will" or "mind objectified." A genuine state exists only when the self-interested individuals of civil

28 Ibid., p. 155.
29 Ibid., p. 156.
30 Ibid.

society "pass over of their own accord into the interest of the universal, and, for another thing, they know and will the universal; they even recognize it as their own substantive mind; they take it as their end and aim and are active in its pursuit." [31] As Hegel puts it on another occasion, "The state is actual only when its members have a feeling of their own self-hood and it is stable only when public and private ends are identical." [32] When this happens, the individual achieves his highest freedom and happiness. Furthermore, "This final end has supreme right against the individual, whose supreme duty is to be a member of the state." [33]

Now if one rejects the notion of a "universal will" or "objectified mind," the Hegelian position plainly collapses. But Hegel is totally convinced of the correctness of these notions, and he sees the error of many political theorists who attempt to base the state on a social contract or on consent as that of recognizing only the individual will (or a "general" will as in Rousseau). "The result," Hegel claims, is the reduction of "the union of individuals in the state to a contract and therefore to something based on their arbitrary will, their opinion, and their capriciously given consent. . . ." [34] This destroys the "absolutely divine principle of the state, together with its majesty and absolute authority" (which was at least in part exactly what some contract theorists and utilitarians wanted to do).[35] For Hegel, the state is not simply a utilitarian device for maximizing the happiness of individuals or of assuring rights. It is a natural and metaphysical entity, without which the private ends of individuals and social groups have no meaning.

Freedom

We have seen that the norm of freedom (and rationality) is the central one in Hegel's political philosophy, just as it is in the philosophy of John Stuart Mill. But what Hegel means by freedom is quite different from Mill. Individual freedom, the right to do what one pleases without state interference, is not the Hegelian concept of freedom. On the contrary, it is by following the direction of the state, by immersing oneself in one's role as citizen, by fulfilling one's role

[31] Ibid., p. 160.
[32] Ibid., p. 281.
[33] Ibid., p. 156.
[34] Ibid., p. 157.
[35] Ibid.

within the overall purpose of the state that the individual finds his true freedom (as well as his happiness and rationality). It is only through political institutions and hence state interference with the actions of individuals that real freedom is possible, for Hegel. In a sense this is also true of Mill, Bentham, Locke, and Hobbes, but only in the limited sense that political institutions permit autonomous individuals to live together cooperatively and fulfill their individual and mutual interests. For Hegel, however, the relationship of freedom to political institutions is much stronger. It includes this limited sense but goes on to claim that one cannot really be a man, and fulfill himself as a man, without political institutions; for both men and their institutions are part of the Idea or plan of history within which everything has its being and significance. Only when one accepts his moral and political obligations within the state is one a free and rational person. Freedom, then, is not so much a property of the individual per se as it is a property of an overall social and political system to which the individual is attached and in which he participates when he fulfills his station in that system. Apart from such a system, Hegel maintains, there is an absence of constitutional law, hence there is ethical anarchy in which self-seeking persons act on mere desires and caprice.

Plainly there is a fundamental disparity between Hegel and the utilitarians (and other political philosophers) on both the nature of the state and of freedom. For the utilitarians, the state is merely an instrument for maximizing, and to some extent, equalizing, happiness or welfare. The basic objective is to provide the conditions whereby the needs and ends of individuals can be satisfied. For Hegel the state is an end in itself and individuals are instruments of it. The good of the state is not merely the sum of the private goods of individuals achieved through social organization but the development of an organic unity as an instantiation in history of the universal spirit. Concomitantly, freedom is not merely the right to pursue one's private ends within a set of social institutions which mutually restrict all members of society; rather it is identification of one's private interests and goals with those of the state, and, through the state, with universal spirit itself.

Forms of Government and Constitutions

What is the best form of government? Who is to frame the constitution for the state? Hegel treats both of these questions as odd or ill-formed, as indeed they are for anyone within the Hegelian metaphysic. He recognizes the traditional divisions of governments and constitutions into monarchy, aristocracy, and democracy, but insists that "the Idea is indifferent to them, . . . because everyone of them is inadequate to it in its rational development and in none of them, taken singly, would the Idea attain its right and actuality." [36] All of these forms are proper at different times in the development of the Idea; "consequently, it is quite idle to inquire which of the three is most to be preferred. Such forms must be discussed historically or not at all." [37] Thus Hegel agrees with Fichte that all of these forms are justified if they function as means for introducing and maintaining universal rights into the state. But this function is not enough, Hegel declares, and those who maintain that it is have a "superficial conception" of the state.

Concerning the question, "Who is to frame the constitution for the state?", Hegel argues that this question on close inspection is "meaningless, for it presupposes that there is no constitution there but only an agglomeration of atomic individuals." [38] With agglomerations of atomic individuals, the question would make good sense but the state is not such an agglomerate and the constitution "must be treated rather as something simply existent in and by itself, as divine therefore, and constant. . . ." [39] In fact "it is absolutely essential that the constitution should not be regarded as something made, even though it has come into being in time." [40] Obviously then, if the constitution is not something made, it makes no sense to ask who should frame it. Any proposal to simply present a constitution to a nation overlooks this fact and the fact "that the constitution of any given nation depends in general on the character and development of its self-consciousness." [41] Therefore, Hegel insists, "every nation has the constitution appropriate to it and suitable for it." [42] For constitutions at least, this seems to be the thesis that what *exists* is *right*, and some think that this holds for all normative issues within Hegel's philosophy.

Divisions of Power in the State

For Hegel there should be three basic divisions of power within the state. This division, "is of the highest importance and, if taken

[36] Ibid., p. 177.
[37] Ibid.
[38] Ibid., p. 178.
[39] Ibid.
[40] Ibid.
[41] Ibid., p. 179.
[42] Ibid.

in its true sense, may rightly be regarded as the guarantee of public freedom." [43] In fact he declares that if these powers become self-subsistent, then "the destruction of the state is forthwith a *fait accompli*." [44] The function of the legislative power is "to determine and establish the universal," that of the executive is to subsume or decide particular cases under the universal, and that of the Crown is "the power of ultimate decision," a synthesis of the legislative and executive powers or "an individual unity which is thus at once the apex and basis of the whole, i.e. of constitutional monarchy." [45] Hegel is most definitely committed to constitutional monarchy as the most viable form of government. "The development of the state to constitutional monarchy," he tells us, "is the achievement of the modern world, a world in which the substantial Idea has won the infinite form. . . ." [46] The monarch expresses the unity of the nation and he is the sovereign power.

Hegel is not always clear when he speaks of "sovereignty," but it is clear that it excludes individual arbitrariness and caprice on the part of the monarch. Such arbitrariness would be despotism. Real sovereignty involves commitment to "the universality of the constitution and laws" in which "the individual functionaries and agents are attached to their office not on the strength of their immediate personality but only on the strength of their universal and objective qualities." [47] The authority of the crown is derived from the fact that it exemplifies the Idea or the universal in history, and "it is precisely in legal, constitutional, government that sovereignty is to be found at the moment of ideality. . . ." [48]

Does the sovereignty of the monarch mean that he initiates law and makes policy? What is the role of the legislature within this sovereign power? Hegel gives no clear answer to these questions. It is plain that the executive power merely executes and applies the monarch's decisions, existing law and so on.[49] And Hegel states that we should not demand "objective qualities" in a monarch, for "he has only to say 'yes' and dot the 'i'. . . . In a well-organized monarchy, the objective aspect belongs to law alone, and the monarch's part is merely to set to the law the subjective 'I will.' " [50] This would appear

43 Ibid., p. 175.
44 *Ibid.*
45 Ibid., p. 176.
46 Ibid.
47 Ibid., p. 179.
48 Ibid., p. 180.
49 Ibid., p. 188.
50 Ibid., p. 289.

at first blush to leave heavy responsibility for drafting laws and making policies to the legislature and to public opinion. But this is not so, for we are told that "in the legislature as a whole the other powers are the first two moments which are effective (i) the monarchy as that to which ultimate decisions belong; (ii) the executive as the advisory body. . . ."[51] The link between the general public and the making of law is through the "Estates" which he calls the "last moment of the legislature." The function of the Estates is that of "bringing into existence . . . the public consciousness as an empirical universal, of which the thoughts and opinions of the many are particulars."[52] They function as "a middle term preventing the extreme isolation of the power of the crown, which otherwise might seem a mere arbitrary tyranny, and also the isolation of the particular interests of persons, societies, and corporations."[53]

Hegel here is insisting that the monarch cannot rule adequately without close contact with the will of the people through the Estates, but the Estates are not given the power to propose legislation or to change or reject the policies of the monarch—as in representative government. The Estates he sees as "a guarantee of the general welfare and public freedom." But he insists that "a little reflection will show that this guarantee does not lie in their particular power of insight, because the highest civil servants necessarily have a deeper and more comprehensive insight into the nature of the states organization and requirements. They are also more habituated to the business of government and have greater skill in it, so that even without the Estates they are able to do what is best, just as they also continually have to do while the Estates are in session. No, the guarantee lies on the contrary in the additional insight of the deputies, insight in the first place into the activity of such officials as are not immediately under the eye of the higher functionaries of state, and in particular into the more pressing and more specialized needs and deficiencies which are directly in their view. . . ."[54]

Hegel on Democracy and Constitutional Monarchy

Hegel is opposed to democracy or to free unrestricted elections and universal participation in government on several grounds. First, all of these, he thinks, lend credence to the view that the state is merely

[51] Ibid., p. 195.
[52] Ibid.
[53] Ibid., p. 197.
[54] Ibid., p. 196.

an agglomeration of individuals merged under a social contract for utilitarian purposes. This is a false conception of the State. Second,

> to hold that every single person should share in deliberating and deciding on political matters of general concern on the ground that all individuals are members of the state, that its concerns are their concerns, and that it is their right that what is done should be done with their knowledge and volition, is tantamount to a proposal to put the democratic element without any rational form into the organism of the state, although it is only in virtue of the possession of such a form that the state is an organism at all.[55]

Most persons are not intelligent or well educated enough to know about the needs, conditions, and problems of different strata of society. Elected deputies must represent and intelligently speak for "one of the essential spheres of society and its large-scale interest" but "the idea of free unrestricted election leaves this important consideration at the mercy of chance." [56] For this reason Hegel advocated a restricted franchise. One-man, one-vote political equality is out, for what is important in Hegel's view is not the fact of political participation but the organic unity of the State and the self-fulfillment (in Hegel's sense) of the individual. "The single person attains his actual and living destiny for universality only when he becomes a member of a Corporation, a society, etc., and thereby it becomes open to him on the strength of his skill, to enter any class for which he is qualified, the class of civil servants included." [57] But just as a person does not have the right to participate in a Corporation (in Hegel's sense) without being a qualified member, so also one cannot participate as a voting member in the body politic without qualifying for membership. Hegel advocates equality of opportunity to qualify for such membership. In this sense and in the sense that each person, just because he is a person, possesses certain abstract rights, Hegel is an egalitarian. But he rejects a straightforward political egalitarianism because he believes that a universal franchise would subvert the ends of the state. On this point Hegel and Mill agree, though they differ radically on what are the ends of the state. Third, "popular suffrage . . . leads inevitably to electoral indifference, since the casting of a single vote is of no significance where there is a multitude of electors. . . . Thus the result of an institution of this kind is more likely to be the opposite of what was intended; election actually falls into the power of a few, of a caucus,

[55] Ibid., p. 200.
[56] Ibid., p. 202.
[57] Ibid., p. 201.

and so of the particular contingent interest which is precisely what was to have been neutralized.[58]

Hegel firmly believes that constitutional and hereditary monarchy is the only effective means of assuring the organic unity of the state and hence of assuring public freedom.[59] Talk about the "sovereignty of the people" he characterizes as "one of the confused notions based on the wild idea of the 'people.' Taken without its monarch and the articulation of the whole which is the indispensible and direct concomitant of monarchy, the people is a formless mass and no longer a state." [60] People, as formless masses, are to be feared, for without organic unity such masses can lead to chaos and despotism (the absence of constitutional law).

Public Opinion and Freedom of Speech

Although Hegel was not a proponent of democracy, he strongly advocated some values which are central to democracy, though always with qualifications. For example, he places great stock in public opinion as "a repository not only of the genuine needs and correct tendencies of common life, but also, in the form of common sense (i.e. all-pervasive fundamental ethical principles disguised as prejudices), of the eternal, substantive principles of justice, the true content and result of legislation, the whole constitution, and the general position of the state." [61] This is very high praise of public opinion. On the other hand, he notes that public opinion can become infected with ignorance and perversity, for which it is to be "despised." Public opinion "in itself . . . has no criterion of discrimination. . . , thus to be independent of public opinion is the first formal condition of achieving anything great or rational whether in life or in science." [62] But how independent of it should one be?

Hegel advocated freedom of speech, for two main reasons. First, ". . . opining and talking should be held in high esteem and respect— the opining because it is personal property and in fact pre-eminently the property of mind; the talking because it is only this same property being expressed and used." [63] Here Hegel's advocacy of free speech seems to be tied to his concept of what it means to be human (a free

[58] Ibid., p. 203.
[59] Ibid., p. 188.
[60] Ibid., p. 183.
[61] Ibid., p. 204.
[62] Ibid., p. 205.
[63] Ibid., p. 206.

and rational being) and to the abstract right that all humans are to be treated as persons. Second, when free speech is practiced, especially in the Estates Assemblies, it results in "sound and mature insight into the concerns of the state," that is, responsible and informed criticism. Hegel recognizes that there will be uninformed and irresponsible uses of freedom of speech, but thinks that the practice of free speech itself is, in spite of the hazards, a "safeguard" against irresponsibility, for "indifference and contempt [are] speedily and necessarily visited on shallow and cantankerous talking." [64]

However, freedom of speech must be limited. "To define freedom of the press as freedom to say and write whatever we please is parallel to the assertion that freedom as such means freedom to do as we please. Talk of this kind is due to wholly uneducated, crude, and superficial ideas." [65] The limitations exclude "slander, abuse, the contemptuous caricature of government, its ministers, officials and in particular the person of the monarch, defiance of the laws, incitement to rebellion, etc." [66] All of these Hegel views as crimes or misdemeanors, as indeed most of them are still regarded.

Justice and Power (Is and Ought)

What is the difference between justice and power for Hegel? Is there any difference, or does might make right? These questions are difficult to answer. Quite clearly, for Hegel, justice in the sense of abstract right, a kind of egalitarianism in which each person is respected because he is human, exists independently of the power of the state. But Hegel makes it plain that it is only through the organic unity of the state that man's moral life and standards of justice can be truly characterized as "ethical life." The justice of the state is supreme over the justice exemplified in individual conscience. "The welfare of the state," he insists, "has claims to recognition totally different from those of the welfare of the individual. . . . When politics is alleged to clash with morals and so to be always wrong, the doctrine propounded rests on superficial ideas about morality, the nature of the state, and the state's relation to the moral point of view." [67] One's highest duty and his highest freedom are simultaneously realized in the state as an instantiation of the Idea or Spirit in history.

[64] Ibid.
[65] Ibid.
[66] Ibid., p. 207.
[67] Ibid., p. 215.

Still, not all states or all laws should be obeyed. A despotic government vitiates law and does not deserve obedience; so justice is not equated merely with existing law. "Whether a state is in fact something absolute depends on its content, i.e. on its constitution and general situation. . . ." [68] This means that right cannot be identified with might or mere existence; for, as Hegel emphasizes, "world history is not the verdict of mere might, i.e. the abstract and non-rational inevitability of a blind destiny." [69]

But how are we to distinguish those states which instantiate the Idea or universal, and hence command our complete obedience, from those which do not? Two points must be made here. First, Hegel holds that each stage of world-history "is the presence of a necessary moment in the Idea of the world mind, and that moment attains its absolute right in that stage." [70] Taken without qualification, this implies that whatever state exists at any given time is "necessary" and has absolute right to obedience. But Hegel does qualify this assertion. Not all nations embody a "necessary moment in the Idea." Only that "nation to which is ascribed a moment of the Idea in the form of a natural principle is entrusted with giving complete effect to it in the advance of the self-developing self-consciousness of the world mind. This nation is dominant in world history during this one epoch, and it is only once . . . that it can make its hour strike. In contrast with this its absolute right of being the vehicle of this present stage in the world mind's development, the minds of the other nations are without rights, and they, along with those whose hour has struck already, count no longer in world history." [71] But which nation is to be seen as "counting" in world history? What are Hegel's criteria for counting? Except in the most general terms these are never spelled out. Furthermore, one is led back to the view that Hegel identifies right with might when he states that "it is the absolute right of the Idea to step into existence . . . whether this right be actualized in the form of divine legislation and favour, or in the form of force and wrong. This right is the right of heroes to found states." [72] But if "force and wrong" are legitimate in founding states, how can one distinguish a legitimate state from an illegitimate one?

Second, Hegel states that "justice and virtue, wrongdoing, power

68 Ibid., p. 212.
69 Ibid., p. 216.
70 Ibid., p. 217.
71 Ibid., pp. 217–218.
72 Ibid., p. 219.

and vice, talents and their achievements, passions strong and weak, guilt and innocence, grandeur in individual and national life, autonomy, fortune and misfortune of states and individuals, all these have their specific significance and worth in the field of known actuality; therein they are judged and therein they have their partial, though only partial justification. World-history, however, is above the point of view from which these things matter." [73] But if world-history is above the point of view from which justice and injustice, rightdoing and wrongdoing, guilt and innocence even matter, and if one's evaluative perspective should be from the point of view of world-history and its necessary evolution, does not this mean that there can be no standard of justice by which we can distinguish a nation which is powerful but unjust from one which is powerful and just? Are we not forced to the conclusion that might makes right or that what is, ought to be? Hegel's own criterion (or prejudice?) is well known: the Germanic peoples have been "entrusted" with the unity of the divine and the human.[74]

War and International Relations

Hegel's position on war is that it "is not to be regarded as an absolute evil and as a purely external accident, which itself has some accidental causes, be it injustice, the passions of nations or the holders of power, etc. or in short, something or other which ought not to be." [75] Quite the contrary, war has an "ethical moment" and is necessary: " . . . by its agency, the ethical health of peoples is preserved in their indifference to the stabilization of finite institutions; just as the blowing of the winds preserves the sea from the foulness which would be the result of a prolonged calm, so also corruption in nations would be the product of prolonged, let alone 'perpetual' peace." [76] Custom he views as an enemy of progress, and war changes customs. It is doubtful that Hegel would support the necessity or "ethical moment" of war today, given the catastrophic results; it would not only change customs, but would obliterate the possibility of having *any* customs.

On the possibility of international law Hegel by no means adopted the position to which his metaphysic would seem to commit him. Absolute spirit, as manifest in the thought and activities of men, is basi-

---

[73] Ibid., p. 217.
[74] Ibid., p. 222.
[75] Ibid., p. 209.
[76] Ibid., p. 210.

cally a unity. It evolves toward complete self-consciousness, freedom, and rationality. Would not this occur more fully in an international community of men, in which there is international law and justice, as opposed to mere national communities? Hegel does not conclude that this is so. The nation-state he sees as the highest manifestation of the Idea. He does acknowledge that there ought to be international law. However, he identifies the "fundamental proposition of international law" as merely the keeping of treaties and holds that the rights of nations "are actualized only in their particular will and not in a universal will with constitutional powers over them." [77] "The relation between states is a relation between autonomous entities which make mutual stipulations but which at the same time are superior to these stipulations." [78] Since this is so, and since national welfare is "the highest law governing the relation of one state to another," Hegel concludes that "if states disagree and their particular wills cannot be harmonized, the matter can only be settled by war." [79] The universal absolute mind he recognizes to be a "higher judge." [80] However, he never conceives of universal mind as an international community of men and nations.

Critique

Clearly, almost any evaluation of Hegel's political philosophy hangs on the acceptance or rejection of his metaphysics. We say "almost any" for as indicated earlier there may be considerable truth and value in parts of Hegel's political theory quite independent of the metaphysical trappings which he places about that theory. For example, look at his theses about the nature of man, morality, and society. Hegel maintains that the extreme individualism of the utilitarians falsifies our views of man, morality, and society. Men are not isolated, atomic individuals. They are psychologically structured by the mores, laws, and institutions of their respective societies. Man's moral and valuational perspective is shaped by that social structure and by historical conditions. In this sense one cannot understand man without understanding society. Hegel presses this thesis strongly—a point now quite common among social scientists—and surely he is correct. Furthermore, although there is a sense in which morality is individual

[77] Ibid., p. 213.
[78] Ibid., p. 297.
[79] Ibid., p. 214.
[80] Ibid., p.297.

(recall Hegel's talk about "conscience"), Hegel's thesis that morality is basically a community or corporate enterprise or activity seems to be correct. Most moral concepts and rules have their homes or their principal function in communities. Hegel, I believe, is correct on these points (and, of course, the utilitarian certainly need not deny them).

However, when Hegel goes further and insists that the individual can be fully moral and rational only by identifying with the State and by complete obedience to it, this seems to be going too far. Surely there are senses in which the state is not the answer to all of our ethical problems. The state does not always make men more moral and rational. (Nor can it be viewed merely as an extension of oneself.) It sometimes does just the opposite. When it does, the state must itself be morally evaluated, and it is not clear that this is even possible in Hegel's theory. Where would one stand to perform such an evaluation? There can be no appeal to natural law or natural rights, for Hegel rejects this doctrine. Nor is the principle of utility available, for Hegel not only rejects the view that the history of the world is "the theatre of happiness"; he also maintains that "as a general rule, individuals come under the category of means to an ulterior end," namely, the evolution of absolute spirit. Some states Hegel clearly thinks are despotic and inferior, and others are superior. But finite human beings cannot see things from the point of view of universal spirit or the Absolute. The spirit works through us without our knowing it. Even the "hero" who founds states is a mere tool of spirit. As suggested earlier, the right or the ideal is indistinguishable from whatever exists and all states and institutions would appear to be necessary stages in the dialectical evolution of spirit. Thus, Hegel seems to identify what ought to be with what is and to reduce morality and moral critique to mere description of history and to historical understanding.

These objections to Hegel's treatment of the concept of morality, to his analysis of what it means to be a human, and to his view of the role of the state involve correlative objections on a normative level. For his analysis of these concepts—man, morality, the State—leads to the normative conclusions that individuals really do not matter (in spite of his insistence on the universality of abstract rights). The desires, interests, and, indeed, the rights of individuals are properly sacrificed, according to Hegel, for the larger goals of the state. Thus, all of the evils of totalitarianism lies implicit in his political theory.

It must be admitted that, in a sense, these criticisms of Hegel beg the question; for Hegel's political theory presupposes the truth of his metaphysics, and these criticisms implicitly deny that metaphysic. A forthright critique of Hegel requires a head-on confrontation with his metaphysic. Is Absolute Spirit something real or merely a figment of Hegel's mind? Is all of history and all change a dialectical process in which Spirit becomes self-conscious, as Hegel claims?

Both of these tenets of Hegel—his metaphysical idealism and his theory of dialectic—have been severely challenged. Just as Hegel fuses the distinction between knowledge and the object of knowledge, he also fuses laws of thought and laws of reality. The dialectic is at the same time a law of logic and a law of reality. But with this fusion it is seldom, if ever, clear what Hegel means by key concepts related to the dialectic, that is, contradiction, consistency, and coherence. When a thesis is "contradicted" by an antithesis, it seems to mean any kind of difference, opposition, causal tendency, and so on. Furthermore, although the dialectic is supposed to provide an explanation of the growth and development of all phenomena, it seems to explain nothing at all. Hegel simply forces all phenomena into the dialectic mold. (In what way, for example, is civil society the negation or contradiction of the family?) And there seems to be no way of testing the so-called explanations of the dialectic. For this reason many philosophers challenge the claim that the dialectic is an essential explanatory device for understanding social change. (Of course, the same scepticism is extended to Marx's and Engels's use of the notion of dialectic.)

This scepticism toward dialectic as a method is often accompanied by doubts about the existence of Absolute Spirit and the Idea. That there is a plan in history and that reality is of the nature of mind or spirit are Hegel's assumptions. He claims that an examination of history bears this out, but many look at the history of man and the world without seeing either a Plan or Spirit. Even Marx and Engels, who accept the dialectic as essential in understanding history and society, insist that Hegel's metaphysic must be turned right side up—from idealism to materialism. To the Marx-Engels brand of historicism we now turn.

Recommended Readings

Bosanquet, B. *The Philosophical Theory of the State*. London, 1899. Chaps. 9, 10.

Findlay, J. N. *Hegel: A Re-examination*. London, 1958.

Foster, M. B. *The Political Philosophies of Plato and Hegel.* Oxford, 1935.

Friedrich, Karl. *The Philosophy of Hegel.* New York, 1954.

Hacker, Andrew. *Political Theory.* New York, 1961. Chapter 11.

Hegel, G. W. F. *Hegel's "Philosophy of Right."* Translated by T. M. Knox. New York, 1952.

Marcuse, H. *Reason and Revolution: Hegel and the Rise of Social Theory.* New York, 1954.

Mure, G. R. G. *An Introduction to Hegel.* Oxford, 1940.

Plamenatz, John. *Man and Society, Vol. 2: Bentham Through Marx.* New York, 1963.

Popper, Karl R. *The Open Society and Its Enemies.* Vol. 2. New York, 1962.

Reyburn, H. A. *The Ethical Theory of Hegel: A Study of the Philosophy of Right.* Oxford, 1921.

Sabine, G. *A History of Political Theory.* New York, 1961. Chapter 30.

chapter 8
Karl Marx and Friedrich Engels
1818-1883
and 1820-1895

Born in the Rhineland area of Germany, Marx studied history and philosophy at several universities, including Berlin. Because of his radical views, he was unable to obtain an academic position. He turned to journalism but the Prussian government expelled him from the country for his journalistic activities. He was later forced to leave France as well. He moved to England in 1849 where he remained until his death.

Engels, the son of a wealthy textile-manufacturing family, was born in Barmen, Germany. He did not attend a university and took a business position early. Strongly influenced by the radical political views of his day, he subsequently played an active role in the working-class movement, authoring his Conditions of the Working Class in England *in 1845.*

Marx and Engels met in Paris in 1844 and, though from widely different social origins, developed a life-long friendship. They co-authored the Communist Manifesto *in 1847 and played active roles in the revolution of 1848. Marx then went to live in England; Engels, back to his post in Manchester. Engels supported Marx for many years enabling Marx to write* Capital, *the first volume of which appeared in 1867. Marx died before the last two volumes were completed and Engels compiled them from Marx's notes. They also jointly authored* The Holy Family (1845) *and* The German Ideology *(1846). Both philosophers worked with the First and Second Internationals, and attempted to develop an international working-class party.*

Other important writings of Marx include the Economic and Philosophic Manuscripts of 1844, Early Writings, The Poverty of Philosophy *(1849) and* A Contribution to the Critique of Political Economy *(1859). Other writings of Engels include his* Anti-Dühring: Herr Eugen Dühring's Revolution in Science *(1878),* The Origin of the Family, Property and the State *(1844) and* Feuerbach and the End of Classical German Philosophy *(1888).*

The Hegelian Heritage

The philosophy of Marx and Engels,[1] like that of Hegel, is a philosophy of history. It owes a great deal to Hegel, and Marx and Engels frequently acknowledge this debt. They accept the Hegelian dialectic, but reject the metaphysical idealism within which Hegel casts the dialectic. Materialism they substitute for idealism, and they conceive of the dialectical process as operative in the world of nature. Marx contrasts his dialectic and that of Hegel in *Capital*:

> My dialectic method is not only different from the Hegelian, but is its direct opposite. To Hegel, the life-process of the human brain, i.e., the process of thinking, which, under the name of 'Idea' he even transforms into an independent subject, is the demiurgous of the real world, and the real world is only the external, phenomenal form of 'the Idea.' With me, on the contrary, the Ideal is nothing else than the material world reflected by the human mind, and translated into forms of thought. . . . The mystifying side of Hegelian dialectics I criticized nearly thirty years ago, at the time when it was still the fashion . . . the mystification which dialectics suffers in Hegel's hand by no means prevents him from being the first to present its general form of working in a comprehensive and conscious manner. With him it is standing on its

[1] It is certainly possible to differentiate between the philosophy and the work of Marx and that of Engels. However, for our purposes this effort will not be made. There are differences of emphasis in their views, and Marx appears to present his philosophical thesis in a more careful and refined manner; but they did jointly author *The Holy Family, The German Ideology* and *The Communist Manifesto*. They also maintained what Marx calls a "constant exchange of ideas by correspondence." Whatever differences exist between their philosophies, they agree on the most fundamental philosophical issues.

head. It must be turned right side up again, if you would discover the rational kernel within the mystical shell.[2]

The essential point of Marx and Engels is that it is matter, not mind, which is the basic causal factor in the historical process and in the evolution of social and political systems. They fully accept the dialectic but chide Hegel on his inversion of reality and on his apparent need to terminate the dialectical process at some stage. The value of the dialectic, as Marx and Engels see it, is that it deals "the death blow to the finality of all products of human thought and action." [3] It leads us to see that "all successive historical situations are only transitory stages in the endless course of development of human society from the lower to the higher." [4] It leads us to see that "each stage is necessary, therefore justified for the time and conditions to which it owes its origin. But in the newer and higher conditions which gradually develop in its own bosom, each loses its validity and justification. It must give way to a higher form which will also in its time decay and perish." [5] All this, according to Marx and Engels, is the tremendous value of the Hegelian dialectic. But Hegel himself subverts it by the dogmatic view that the process has a definite end in the Absolute Idea. This also leads Hegel to neglect the revolutionary side of the dialectic and to endorse "extremely tame political conclusions."

Once Hegel's idealism is placed right-side-up and is made into materialism, and once the dialectic is seen as a never-ending process operative in the material world and with a material base, we are well on our way to what Engels calls "a task which openly amounts to the discovery of the general laws of society." [6] For "what is true of nature, is also true of the history of society in all its branches and of the totality of all sciences which occupy themselves with things human. . . ." [7] Dialectical materialism is the key to understanding all reality, Marx and Engels hold—in particular, human and social reality.

Dialectical Materialism and Economic Determinism

What do Marx and Engels mean by dialectical materialism? They do not mean by materialism the reductionistic materialism of Baron

[2] Karl Marx, *Capital*, Vol. I (1867), ed. Friedrich Engels, trans. Samuel Moore and Edward Aveling (London: Lawrence and Wishart, 1961), p. 19.
[3] Friedrich Engels, *Ludwig Feuerbach and The End of Classical German Philosophy*, in *Karl Marx, Selected Works*, Vol. I, ed. C. P. Dutt (New York: International Publishers, Inc. n.d.), p. 420.
[4] Ibid., p. 421.
[5] Ibid.
[6] Ibid., p. 457.
[7] Ibid.

Holbach in which physics and chemistry are the basic sciences and in which the mechanical explanation paradigmatic of these sciences is extended to man and society. Quite the contrary, although mechanism fits physics and chemistry, it does not fit man, society, and history. Classical materialism emphasized that nature shapes man. Marx and Engels agree that this is so, but Marx in particular insists that man shapes nature as well, that human activity is causally significant, and that we cannot understand human history without understanding man's interaction with the forces and objects of nature. Furthermore, man's history and his economic and social institutions involve "tendencies that work out with an iron necessity toward an inevitable goal." Since there is a goal or purpose in history, it cannot be understood on a purely mechanical model. What is required to understand the necessity of social life and history is the dialectical model of explanation. The Marx-Engels materialism is the view that the material and economic conditions of man's existence determine basically his social and political existence. They state: "The way in which men produce their means of subsistence depends first of all on the nature of the actual means they find in existence and have to reproduce. This mode of production . . . is . . . a definite form of expressing their life. . . . As individuals express their life, so they are. What they are, therefore, coincides with their production, both with what they produce and with how they produce. The nature of individuals thus depends on the material conditions determining their production." [8]

The social and psychological conditions of man, as well as his legal and political institutions, are determined by economic conditions. Marx does not maintain that economic causes are the only causes but that they are the basic causes and are efficacious in the long run. Even man's intellectual life, his ideas—whether they be religious, political, artistic, or moral—are causally determined, basically, by the conditions of his economic existence. Thus Marx and Engels are properly characterized as economic determinists, but it must be kept in mind that they do not deny there are also noneconomic causes and aspects of our social life and that man's activity is causally and historically significant.

Marx states his theory quite clearly in this passage:

> In the social production of their life, men enter into definite relations that are indispensible and independent of their will, relations

8 Karl Marx and Friedrich Engels, *The German Ideology* (1846), ed. R. Pascal (New York: International Publishers, Inc., 1947), p. 7.

of production which correspond to a definite stage of development of their material productive forces. The sum total of these relations of production constitutes the economic structure of society, the real foundation, on which rises a legal and political superstructure and to which correspond definite forms of social consciousness. The mode of production of material life conditions the social, political, and intellectual life process in general. It is not the consciousness of men that determines their being, but, on the contrary, their social being that determines their consciousness.[9]

Marx's basic thesis, then, is that the method of economic production—the forces and modes of production—and the ways of distributing the products of the economic system are causally responsible for the "relations of productions," that is, the existence and structure of social classes and the social, legal, and political system within which that structure operates. The entire social life of any society at any time in history can be causally explained by explaining the forces and modes of production which were operative at the time. As Marx says in *The Poverty of Philosophy*, "The windmill gives you society with the feudal lord; the steam-mill society with the individual capitalist." If the basic mode of production at a given time is a plow and the mule, then the social structure will be organized in a certain way (and indeed the character of the people will be of a certain type); if the basic mode of production is the factory system, both the character of the people and their social structures will be quite different; and in an era of computers and high technology, the social structure and character of the people or classes in that society will be different yet. Presumably, with enough information about developing changes in the forces and modes of production, one could predict with certainty the relations of production or social organization of the future. And Marx, of course, engages in prediction of just this type. Such prediction of the "iron necessities" of history is what his philosophy of history is all about. Dialectical materialism enables one to grasp the social and political significance of ever-changing forces and relations of production.

All of man's social history (or "pre-history" for Marx, since man's *real* history begins only with the advent of the classless society) is a tension between existing (but ever-changing) forces of production and relations of production. He states:

---

[9] Karl Marx and Friedrich Engels, *Preface to A Contribution To The Critique of Political Economy* (1859), in Karl Marx and Friedrich Engels, *Selected Works* (London; Lawrence and Wishart, 1962) I, 362.

At a certain stage of their development, the material productive forces of society come in conflict with the existing relations of production, or—what is but a legal expression for the same thing—with the property relations within which they have been at work hitherto. From forms of development of the productive forces these relations turn into their fetters. Then begins an epoch of social revolution. With the change of the economic foundation the entire immense superstructure is more or less rapidly transformed. In considering such transformations a distinction should always be made between the material transformation of the economic conditions of production, which can be determined with the precision of natural science, and the legal, political, religious, aesthetic or philosophic—in short, ideological forms in which men become conscious of this conflict and fight it out.[10]

In *The Communist Manifesto* Marx and Engels spell out in some detail the way in which men become conscious of the conflict and fight it out. Before examining that account, however, we must again stress the necessity or inevitability of the multiple and successive historical changes in the social order. As Hegel would put it, each social order has its own time on the stage of history. It comes when its time is ripe and perishes when the conditions necessary for its continued existence are gone. The difference between Marx and Hegel lies not on the necessity of social change but in the nature of efficacious causes. For Marx they are material and economic, not spiritual and ideal. But just as Hegel insists that a new stage in the development of spirit cannot be reached until the older stage is played out, so also Marx insists that "no social order ever perishes before all the productive forces for which there is room in it have developed; and new, higher relations of production never appear before the material conditions of existence have matured in the womb of the old society itself." [11] This means that every social system, no matter how many class distinctions there are or how unequally the social products are distributed, has its place in the progressive evolution of economic and social systems (the long-run optimism, indeed messianic character of Marx's thought should not be forgotten), just as each nation for Hegel, no matter how brutal or tyrannical, plays a necessary role in the evolution of spirit. Marx states: "In broad outlines Asiatic, ancient, feudal, and modern bourgeois modes of production can be designated as progressive epochs in the economic formation of society. The bourgeois relations of production are the last antagonistic form of the social

[10] Ibid., p. 363.
[11] Ibid.

process of production—antagonistic not in the sense of individual antagonism, but of one arising from the social conditions of life of the individuals; at the same time the productive forces developing in the womb of bourgeois society create the material conditions for the solution of that antagonism. This social formation brings, therefore, the prehistory of human society to a close." [12] Prehistory is over when the classless society of ideal communism evolves. But that ideal society cannot evolve or exist without the prior and necessary existence of the evils of capitalism, feudalism, and so on. In this sense, evil is a necessary prerequisite for good.

Classes and Class Struggles

The Communist Manifesto summarizes Marx's and Engels's theory of history. We have seen that the dialectical movement of history is driven onward and forward by the tensions and conflicts between the forces of production and the relations of production. In *The Communist Manifesto* Marx and Engels explicitly link the concepts of class and class struggle to the dialectic:

> The history of all hitherto existing society is the history of class struggles.

> Freeman and slave, patrician and plebeian, lord and serf, guild-master and journeyman, in a word, oppressor and oppressed, stood in constant opposition to one another, carried on an uninterrupted, now hidden, now open fight, a fight that each time ended, either in a revolutionary reconstruction of society at large, or in the common ruin of the contending classes.[13]

Marx and Engels do not provide detailed analyses of the notion of class. They make it clear that the essential criterion for class membership is ownership of property and the type of property owned. No attention is given other senses of "class" in which membership is determined by education, religion, race, and so on. If one must sell his labor for wages in order to live and if one does not own the resources and instruments of production, one is classified as a member of the proletariat. If, on the other hand, one does own property—the materials and instruments of production—and employs other persons, one is a member of the capitalist or bourgeois class.

[12] Ibid., p. 364.
[13] Karl Marx and Friedrich Engels, *The Communist Manifesto* in *Selected Works*, (London, 1962) I, 109.

Marx and Engels, of course, knew that there were other ways of conceptualizing classes, and they knew that the simple bourgeoisie-proletariat distinction left problems in classifying some persons. Engels sometimes spoke of "three great classes" whose conflicts of interests are the "driving force of modern history"—the landed aristocracy, the middle class, and the proletariat. But both Marx and Engels make it quite clear that the significant basis for determining class is economic, and that more complex distinctions of class strata are irrelevant for their purposes. Marx states:

> In England, modern society is indisputably most highly and classically developed in economic structure. Nevertheless, even here the stratification of classes does not appear in its pure form. Middle and intermediate strata even here obliterate lines of demarcation everywhere (although incomparably less in rural districts than in the cities). However, this is immaterial for our analysis. We have seen that the continued tendency and law of development of the capitalist mode of production is more and more to divorce the means of production from labour, and more and more to concentrate the scattered means of production into large groups, thereby transforming labour into wage-labour and the means of production into capital.[14]

Those persons who could not be directly classified as bourgeoisie or proletarians on the basis of ownership of property were apparently placed in one of the two categories on the basis of their function or status (income, family heritage, type of employment—some of our other ways of defining classes) which link them closer to one or the other category.

It is important to note that the notions of hostility, conflict, and "battle" are essential to Marx's and Engels's concept of a class. Marx notes that "the separate individuals form a class only in so far as they have to carry on a common battle against another class; otherwise they are on hostile terms with each other as competitors. On the other hand, the class in its turn achieves an independent existence over against the individuals, so that the latter find their conditions of existence predestined, and hence have their position in life and their personal development assigned to them by their class, become subsumed under it."[15] Again he insists that "in so far as millions of

---

[14] Engels, *Ludwig Feuerbach and The End of Classical German Philosophy*, p. 457.

[15] Karl Marx, *Capital*, Vol. III (1894), ed. Friedrich Engels (London: Lawrence and Wishart, 1962).

families live under economic conditions of existence that separate their mode of life, their interests, and their culture from those of other classes, and put them in hostile opposition to the latter, they form a class. In so far as there is merely a local interconnection among these small-holding peasants, and the identity of their interests begets no community, no natural bond and no political organization among them, they do not form a class." [16]

There must be a sense of community and of common interests for a class to exist. Perhaps Marx means that an effective class, one which can change the world, does not exist without a sense of common interests, community, and a political organization. This would certainly appear to be true, but surely there can be classes, perhaps ineffective ones but nonetheless based on Marx's economic criteria, without class consciousness or political organization. Such consciousness and political clout, however, are fundamental to Marx's concept of class and class conflict. Both economic and political interests and awareness are required for a group to really be a class. Perhaps this is why Marx and Engels show less interest in the conflict between the landed aristocracy and the bourgeoisie than in that between the bourgeoisie and proletariat. The landed aristocracy and bourgeoisie were political adversaries. They struggled for political power. But they were not in direct economic conflict, for the type of property each group owned and their means of production were different and unrelated. In the case of the bourgeoisie and proletariat, however, the conflict is both political and economic.

With this brief characterization of Marx's and Engels's concept of a class, we are now in a position to see more clearly what they mean when they say that "the history of all hitherto existing society is the history of class struggles," and that "all political struggles are class struggles, and all class struggles for emancipation in the last resort, despite their necessarily political form—for every class struggle is a political struggle—turn ultimately on the question of economic emancipation." [17] Marx and Engels attempt to illustrate and document this theory of social history by analyzing the historical evolution of bourgeois society from feudal society. The economic system of feudalism was based on production in the home and on local crafts. Production of goods and the perpetuation of the crafts were controlled by

[16] Marx and Engels, *The German Ideology*, p. 49.
[17] Karl Marx and Friedrich Engels, "The Eighteenth Brumaire of Louis Bonaparte," in *Selected Works* (London: Lawrence and Wishart, 1962), I, 334.

guilds, whose members were the skilled craftsmen in the various crafts. For a considerable period of time there was harmony between the guild system of economic control and organization (relations of production) and the forces of production operative at the time (the existing tools, status of skilled labor, market demand for goods, and so on). But changes in those forces of production soon created internal tensions requiring changes in the relations of production or the guild system. Increased population, a greater demand for goods and new technological inventions slowly made the guild system, with its method of economic and social control, obsolete. As Marx and Engels put it, "The feudal system of industry, under which industrial production was monopolized by closed guilds, now no longer sufficed for the growing wants of the new markets. The manufacturing system took its place. The guild-masters were pushed on one side by the manufacturing middle class; division of labour between the different corporate guilds vanished in the face of division of labour in each single workshop." [18]

But the small factory system, which superseded the feudal system, was also not adequate to the demands. The forces of production continued to develop, "the markets kept ever growing, the demand ever rising. Even manufacture no longer sufficed. The place of manufacture was taken by the giant, Modern Industry, the place of the industrial middle class, by industrial millionaires, the leaders of whole industrial armies, the modern bourgeois." [19]

For Marx and Engels this entire process of historical change is both necessary and dialectical. The pattern is part of nature and it works itself out with an iron necessity (much as Hegel's Idea or plan in history), sometimes on a conscious level, sometimes not. Speaking of the proletariat as an emerging class, Marx declares that "the question is not what this or that proletarian or even the whole of the proletariat at the moment *considers* as its aim. The question is, *what the proletariat is*, and what, consequent on that *being*, it will be compelled to do. Its aim and historical action is irrevocably and obviously demonstrated in its own life situation as well as in the whole organization of bourgeois society today. There is no need to dwell here upon the fact that a large part of the English and French proletariat is already *conscious* of its historical task and is constantly working to

[18] Engels, *Ludwig Feuerbach and The End of Classical German Philosophy*, p. 462.
[19] Karl Marx and Friedrich Engels, *Manifesto of The Communist Party* (1848), trans. Samuel Moore (Moscow: Foreign Languages Publishing House, n.d.), p. 46.

develop that consciousness into complete clarity." [20] And just as the emerging bourgeois society and "the forces of production represented by the bourgeoisie rebelled against the order of production represented by the feudal landlords and the guildmasters," resulting in the smashing of all "feudal fetters" (the feudal relations of property), so also large industry comes into conflict with the small factory system and the concomitant bourgeois order of production which took the place of the feudal system. That is, just as modern bourgeois society "has sprouted from the ruins of feudal society," so also modern proletarian society will sprout from the ruins of bourgeois society. As Engels puts it, "tied down by this order, by the narrow limits of the capitalist mode of production, big industry produces on the one hand an ever increasing proletarianization of the great mass of the people, and on the other hand an ever greater mass of unsaleable products. Over-production and mass misery, each the curse of the other—that is the absurd contradiction which is its outcome and which of necessity calls for the liberation of the productive forces by means of a change in the mode of production." [21] Marx's assumption seems to be that throughout history, at least up until the establishment of the proletarian society and of communism, the modes or forces of production develop too rapidly to be long contained within whatever relations of production are operative. The tension and the dialectic process terminate only when the forces of production and relations of production are harmonized and when the conflict of economic classes ceases. We will see how Marx characterized this harmonious condition in a moment. But first let us see in more detail what the bourgeois revolution or negation of feudalism accomplished.

In *The Communist Manifesto*, Marx and Engels describe the effects of the bourgeois revolution in these words:

> The bourgeoisie, wherever it has got the upper hand, has put an end to all feudal, patriarchal, idyllic relations. It has pitilessly torn asunder the motley feudal ties that bound man to his 'natural superiors' and has left remaining no other nexus between man and man than naked self-interest, than callous 'cash payment'. It has drowned the most heavenly ecstasies of religious fervour, of chivalrous enthusiasm, of philistine sentimentalism in the icy waters of egotistical calculation. It has resolved personal worth into exchange value, and in place of the numberless indefeasible

[20] Ibid., p. 47.
[21] Karl Marx and Friedrich Engels, *The Holy Family* (1845) (London: Lawrence and Wishart, 1956), p. 53.

chartered freedoms, has set up that single, unconscionable freedom—Free Trade. In one word, for exploitation, veiled by religious and political illusions, it has substituted naked, shameless,
direct, brutal exploitation.[22]

Much of this description of the effects of the bourgeois revolution is *in a sense* negative, for Marx and Engels are firmly opposed to
brutal exploitation and the reduction of the worth of persons to mere
exchange value. But they also recognize the essential role played by
the bourgeoisie in the dialectical process of history and the positive
accomplishments of this class. This class, they state, is "the first to
show what man's activity can bring about. It has accomplished won-
ders far surpassing Egyptian pyramids, Roman aqueducts, and Gothic
cathedrals; it has conducted expeditions that have put in the shade all
former Exoduses of nations and crusades." [23] Marx and Engels are
admirers of the capitalist's imaginative development and use of technology to conquer nature. Capitalists exploit other human beings in
their ceaseless drive for personal wealth. This is undesirable in the
long run (the end of which is a classless, nonexploitative society) but
apparently necessary, and hence, in that sense, desirable in the short
run. The bourgeoisie, through its technological revolutionizing of the
forces of production, gives "a cosmopolitan character to production
and consumption in every country" and "draws all, even the most
barbarian, nations into civilization." [24] Potentialities for consumption
and for the quality of economic existence undreamed of by earlier
classes are made actual by the capitalist. Furthermore, by wiping out
"all fixed, fast-frozen relations, with the train of ancient and vener-
able prejudices and opinions," he forces man to face reality: "man
is at last compelled to face with sober senses, his real conditions of
life, and his relations with his kind." [25] That reality is the necessary
conflict of economic classes. The distinctive feature of the epoch of
the bourgeoisie, Marx and Engels claim, is that "it has simplified class
antagonisms. Society as a whole is more and more splitting up into
two great hostile camps, into two great classes directly facing each
other: Bourgeoisie and Proletariat." [26] This direct confrontation is a
historical necessity for progress, for it is the beginning of the end of

22 Engels, *Ludwig Feuerbach and The End of Classical German Philosophy*,
p. 461.
23 Ibid.
24 Marx and Engels, *Manifesto of The Communist Party*, p. 50.
25 Marx and Engels, *Selected Works* (London, 1962), I, 37.
26 Marx and Engels, *Manifesto of The Communist Party*, p. 53.

class conflict, human alienation (of which we will say more later), and exploitation. Just as Hegel saw tyranny and war as necessary for the progressive evolution of spirit in world-history, so Marx and Engels see the exploitation and repression of the proletariat by the bourgeoisie as necessary in the dialectical evolution of social systems; and, at least in some countries, the resolution of the bourgeois-proletarian class conflict will be a violent revolution. "Is it at all surprising," Marx asks, "that a society founded on the opposition of classes should culminate in brutal *contradiction*, the shock of body against body, as its final denouement?" [27]

We have seen in some detail the nature of the bourgeois class and its role in history. What is the nature of the proletarian class and its role in history? The proletariat is described by Marx and Engels as the exploited, laboring class, as the revolutionary class, and as the universal class. What do these characteristics denote?

First, as the exploited, laboring class. There are several senses in which the proletarian is exploited and is a slave. He owns no productive property and must sell his labor in order to live. He is at the mercy of the capitalist. As Marx states in *Capital*,

> The labourer is nothing else, his whole life through, than labour-power, that therefore all his disposable time is by nature and law labour-time, to be devoted to the self-expansion of capital. Time for education, for intellectual development, for the fulfilling of social functions and for social intercourse, for the free-play of his bodily and mental activity, even the rest time of Sunday (and that in a country of Sabbatarians!)—moonshine! But in its blind unrestrainable passion, its werewolf hunger for surplus labour, capital oversteps not only the moral, but even the merely physical maximum bounds of the working-day. It usurps the time for growth, development, and healthy maintenance of the body. It steals the time required for the consumption of fresh air and sunlight. It higgles over a meal-time, incorporating it where possible with the process of production itself, so that food is given to the labourer as to a mere means of production, as coal is supplied to the boiler, grease and oil to the machinery.[28]

Within capitalism the proletarian is a mere means of production. He has no intrinsic worth and is an object to be manipulated, efficiently and at minimum cost. He is a slave not only of the individual bourgeois manufacturer but of the bourgeois class, which benefits

[27] Ibid., pp. 51–52.
[28] Ibid., p. 46.

as a whole by the system of exploitation, and of the bourgeois state which provides a social and legal system which supports and perpetuates the system of exploitation.[29] It goes without saying that the proletarian is also a slave of the machine, for the existence of the machine is the essential causal factor responsible for the division of labor, hence for private property and capitalism. "Division of labour and private property", Marx states, "are . . . identical expressions: in the one the same thing is affirmed with reference to activity as is affirmed in the other with reference to the product of the activity." [30]

Aside from being a slave of the individual bourgeois manufacturer, of the bourgeois class, of the bourgeois state, and of the machine, the proletarian is a slave of himself and of his fellow workers, for "driven by want, . . . he still further increases the evil effects of the division of labour. The result is that the more he works the less wages he receives, and for the simple reason that he competes to that extent with his fellow workers, hence makes them into so many competitors who offer themselves on just the same bad terms as he does himself, and that, therefore, in the last resort he competes with himself, with himself as a member of the working class." [31] In effect he is the slave of a complete economic system. Given that system, the exploitation of the proletariat (and, in a different sense, of the bourgeoisie as well) is necessary and unavoidable. And given the necessity of capitalism as a stage in the dialectical evolution of economic and social systems (an evolution which eventually reaches communism and a classless society), the proletarian can also be seen (as can everything else) as a slave of the historical process.

That the exploited, slave-status of the proletariat is due entirely to the capitalist system of production Marx and Engels make perfectly clear in the following passage:

> The cry for an equality of wages rests, therefore, upon a mistake, is an insane wish never to be fulfilled. It is an offspring of that false and superficial radicalism that accepts premises and tries to evade conclusions. Upon the basis of the wages system the value of labouring power is settled like that of every other commodity; and as different kinds of labouring power have different values, or require different quantities of labour for their production, they must fetch different prices in the labour market. To clamour for

---

29 Karl Marx, *The Poverty of Philosophy* (1847), (London: Lawrence and Wishart, n.d.), p. 175.
30 Marx, *Capital*, in *Selected Works* (London, 1962), I, 265.
31 Marx and Engels, *Manifesto of The Communist Party*, p. 59.

equal or even equitable retribution on the basis of the wages system is the same as to clamour for freedom on the basis of the slavery system.[32]

Given the capitalist system the slavery of the proletariat is necessary, and it is foolish, normatively naive, and conceptually absurd to think that equality or equality of distribution of products can take place within that system. Genuine equality can occur only in a classless society which presupposes the negation and demise of capitalism.

Second, the proletariat is a revolutionary class. Discontented with their exploited status and with the knowledge that past revolutionary ideals were in effect masks used to enhance and perpetuate the interests of the bourgeois class, the proletariat develops a sense of class interest and class consciousness. Until this mass condition of the proletariat occurs, "the proletariat is not yet sufficiently developed to constitute itself as a class and consequently . . . the struggle . . . of the proletariat with the bourgeoisie has not yet assumed a political character. . . ." [33] But when this consciousness develops, and when "the material conditions necessary for the emancipation of the proletariat" develop "in the bosom of the bourgeoisie itself," the proletariat is ready to perform its revolutionary role, a role which is historically inevitable.[34] Those theorists who think that the exploited state of the proletariat can be rectified prior to the emergence of these historical conditions are utopian dreamers, Marx declares.

Third, the proletariat is the "universal" class. This is so in several senses. First, "all previous historical movements were movements of minorities, or in the interest of minorities. The proletarian movement is the self-conscious, independent movement of the immense majority, in the interest of the immense majority." [35] Second, in addition to being in the interest of the majority, the proletarian class arouses the enthusiasm of society at large and becomes recognized as the "general representative" of society. Third, and most important, the proletariat is a "universal" class in the sense that it is the tool of the historical process which is responsible for the abolition of classes. As Marx argues,

[32] Marx and Engels, *The German Ideology*, p. 22.

[33] Karl Marx and Friedrich Engels, "Wage Labour and Capital" (1847) in *Selected Works* (London, 1962), I, 103.

[34] Karl Marx and Friedrich Engels, "Wages, Price and Profit," in *Selected Works*, Vol. I, p. 426.

[35] Marx, *The Poverty of Philosophy*, p. 140.

in all revolutions up till now the mode of activity always remained unscathed and it was only a question of a different distribution of this activity, a new distribution of labour to other persons, whilst the communistic revolution is directed against the preceding mode of activity, does away with labour, and abolishes the rule of all classes with the classes themselves, because it is carried through by the class which no longer counts as a class in society, is not recognized as a class, and is in itself the expression of the dissolution of all classes, nationalities, etc., within present society. . . .[36]

Shlomo Avineri correctly notes that for Marx "the proletariat was never a particular class, but the repository of the Hegelian "universal class." [37] But whereas for Hegel the universal class, the class which was the instrument of the self-conscious development of Spirit in world-history, was the political bureaucracy, for Marx it is the proletariat which moves history on toward its ultimate goal. The proletariat is "a class *in* civil society which is not a class *of* civil society. . . ." [38] It "claims no traditional status but only a human status"; it represents "a sphere of society which has universal character because its sufferings are universal, and which does not claim a particular redress because the wrong which is done to it is not a particular wrong but wrong in general." [39] The wrongs which it suffers are the result of the entire economic system, which must be abolished. By such abolition the proletariat not only redeems itself but provides a "total redemption of humanity." [40] It changes the social and economic system which not only alienates the proletariat but destroys the humanity of the bourgeoisie as well.

Alienation and Freedom

For Marx both the bourgeoisie and the proletariat exist in a state of alienation. In fact all past human societies (and all those which will come into existence prior to communism) exist in a state of alienation. But what does Marx mean by "alienation"? To some extent this concept has been explicated in the above description of the proletarian class. However, more must be said to characterize this concept

---

[36] Ibid.
[37] See Shlomo Avineri's discussion of this in his *The Social and Political Thought of Karl Marx* (Cambridge: Cambridge University Press, 1968), p. 62.
[38] Marx and Engels, *Manifesto of The Communist Party*, p. 66.
[39] Marx and Engels, *The German Ideology*, p. 69.
[40] Avineri, *Social and Political Thought of Karl Marx*, p. 62.

adequately, for it is central to Marx's entire philosophy—to his philosophy of history, his theory of economic systems, his theory of the State, his account of morality, and his philosophy of man.

There are several senses in which man is alienated (and there also are apparently degrees of alienation for Marx). Basically, man is alienated from his labor. It is labor which distinguishes man from the animals. His ability to work and create makes man what he is. Rephrasing Descartes a Marxist might properly say, "I work, therefore I am." But man's work has become a process of alienation. Why is this the case? It is because, under existing conditions,

> The work is external to the worker, that it is not part of his nature; and that, consequently, he does not fulfill himself in his work but denies himself, has a feeling of misery rather than well-being, does not develop freely his mental and physical energies but is physically exhausted and mentally debased. The worker, therefore, feels himself at home only during his leisure time, whereas at work he feels homeless. His work is not voluntary but imposed, *forced labour*. It is not satisfaction of a need, but only a *means* for satisfying other needs. Its alien character is clearly shown by the fact that as soon as there is no physical or other compulsion, it is avoided. . . .
>
> We arrive at the result that man (the worker) feels himself to be freely active only in his animal function—eating, drinking and procreating, or at most also in his dwelling and in personal adornment—while in his human functions he is reduced to an animal. The animal becomes human and the human animal.[41]

Working merely in order to survive, man's labor, and hence a large portion of his life, is a commodity turned over to the capitalist. This animalizes and dehumanizes man, for his creative work is no longer his own, and only animal functions remain. In the capitalist system man sells his soul—his creative work—in the marketplace and becomes a mere commodity. Everything becomes a commodity or a saleable item. All aspects of the culture become capitalistically oriented, with a monetary or product value assigned to everything, and even the very desires and needs of men are oriented to fit the products produced. Marx speaks of this as the "fetishism of commodities," in which everyone—capitalist and proletarian alike—is stripped of his personality and humanity:

> A commodity is therefore a mysterious thing, simply because in it the social character of men's labour appears to them as an

[41] Ibid., p. 59.

objective character stamped upon the product of the labour; because the relation of the producers to the sum total of their own labour is presented to them as a social relation, existing not between them but between the products of their labour. . . . There is a definite social relation between men that assumes, in their eyes, the fantastic form of a relation between things. In order, therefore, to find an analogy, we must have recourse to the mist-enveloped regions of the religious world. In that world the productions of the human brain appear as independent beings endowed with life and entering into relation both with one another and the human race. So it is in the world of commodities with the products of men's hands. This I call the Fetishism which attaches itself to the products of labour. . . .[42]

Just as religion envelops the world in mist and endows the religious products of the human brain with reality, capitalism inverts humans and human relationships into commodities and commodity relationships. Both result in irrationality, the former in our not seeing the world as it really is, the latter in a dehumanized conceptualization of man with all of the attendant irrational practices. With everything in the system given a price, persons become things having no intrinsic value but only extrinsic or instrumental value. (Students, for example, become conceptualized as *products* of an educational institution, as items which command $12,000 or $14,000 on the marketplace, depending on their field.) Everything becomes "consumer" oriented, with labor and the products of labor no longer being the servants of man and his needs but the master of man. The "needs" and goals of men are manipulated by the capitalist system in the interest of greater profits, not in the interests of men.

Man, then, for Marx and Engels, becomes a manipulated object within an economic system which has complete control over him economically, and within a political system which reflects and perpetuates that system. Thus man is not only alienated from his own labor and the products of that labor; he is also alienated from other men—from proletariat and bourgeoisie alike—as a result of the competitive nature of the economy of capitalism. Furthermore, he is alienated from society and social institutions, for those institutions, as they presently exist, are tools which perpetuate economic exploitation and class conflicts. Whether the alienation is man from his labor, man from other men, or man from society, it cannot be adequately overcome without changing the entire economic system. For Marx

42 Ibid.

and Engels we must negate the capitalist system in which the relations of production force one to conceptualize man as a commodity and which make human relationships into relationships between objects and commodities.

What is a nonalienated condition? a nonalienated man? Such a man is one who "owns" his own labor, whose labor is not a *mere* means to his survival or a commodity sold in the marketplace, one who is respected as a person and who is conceptualized as having intrinsic worth both by himself and others. A nonalienated man is a free and a rational man, but he is not free in the sense that his life is unconditioned and his actions *completely* self-determined. This utopian sense of freedom—and the concomitant sense of alienation as complete determination of man's actions by factors outside of his control—sometimes appears in Marx's writings, but he recognizes that man's freedom exists only within a conditioned environment. And man is not rational in the sense that he always acts rationally, although again in his utopian moments Marx entertains the possibility of such complete rationality. Rather, the freedom and rationality of a non-alienated man exists *within* causal and conditioned circumstances—there is no escaping nature for Marx—but *within* a social and economic system which permits him to exercise creative autonomy. As long as capitalism and class conflicts exist, such autonomy is not possible. Only with the advent of communism and the death of private property and class distinctions are genuine freedom and rationality possible. Furthermore, the communism must be fully developed, for although alienation does not exist in primitive communism, primitive conditions preclude the kind of productivity essential for the development of human capacities and the fulfillment of human needs. As Marx and Engels put it in *The Communist Manifesto*: "In place of the old bourgeois society, with its classes and class antagonisms, we shall have an association, in which the free development of each is the condition for the free development of all." [43]

Stated in terms of a notion which appears in Marx's *Early Writings*, real freedom and rationality or the preclusion of alienation requires that man behave as a "species-being" or *Gattungswegen*. "The practical construction of an *objective world*, the *manipulation* of inorganic nature, is the confirmation of man as a conscious species being, i.e. a being who treats the species as his own being or himself as a species-being." [44] Although this is put forth as a descriptive, anthropo-

[43] Ibid., p. 60.
[44] Marx and Engels, *Selected Works* (Moscow, 1962), I, 363.

logical claim, it is also plainly normative. Indeed it smacks of the Golden Rule and of Kant's categorical imperative, in which men are not treated as mere means but as having intrinsic worth and dignity.[45] A society of species-beings—a nonalienated society—must be a class-less society and a communistic one. For Marx this does not mean that man is swallowed up in society or the state. For him there is no problem of choice between individualism and collectivism, no necessary tension between the individual and society, for "the individual is the social being. . . ." A man fully becomes himself only through his social relations. In communistic society, the State (with its traditional role of perpetuating a repressive and alienating social and economic system) will have "withered away" and man's individual and social characteristics will be reunited. Man will have become *really human.*

The State

The State, for Marx and Engels, is a manifestation of alienation, and it is a device which perpetuates alienation. This is particularly true of capitalist society, but the Marx-Engels thesis is that all states, those which have existed in history and those that will come into exis-

[45] This same norm is fundamental to Marx's evaluation of the relationship between man and woman. He argues that
the bourgeois sees in his wife a mere instrument of production. . . . On what foundation is the present family, the bourgeois family, based? On capital, on private gain. . . . The bourgeois clap-trap about the family and education, about hallowed co-relation of parent and child, becomes all the more disgusting the more, by the action of modern industry, all family ties among the proletarians are torn asunder, and the children transformed into simple articles of commerce and instruments of labour. (Capital, Vol. I, pp. 73–74.)
Proper sexual and family relationships, however, cannot be exploitative. They cannot exemplify class distinctions and divisiveness. They must be founded on the norm that each partner is a person with intrinsic worth, and upon a relationship of mutual respect and reciprocity. This does not preclude differences in roles but it does preclude treating one's mate as a sex object or as provider-object. In fact, Marx makes it plain in the following passage that ideal family relationships exemplify both the norms and the behavior of an ideal society:
The immediate, natural and necessary relation of human being to human being is also the *relation of man* to *woman*. In this *natural* species-relationship man's relation to nature is directly his relation to his own *natural* function. Thus, in this relation it is sensuously revealed, reduced to an observable *fact*, the extent to which human nature has become nature for man to which nature has become human nature for him. From this relationship man's whole level of development can be assessed. It follows from the character of this relationship how far *man* has become, and has understood himself as, a *species-being*, a *human being*. (*Early Writings*, pp. 127–28.)

tence prior to communism, and the laws, moralities, and conventions (and forms of government—democracy, aristocracy, and monarchy) that constitute the superstructure of states, are reflections of class-struggles and the domination of a class or classes. States, with their different superstructures, come into existence and pass out of existence as a result of economic and dialectical tensions. Each society itself internally creates the conditions required for its own overthrow. Capitalist society, for example, creates a large, exploited proletarian class, which in time becomes sensitized to its condition and its historical role. What then happens?

> The proletariat seizes the state power, and transforms the means of production in the first instance into state property. But in doing this, it puts an end to all class differences and antagonisms, it puts an end also to the state as the state. Former society, moving in class antagonisms, had need of the state, that is, an organization of the exploiting class at each period for the maintenance of its external conditions of production; that is, therefore, for the forcible holding down of the exploited class in the conditions of oppression (slavery, villeinage or serfdom, wage labour) determined by the existing mode of production. The state was the official representative of society as a whole, its embodiment in a visible corporation; but it was this only in so far as it was the state of that class which itself, in its epoch, represented society as a whole; in ancient times, the state of the slaveowning citizens; in the Middle Ages, of the feudal nobility; in our own epoch, of the bourgeoisie.[46]

With the proletariat as the genuine representative of society and with the abolition of classes and class distinctions, there is no further need of a state:

> As soon as there is no longer any class of society to be held in subjection; as soon as, along with class domination and the struggle for individual existence based on the former anarchy of production, the collisions and excesses arising from these have been abolished, there is nothing more to be repressed which would make a special repressive force, or state, necessary. The first act in which the state really comes forward as the representative of society as a whole—the taking possession of the means of production in the name of society—is at the same time its last independent act as a state. The interference of the state power in social relations becomes superfluous in one sphere after another,

[46] Karl Marx and Friedrich Engels, *Economic-Philosophical Manuscripts* in *Selected Works* (Moscow, 1962), I, 50–51.

and then ceases of itself. The government of persons is replaced by the administration of things and the direction of the process of production. The state is not "abolished", it withers away.[47]

When the state withers away, so also does the superstructure of ideas, law, morality, and conventions—the ideological and valuational base of the state. Society is no longer dominated by a class or a "consumer" value system in which persons are treated as things. Political power, which Marx and Engels define as "the organized power of one class for oppressing another" withers away, for there are no longer any classes. The state is replaced by a science of administration.

The revolution of the proletariat will differ in different countries. In some it will be evolutionary and perhaps nonviolent; in others, necessarily violent. The following are policies which the proletarian government will instantiate:

> The proletariat will use its political supremacy to wrest, by degrees, all capital from the bourgeoisie, to centralise all instruments of production in the hands of the state, i.e. of the producers organised as the ruling class; and to increase the total of productive forces as rapidly as possible.
>
> Of course, in the beginning, this cannot be effected except by means of despotic inroads on the rights of property, and on the conditions of bourgeois production; by means of measures, therefore, which appear economically insufficient and untenable, but which, in the course of the movement, outstrip themselves, necessitate further inroads upon the old social order, and are unavoidable as a means of entirely revolutionizing the mode of production.
>
> These measures will of course be different in different countries.
>
> Nevertheless in the most advanced countries, the following will be pretty generally applicable.
>
> 1. Abolition of property in land and application of all rents of land to public purpose.
> 2. A heavy progressive or graduated income tax.
> 3. Abolition of all rights of inheritance.
> 4. Confiscation of the property of all emigrants and rebels.
> 5. Centralisation of credit in the hands of the State, by means of a national bank with State Capital and an exclusive monopoly.

[47] Karl Marx, *Early Writings*, trans. and ed. T. B. Bottomore (New York: McGraw-Hill Book Company, 1964), p. 154.

6. Centralisation of the means of communication and transport in the hands of the State.
7. Extension of factories and instruments of production owned by the State; the bringing into cultivation of waste-lands, the improvement of the soil generally in accordance with a common plan.
8. Equal liability of all to labour, Establishment of industrial armies expecially for agriculture.
9. Combination of agriculture with manufacturing industries; gradual abolition of the distinction between town and country, by a more equable distribution of the population over the country.
10. Free education for all children in public schools. Abolition of children's factory labour in its present form. Combination of education with industrial production, &c., &c.[48]

The purpose of the socialist or proletarian dictatorship is not *political* power. It is not used to enhance narrow or particular interests but to realize universal interests. Common objectives and cooperation replace class antagonism and conflict. With the death of capitalism and class conflicts, the historical dialectic reaches a new level. Man's real history—the circumstances in which his creative autonomy and rationality can prevail—begins. Everything prior to this is "prehistory."

The Socialist Dictatorship

The socialist dictatorship, however, is seen by Marx and Engels to be a transitional period in man's history. It is not yet communism but contains the seeds and the historically enabling conditions for communism to develop. But as the synthesis of the clash between the bourgeois state and the proletarian movement, it will necessarily contain many features which are far from ideal—economically, morally, and socially. Dictatorial techniques must be used and will be essential to prevent a counterrevolution. Private industry and economic inequality will continue to exist, although controlled by the universal objectives of the socialist state. Nor will the values and attitudes of capitalist society be wiped out overnight. The socialist dictatorship will be a period in which changes are slowly wrought, in which the historical conditions necessary for communism are gradually developed.

A primary function of the socialist state will be the education of

[48] Friedrich Engels, *Anti-Duhring* (Moscow: Foreign Languages Publishing House, 1954), pp. 388–89.

the new generation. The capitalist ethic and value system will be historically phased out, and the ethic of communism will replace it, creating the attitudes and responses necessary for a cooperative, reciprocative society of "species-beings." When the proletarian victory is complete, a true democracy will exist. The latter leads to communism but does not constitute it, for with communism the need for universal suffrage and a state is transcended. Democracy and its values are not the *summmum bonum* for Marx. They are a means to a non-political society.

Marx characterizes early communism as "crude." Property is nationalized and wages are distributed on a more equitable basis, but the prime emphasis is narrowly on materialistic values. It ignores other values, "negates the personality of man in every sphere. . . . and is only the culmination of . . . envy and leveling down on the basis of a preconceived minimum." [49]

> The domination of material property looms so large that it aims to destroy everything which is incapable of being possessed by everyone as private property. It wishes to eliminate talent, etc. by force. Immediate physical possession seems to it the unique goal of life and existence. The role seems to it the unique goal of life and existence. The role of the worker is not abolished, but is extended to all men. The relation of private property remains the relation of the community to the world of things.[50]

In crude communism, the reciprocity and creative autonomy of ideal communism exists only in germinal form. In fact, strong remnants of the old bourgeois system of property rights remain. As Marx states, "*equal right* here is still in principle—*bourgeois right*, although principle and practice are no longer at loggerheads. . . . In spite of this advance, this *equal right* is still constantly stigmatized by a bourgeois limitation. The right of the producers is *proportional* to the labour they supply; the equality consists in the fact that the measurement is made with an *equal standard*, labour." [51] Under this modified system of bourgeois rights, a person is conceptualized basically as a worker or producer. Goods are distributed according to the amount and quality of one's labor, but not according to the peculiar needs and wants of individuals. Thus, a certain kind and degree of alienation still exists.

[49] Ibid.
[50] Marx and Engels, *The Communist Manifesto* in *Selected Works* (London, 1962), I, 53–54.
[51] Marx, *Early Writings*, p. 153.

Mature Communism and Social Justice

In developed or mature communism, on the other hand, all remnants of bourgeois ideology and values are extinct. In place of a system of rights rooted in class distinctions, even that in which labor is the criterion for the distribution of goods and services, we have a system of need fulfillment:

> In a higher phase of communist society, after the enslaving subordination of the individual to the division of labour, and therewith also the antithesis between mental and physical labour, have vanished; after labour has become not only a means of life but life's primary want; after the productive forces have also increased with the all-round development of the individual, and all the springs of co-operative wealth flow more abundantly—only then can the narrow horizon of bourgeois right be crossed in its entirety and society inscribe on its banners: 'From each according to his ability, to each according to his needs.' [52]

And the needs of persons are not defined by the system but by the uniqueness of each person. With the springs of cooperative wealth flowing abundantly, the competitive element in need-fulfillment ceases. Under such conditions there is no need for a system of rights—a characteristic essential in past societies—for there is no problem of distribution. Man is no longer alienated from other men in this non-competitive society. Nor is he alienated from his work, for his labor is no longer forced but autonomous and self-fulfilling.

> In communist society where nobody has one exclusive sphere of activity but each can become accomplished in any branch he wishes, society regulates the general production and thus makes it possible for me to do one thing today and another tomorrow, to hunt in the morning, to fish in the afternoon, rear cattle in the evening, criticise after dinner, just as I have a mind, without ever becoming hunter, fisherman, shepherd or critic. This fixation of social activity, this consolidation of what we ourselves produce into an objective power above us, growing out of control, thwarting our expectations, bringing to naught our calculations, is one of the chief factors in the historical development up til now.[53]

The result of communism is the fulfillment of the whole man,

> . . . The return of man to a social, i.e. really human, being, a complete and conscious return which assimilates all the wealth of

[52] Ibid.
[53] Ibid.

previous development. Communism as fully developed naturalism is humanism and as fully developed humanism is naturalism. It is the definite resolution of the antagonism between man and nature, and between men and men. It is the true solution of the conflict between existence and essence, between objectification and self-affirmation, between freedom and necessity, between individual and species. It is the solution of the riddle of history and knows itself to be this solution.[54]

Nor is man alienated from society and social institutions in mature communism. Society is not seen as a force which confronts man or as a power which exploits or restricts him. It is seen as an extension of man as a social being, as the instrument of man as a species-being, an instrument which enlarges the freedom and creative autonomy of everyone. Mature communism permits all of man's "relations to the world—seeing, hearing, smelling, tasting, touching, thinking, observing, feeling, desiring, acting, loving—in short, all the organs of his individuality" to develop.[55] It permits the complete *human* development of man, not merely his economic development. Man's dominant characteristics are no longer those of an acquisitive, egoistic, possessive, hedonistic being but those of a "species-being," a benevolent, autonomous creature who fulfills his human capacities for freedom and rationality and his unique needs within a social system which permits the same fulfillment for everyone else. Mature communism is the only truly egalitarian and nonalienating society.

Critique

There is no question that the ethic of ideal communism is utopian. Many argue that the ideal of a society of completely free and rational beings, spontaneously creative beings who both adapt to nature and control it, who define their own needs and purposes within their potentialities, who determine their own future, instead of being determined by external forces, who are benevolently motivated and species-oriented, instead of being egoistic and acquisitive, who have no need for a system of rights because of that species-orientation and because of the abundance of need-fulfilling resources made available by technology and control of nature—all this, they argue, is an unrealizable ideal. Even given the elimination of private property and of class conflicts (in Marx's sense of classes), there still appear to be basic value differences among humans which can cause conflict.

[54] Karl Marx and Friedrich Engels, *Critique of The Gotha Programme* in *Selected Works*, II, 234.

[55] Ibid., p. 24.

Marx and Engels, however, see ideal communism not as utopian but as necessary or inevitable. It is the immanent goal of human history. The morality of ideal communism they consider to be not merely a prescription of a desirable state of affairs but a scientifically justified theory. It is the inevitable result of historical laws that determine man's development and that of society (at least up to the point where bondage and alienation are overcome). All moralities and social systems (up to this point)—feudal, bourgeois, and proletarian alike —are determined by economic class and environmental conditions. Each morality and social structure is a reflection of those conditions, and each in this sense is a relativistic code. Declarations of rights are historical productions, reflecting the interests and demands of specific classes. Thus, just as St. Thomas's ethic sanctioned the class privileges of feudal society, Locke's emphasis on property rights sanctioned, via natural law theory, the class privileges of bourgeois society. Such declarations and moralities are not immutable truths, but, at best, historically relative reactions to current alienating conditions and the effort to overcome them. Marx and Engels thus do Ruth Benedict one better, for morality as they conceive it is not only relative to culture but relative to economic system and class structure. But they are not consistent relativists, for they admit that the morality of the bourgeoisie represents progress over that of feudal society, that of the proletariat represents progress over that of the bourgeoisie, and that of mature communism represents progress over proletarian morality. This is an element of moral absolutism in Marx and Engels. The moral truths of ideal communism are not eternal truths inscribed on stone and delivered to man as part of the moral furniture of the universe, for the historicist theory rules out the existence of an objective or nonhistorical moral perspective. They therefore reject the natural law theory, for all moral truths are historical evolutions and human formulations. There is no denying, however, the absolutistic function of the ethic of ideal communism in Marx and Engels. That ethic is the criterion for moral progress (even though Marx allows for further human evolution). It is an absolute, not relative, standard of evaluation and an ultimate moral commitment.

What Marx and Engels appear to do is to disguise this absolute moral standard as a scientific, sociological fact about man and his evolutionary development. They presume to be describing, explaining, and predicting social facts and the laws which govern them; for the emergence of proletarian morality and of communism is set forth as a scientific judgment, not a moral one—in effect a prediction of the results of the natural laws which govern the evolution of social systems.

But much of what Marx and Engels did and said belied the claim that they were merely doing "science." Their passionate commitment to the improvement of the human condition and to the basic ideals of freedom and equality led them to socialism. When Marx and Engels speak of the inhuman morality of capitalist society and the *really* human morality of ideal communism, they are doing much more than presenting a logical, historical analysis or a scientific theory. Of course, there is nothing wrong with prescribing or moralizing, but there is something wrong with confusing this kind of activity with a mere sociology of morals or historical explanation. Why not admit the moral commitment? True, one is left with the philosophical problem of justifying a normative theory that cannot be reduced to a scientific one. And this is a difficult problem. But facing it squarely is surely preferable to conflating those ideals and science.

If the above critique is correct (if to use a current distinction, Marx and Engels offer us a normative ethic under the guise of a metaethic), then the entire problem of the justification of basic norms confronts them. The problem cannot be escaped by conflating the "is" and the "ought" or by pretending that all valuational issues are scientific ones. What is at stake here is the adequacy of dialectical materialism itself, for it is the philosophical underpinning of Marx's so-called "science of society."

The thesis of dialectical materialism and economic determinism is also the basis for the Marx-Engels doctrine that economic factors and class membership determines one's class consciousness and one's morality. Sometimes this doctrine is held in a rather crude form which asserts that economic causes are the sole efficacious ones. Marx and Engels did not adhere to this crude form. They argue, rather, that in the long run economic causes are the overriding and most significant causes of social attitudes and changes, stating that "the mode of production in material life determines the *general* character of the social, political, and spiritual process of life. It is not the consciousness of men that determines their consciousness." This being the case and since "the ruling ideas of each age have ever been the ideas of its ruling class," then economic causes and class membership determine moral systems. So long as economic classes exist, moralities which reflect those classes and their interests will exist.

There is undoubtedly *some* truth in this moderate form of economic determinism. Few would now challenge the usefulness of economic explanation in social and political history. The problem is specifying the amount, which in turn requires the clearer formulation of the moderate form of this doctrine. It seems to be true that moralities and theories of rights often reflect class distinctions and criteria based on economic standards. The thesis of Charles Beard that the United States Constitution was really "an economic document drawn with superb skill by men whose property interests were at stake"—especially with the sanction given to slavery—is well known. But is it not possible to formulate a morality or a theory of rights which is not based merely on class-restrictive criteria (and hence on economic factors)? It would appear that such a theory is possible, and the ethic of ideal communism would be such a theory. Of course, this ethic can exist, Marx and Engels would claim, only when classes are abolished. Hence, it would not constitute counter-evidence to economic determinism, since economic determinism and alienation by definition no longer exist under communism. But it would also appear possible for one to adopt and live by a morality that does not reflect one's economic class in a class-structured society. There are causal factors other than economic ones. Engels, who himself would be classified as bourgeois, might be a good example of one whose moral code or class consciousness was not determined by his class membership. And, as Eugene Kamenka points out, some current Soviet philosophers conceptualize fundamental moral values such as justice as being quite independent of the economic base of any given society.[56] This amounts to an abandonment of a strict economic determinism.

Any critique of Marx must carefully avoid the conflation of his views and those of his current disciples. Though he agreed that violence may occur and may be necessary for communism to evolve, Marx did not advocate systematic violent revolution, nor strong centralized political control as did some professed followers. Communism basically must *evolve* for Marx. The conditions necessary for its emergence must develop historically and dialectically within capitalist society. They cannot be created by fiat overnight by a revolutionary party. Kamenka is surely correct that the Soviet transformation of Marxism into a "dogmatic theology" justifying a one-party system and complete ideological control of society is a "vulgar caricature of Marxist thought." It falsifies "the whole spirit of Marx's life and work" and substitutes "the un-Marxian notion of a dictatorship *over*

[56] Karl Marx and Friedrich Engels, *The German Ideology* (London, 1965), pp. 44–45.

the proletariat in place of a dictatorship *of* the proletariat." [57] Marx
is not a "collectivist" as often charged. On the contrary, individual
freedom is a basic value for him. The state must "wither away," leaving a truly open society of species-oriented, autonomous individuals.

Recommended Readings

Avineri, Shlomo. *The Social and Political Thought of Karl Marx*. Cam-
bridge, Mass., 1968.
Beard, Charles. *An Economic Interpretation of the Constitution of the
United States*. New York, 1949.
Berlin, Isaiah. *Karl Marx*. London, 1948.
Bober, M. M. *Karl Marx's Interpretation of History*. Cambridge, Mass., 1948.
Bottomore, T. B., ed. *Marx, Early Writings*. New York, 1964.
Cole, G. D. H. *The Meaning of Marxism*. London, 1948.
Federn, Karl. *The Materialist Conception of History: A Critical Analysis*.
London, 1939.
Fromm, Erich. *Marx's Concept of Man*. New York, 1961.
Gregor, A. James. *A Survey of Marxism*. New York, 1965.
Hook, Sidney. *From Hegel to Marx*. Ann Arbor, 1962.
Kamenka, Eugene. *Marxism and Ethics*. New York, 1969.
Kamenka, Eugene. *The Ethical Foundations of Marxism*. London, 1962.
Marcuse, H. *Reason and Revolution*. New York, 1954.
Mayo, H. B. *Democracy and Marxism*. New York, 1955.
Plamenatz, John. *German Marxism and Russian Communism*. London, 1954.
Popper, Karl. *The Open Society and Its Enemies*. Princeton, 1950.
Rotenstreich, Nathan. *Basic Problems of Marx's Philosophy*. New York,
1965.
Talman, J. L. *The Origins of Totalitarian Democracy*. London, 1952.
Tucker, Robert C. *Philosophy and Myth in Karl Marx*. Cambridge, 1961.

[57] Marx, *Early Writings*, p. 155.

Conclusion

The above chapters make it plain that there are serious problems confronting the historicist theory of the state, both on a theoretical and practical level. We have already discussed a number of the problems which confront the positions of Hegel, Marx, and Engels. There is no need to repeat them in detail here. The grounds and status of the basic philosophical theses of dialectical idealism and dialectical materialism have been challenged. The conflation of the "is" and the "ought," of science and morality, and the reduction of moral and political critique to historical description have been challenged. The vacuousness of dialectical explanation, the complete absorption of the individual in the state (in particular for Hegel), the utopian nature of communism with Marx, the inadequacy of economic determinism as an explanatory and predictive tool—these are all serious challenges to the adequacy of the historicist moral and political theories of Marx, Engels, and Hegel.

On the other hand, the historicism of Hegel, Marx, and Engels has certainly contributed to an increasingly sophisticated sociology of morals and politics. This is no small contribution to an understanding of social and political phenomena. We have learned much from their insistence that man is not an essence or end standing outside of historical and cultural change, manipulating that change. He is part of that process and can be properly understood as a social and political being only as a part of that process. Furthermore the historicist political philosophers have helped us to see that an adequate analysis and understanding of moral and political concepts—justice, goodness, and obligation—requires an analysis and understanding of complete social systems, their evolution and the causal factors responsible

176

for their existence. Concomitantly, an adequate moral and political critique (assuming for the moment that such is possible for the historicist) must focus not merely on the individual but upon the social and economic *system* within which he exists. The historicism of Hegel, Marx, and Engels enables us to see, in a way in which the utilitarianism of Bentham and Mill and the natural law theories of Hobbes, St. Thomas, and Locke.do not, that injustice is a predicate of an entire social system; that if the system is a bad one, then the acts denominated as right within that system are a sham; that moral and political responsibility require an evaluation of the entire system and its institutions, not merely of isolated acts and exemplifications of that system; and that an adequate political philosophy must include a comparative analysis and evaluation of alternative social and economic systems and institutions.

The dangers which might accompany such a comparative analysis are well-known. If a theorist or a political leader thinks he has the final answers to all of man's normative problems, dogmatism and political authoritarianism are likely results. If he assumes that his *locus standi* is infallible, then dire consequences indeed can follow. But comparative analysis and evaluation of social systems is possible without such dogmatism and authoritarianism, and Marx himself, in most of his work, exemplifies this approach. His *locus standi* involves a basic commitment to certain values—freedom, equality, and justice—but he recognizes that those values must and will evolve, that they will have different signification under different historical conditions, that these values, even in mature communism, will continue to evolve, and that an ethic or value system cannot be holistically imposed upon all of mankind from above.

Recommended Readings

Arendt, H. *The Origins of Totalitarianism.* New York, 1951.
Benn, S. I. and Peters, R. S. *Social Principles and the Democratic State.* London, 1959.
Berlin, I. *Two Concepts of Liberty.* Oxford, 1958.
Bosanquet, B. *The Philosophical Theory of the State.* London, 1920.
Hobhouse, L. T. *The Metaphysical Theory of the State.* London, 1918.
Hook, Sidney. *From Hegel to Marx.* Ann Arbor, Michigan, 1962.
Jordan, Elijah. *Theory of Legislation.* Chicago, 1952.

Olafson, Frederick, ed. *Society, Law and Morality*. Englewood Cliffs, N.J., 1961. Part II.

Popper, Karl. *The Open Society and Its Enemies*. 2 Vols. London, 1950.

Popper, Karl. *The Poverty of Historicism*. London, 1957.

Talmon, J. *The Origins of Totalitarian Democracy*. London, 1952.

part 3
criteria of adequacy for a political philosophy

In Chapter 1 we argued that political theory cannot be reduced to a single component. On the contrary, it embraces at least three distinct but related activities or concerns which we characterized as the empirical, the normative, and the analytic or conceptual. Those who reduce political theory to only one of these concerns provide us with impoverished theories. The behaviorist, we saw, with his commitment to the methodological assumptions and techniques of empirical science and to the value-free status of his theories, insists that the total concern of the political theorist is with the discovery of laws and regularities explaining political behavior and permitting prediction. Although this commitment does not preclude conceptual or analytic concerns—indeed such concerns are required in the formulation of behavioral theories—it does preclude the normative function characteristic of traditional political theory. It thus excludes from the domain of political theory the establishment of rational criteria for evaluating social and political institutions and the ends or goals which those institutions purport to serve. This exclusion renders political theory devoid of the basic function from which the empirical data and regularities discovered derive their significance. The same exclusion of the normative component is effected by the logical positivist as a result of the application of the verifiability criterion of meaning. It is effected by some "ordinary use," analytic philosophers as a result of their view that philosophy is basically analysis and conceptual ground-clearing (not that of giving answers to normative or empirical questions) and the further view that the so-called questions and answers of traditional political theory are conceptually confused and "worthless."

Quite to the contrary, we have argued that the primary concern of political theory is with the normative dimension. The analysis and clarification of concepts, the collection of empirical data, the formulation of hypotheses, the attempt to discover laws or regularities to explain political behavior and institutions and to permit prediction—all this is essential to an adequate political theory but it is subsidiary to the normative task. The normative task, however, is *not* political casuistry, that is, the recommendation of specific solutions to specific normative political issues. Such casuistry is futile, for the solution to specific normative political issues requires specific and detailed knowledge of concrete social and political circumstances. This the political theorist does not have. Thus, his normative task is the justification of *general* (normative) political principles, which might serve as premises for those responsible for formulating specific social and political policies, premises that, when combined with empirical knowledge of context and circumstances, will yield those specific recommendations and policies. The need for contextual decision cannot be avoided, and the political theorist cannot properly make such decisions. But he can provide principles, hopefully justified ones, from which *decisions of principle* (the application and extension of principles) can be made by those who know the contexts and circumstances.[1]

It was further stated in Chapter 1 that the formulation of such general principles is best done against the backdrop of the political theories advanced by influential and classical theorists. The analysis and evaluation of those theories is essential in providing a perspective from which one's own answers to the key questions of political philosophy can be formulated. Thus in Part 2 we examined the views of classical natural law theorists (St. Thomas Aquinas, Thomas Hobbes and John Locke), those of the classical utilitarians (Jeremy Bentham and John Stuart Mill), and those of the influential historicist theorists (Friedrich Hegel, Friedrich Engels, and Karl Marx). We saw that these theorists offered three distinct, though often overlapping, models of justification (with important variations *within* each model), and that these models of justification were rooted in different moral beliefs, metaphysical beliefs, theological beliefs, epistemological beliefs, and scientific beliefs. To understand and appraise these models and the variations upon them required the understanding and appraisal of their essential components. This appraisal was performed in Part 2.

The appraisal of these theories and their parts itself required the use of various norms or standards of evaluation (logical, epistemological, scientific, moral, and so on) which themselves remained unexplicated and unjustified in the context of their use in those chapters. We promised that we would explicate these various norms of appraisal and their grounds in this final chapter, and we must now make good that promise. First, these norms, which fall under all three dimensions (the empirical, the analytic-conceptual, and the normative) and which we argued earlier must be embraced by any adequate political theory, will be sorted out and treated under the general rubric of "criteria of adequacy" for a political theory. We will set about accomplishing this by briefly recapitulating the three models of political justification examined in Part 2 and by recalling some of the criticisms—the virtues and the defects—of these models. Having done this, we will then focus on three issues or concepts fundamental to any political theory: freedom (What is to be meant by political freedom?); equality (What is to be meant by equality of treatment?); and the public interest (What is to be meant by the public interest?). Other concepts or questions are perhaps equally basic—political

[1] See Richard Hare's *The Language of Morals* (Oxford: Clarendon Press, 1952), in particular Part I, Chapter 4.

authority, the rule of law, and political obligation, for example. But these latter concepts can be explained in terms of the former and, historically at least, there are good reasons for focusing on freedom, equality, and the public interest. The criteria of adequacy outlined in our review of the three models will, to some extent, be used in our treatment of these basic concepts or questions. We will argue for a certain interpretation of these norms or concepts, which amounts to a normative defense of a type of democracy. En route to this defense, we will examine alternative interpretations of these norms or concepts, and, hence, of several interpretations of democracy (and, indirectly, of other forms of government).

chapter 9
Criteria of
Adequacy

It was seen in Chapters 2, 3 and 4 that although there are wide differences among the classical natural law theorists, they share the basic belief that there exist valid and objective moral laws or rules which prescribe or prohibit conduct of certain types. These laws or rules are antecedent to and independent of both the consciences of individuals and of the prescriptions and prohibitions of the existing legal order. They are in no sense human contrivances or inventions; on the contrary, the rules of conscience and the legal order should themselves reflect these natural laws. Natural law constitutes the objective standard for the appraisal or evaluation of all existing political institutions and laws. This view still has many strong advocates.

In evaluating our chosen spokesmen for natural law theory—St. Thomas, Hobbes, and Locke—we attempted to ferret out problems or inadequacies of three kinds: conceptual or analytic, normative, and empirical. Recognizing the interrelationships of these three components, we concentrated primarily on conceptual or analytic problems, though normative and empirical inadequacies were also noted. Let us briefly recount some of these problems and inadequacies, primarily conceptual or analytic ones.

All three natural law theorists hold, we saw, to some form of moral cognitivism, the view that moral judgments are truth claims and are capable of being true or false, though they differ on the avenue of cognition and, it seems, on the sorts of facts cognized. Thomas's appeal to revelation as an avenue of knowledge, as in any theologically based ethic or political theory, poses severe problems of testability and meaning. There seems to be no way of adjudicating conflicting revelations rationally. That is, the appeal to revelation straightforwardly rules out intersubjective (public) testability. To the extent that Hobbes and Locke appeal to the existence of God and revelation, the same problem confronts them. (Each of them appeals to God but there is a difference of emphasis.)

The problem of testability is related to that of meaning. How can one who is "outside the faith" know the meaning of the central concepts of Thomas's ethic—eternal happiness, beatitude, or possession of God—and hence the meaning of the moral and political norms which presumably reflect these concepts. Much of contemporary philosophy calls into question the meaningfulness of such concepts and the cognitive status of the claims in which they are used, and we saw that the entire Pandora's box of natural and revealed theology must be opened in any assessment of Thomas's views. His essentialistic theory of man, the view that man has an essential nature—a goal or function uniquely his because he is a man and is God's creature—is simply denied by those who do not share his Christianized version of Aristotle. Man has no "final" end, his critics aver. The empirical evidence (note the appeal to a contrary epistemological principle) indicates rather that man has the potentiality for a wide spectrum of activities and can in fact develop or be molded along many lines.

Locke's appeal to the intuitive, self-evident status of natural rights poses similar problems. How can rival intuitions be rationally resolved? Furthermore, his view that those rights, the protection of which constitutes the *raison d'être* for the state, exist prior to any legal structure and are part of the moral furniture of the universe, seems to be incompatible with his view in the *Essay Concerning Human Understanding* that obligation is a "mixed mode," a human construction with no "archetype" in nature.

Another conceptual problem common to both Locke and Thomas has to do with their mutual claim that ethics can be a "demonstrative science." Neither attempts to demonstrate this in any systematic way. Thomas states that the principle of synderesis ("good is to be done, evil avoided") is the basic premise from which all other moral norms "flow," but he does nothing to establish that. And even assuming that human nature has an essence as Thomas supposes, he must show how moral and political norms can be validly inferred from the qualities constituting that essence. As already noted, critics point out that there is no consensus on the meaning of human nature, and some go on to argue that appeals to this concept, like those of Thomas, are really circular—those functions and activities that philosophers designated as essential to what it means to be a human being are in reality social and political preferences or prejudices which they have built into the concept of human nature. It is then easy enough to infer these moral and political norms from the concept of human nature, but only at the cost of circularity. The "is-ought" question is plainly involved here, and critics of natural law theory often argue that the terms "man," "human nature," and "reason"—from which norms are presumably derived—are not merely descriptive concepts but evaluative or prescriptive ones, which means that the apparent descriptions of man and nature set forth by natural law theorists are, at the very least, recommendations as well.

Locke does no better than Thomas in attempting to set up a system of logical deduction in ethics. Perhaps such a system can be constructed, indeed, in such a way that it allows for changing empirical states of affairs and for what Hare calls "decisions of principle." And perhaps such a logical system can then be deductively related to a set of political norms. Locke and Thomas suggest these possibilities, but they do not develop such a system and attempt to apply it to moral and political experience. Thus their theories are inadequate in terms of their completeness and application, if not applicability.

There is no need to recapitulate all of the conceptual problems cited in the discussion of natural law. And it should be plain by now that the norms or standards which we have invoked in our critique of these theories are traditional ones: logical consistency, coherence, testability, applicability, and completeness or adequacy. Perhaps a few examples from the natural law theorists of normative and empirical problems will make even clearer these standards of theory evaluation. Then we will briefly recapitulate how these same standards were applied to both the utilitarians and the historicists.

Thomas subscribes to several moral principles, we saw, including "equality of proportion" and the "common good." In fact we saw that natural law theorists in general, although they embrace the utilitarian norm, maintain that there are also nonutilitarian reasons relevant to moral decisions, and that an adequate ethic must recognize those dimensions. For Thomas, these nonutilitarian features involve the will of God; for Locke, certain natural rights. Two issues arise, conceptual and normative. Conceptually, the issue is that of criteria of adequacy for a normative ethic. Locke and Thomas alike reject a utilitarian type of reductionism, apparently on the grounds that the nonutilitarian criteria to which they appeal are part of any accurate account of the moral principles used in reaching moral decisions, and that such criteria are required in any adequate moral assessment of an action or a policy of action. Their rejection of a utilitarian sort of reductionism—that is, the recognition that there are some obligations which are binding not merely because of utilitarian reasons—creates a serious normative problem. What if the nonreductive grounds of obligation conflict on occasion? What is one to do? More specifically, to go back to the example in Thomas, what if the "common good" and "equality of proportion" conflict? Thomas would probably deny that the two could conflict, but if they could (and I will argue that they can later in this chapter) and if one must choose between equality and utility, then plainly the normative stakes are high.

A similar sort of conflict of values, we saw, arose for Locke in his doctrine of natural rights. Not only do the rights of some persons seem to conflict with the realization of the same rights of other persons, but it may be that the rights themselves, say, the right to freedom and the right to equality, may conflict (obviously everything depends on the interpretation of these rights, about which we will have more to say later). That is, the extension of equality may require the restriction of freedom, or the extension of freedom may require the restriction of equality. (It may be that an interpretation of these rights can be given so that they *cannot* conflict. H. L. A. Hart's formulation of the basic "natural" right in terms of the "equal right of all men to be free" may accomplish this.[1]) Whatever the value conflict, whether it be between different rights, or between rights (justice) and utility, the issue is the same: a reductionist theory (no matter whether the reduction is in the direction of a teleological theory or a deontological one) seems to violate the criteria of completeness and applicability, but a nonreductionist theory leaves one with principles of choice that conflict at least sometimes, and hence give no clear-cut directive for choice. If some form of nonreduc-

[1] See H. L. A. Hart's "Are There Any Natural Rights?", *Philosophical Review*, 64 (1955); in Frederick Olafson, ed., *Society, Law and Morality* (Englewood Cliffs, N.J.: Prentice-Hall, Inc., 1961).

tionism in ethics is correct, that is, an ethic in which there are several moral principles neither of which can be reduced to the other; and if there are such conflicts between nonreducible values (not only in fact but in principle), then surely an adequate ethical theory, and hence an adequate political theory, must recognize them. We will say more about the plurality of values and inherent value conflicts later, for a consideration of this issue is central to the formulation of an adequate political theory.

As already implied above, determining the meaning or interpretation of any given value or moral principle is essential in discovering whether value conflicts exist (in fact, in principle, or both) and hence in resolving such conflicts. Such resolution is at least one, if not the most fundamental, objective of both moral and political philosophy. This problem of meaning was noted above in the case of Thomas's appeal to the notions of "beatitude" and "possession of God." But it holds also for less esoteric concepts such as the "common good," the "public interest," "equality," and "justice," concepts utilized by nearly all moral and political philosophers. When Thomas speaks of "equality of proportion," we ask: equality in regard to what? and proportional to what? Otherwise this norm is vacuous. The same holds for Locke's appeal to the right to property, to freedom, or equality. Equality in regard to what criteria and for what objective? Freedom to do what? Or freedom from what? Distributive justice, the equitable distribution of goods, requires a distribution of what and on the basis of what criteria? Who is included under "common" in the norm "common interest" or under "public" in "public interest"? And what is an "interest"? Is it the same thing as a right? And what is a "right"? These and similar questions must be asked and answered if these concepts and norms are to be intelligible guides for either moral or public policy decisions. And surely, reasonably clear, intelligible guides to action are at least a necessary condition for an adequate moral and political theory. Perhaps a strictly operational definition of these concepts and norms is not possible. Indeed, I shall argue later that such a request (of normative concepts) is misplaced and indicates a lack of understanding of the uses and functions of such concepts. But some degree of clarity is possible short of strict descriptive definitions. We will attempt to provide this clarity with regard to the concepts of (1) freedom, (2) equality or justice, and (3) the public interest.

We have cited both analytic-conceptual issues and normative ones, and have indicated how the positions of some of the natural law theorists on these issues violate certain criteria of adequacy for a political theory. Briefly now let us recall several challenges to empirical theses held by these philosophers.

Hobbes, we saw, rested much of his political philosophy on the thesis that all men are egoists, and we saw that this presumably empirical thesis is conceptually tied to his account of obligation, which excludes the very possibility of impartiality or of altruistic action. But he offers precious little empirical evidence for psychological egoism. Surely, even if egoism is a correct account of man, a political theory which utilizes egoism as a foundational premise must provide adequate verifying evidence for this belief. In the same way, if a political theorist cites the existence of a social contract as a historical fact in his effort to explain political obligation (as Locke appears to do), he must surely be prepared to provide the documenting evidence for such a fact. Such empirical claims play an essential role in relation to the normative claims of theory and indeed in relation to other descriptive-explanatory components as well. If those claims are not adequately verified, then the political theory itself, to that extent, is inadequate.

What we have done thus far in this recapitulation is to focus on some of the analytic-conceptual, normative, and empirical components of traditional natural law theories and we have indicated certain inadequacies of those theories. Our evaluations have been based on the following general criteria: logical consistency, coherence, clarity, testability and empirical accuracy, completeness, and applicability. Similar sorts of inadequacies we found in the utilitarian theories of Bentham and Mill, and in the historicist theories of Hegel, Marx and Engels. The *empirical accuracy* of Bentham's doctrine of psychological hedonism; the *adequacy* and *applicability* of the hedonistic calculus as an instrument for measuring rightness; the *logical consistency* of the Bentham-Mill move from descriptive premises about man's nature and his desires to the normative conclusion that the principle of utility is the test of rightness (that is, their leap from "is" to "ought")—all of these have been challenged. The *coherence* and *completeness* of the utilitarian ethic—the reduction of all morally relevant considerations to consequential ones—was challenged. This involved questioning the Mill-Bentham subsumption of the principle of justice under the principle of utility. We also saw that greater *clarity* of certain basic concepts in the utilitarian theory—justice and freedom, for example—was needed, as well as a clearer explication of the normative entailments of these principles.

The same criteria—clarity, empirical accuracy and testability, logical consistency, coherence, completeness and applicability—are sometimes violated, we saw, by the historicist. Hegel's metaphysical idealism fails to meet criteria of *clarity* and *testability*. His theory of dialectic, which fuses laws of logic and of reality, results in the muddling of concepts like "contradiction" and "consistency," and although it purports to explain the growth and development of all phenomena, it frequently seems to explain nothing at all; hence it is challenged in terms of *applicability* and *completeness*. His conflation of "is" and "ought" and his identification of the individual with the state and its organic unity involve serious conceptual and normative problems; that conflation makes genuine moral critique impossible and the identification results, normatively, in the conclusion that individuals per se do not really matter and, consequently, in all of the possible evils of totalitarianism.

We saw that Marx's and Engels's brand of historicism also violates these general criteria. The *testability* of the theory of dialectical materialism is often questioned; the *clarity* of the doctrine of economic determinism (Is the doctrine to be understood strictly so that *only* economic causes are efficacious?); the *empirical accuracy* of economic determinism as the explanation of the causes of value conflicts and moral systems; the conflation of science and morality; the *logical consistency* of the relativistic moral code constitutive of their historist position and the apparent absolutism of the ethic of ideal communism; the *completeness* and *applicability* of the ethic of communism (Is the ethic utopian? Are the basic norms both clear and adequate for the resolution of moral and political issues?)—these have all been challenged and found wanting to some extent.

On the other hand we found that each of these three models of justification—the theory of natural law, utilitarianism, and historicism—and each of the individual theories discussed under these models has had something significant to contribute to the normative and conceptual questions of political philosophy and each has made important contributions to our understanding of political reality. The adequacy of a theory is a matter of degree. We do not want merely to focus upon the inadequacies of these models and theories but on their adequacies as well. Consequently in our treatment of these models and of individual theories we also indicated the advantages of each. The natural law theorists' insistence upon the relevance and irreducibility of both utilitarian and deontological criteria in assessing both the morality of acts and the political appropriateness of policies and institutions we found to be a distinct advantage. This insistence meant, we suggested, that this model appears to meet the criteria of completeness and applicability (relative to the normative dimension) to a greater extent than other models (for example, more than the reductionist theory of the utilitarian). The utilitarian model, which conceives of political norms as utilitarian devices or conventions which fundamentally selfish but also rational beings recognize as essential principles of cooperation, the consequences (and hence the rightness) of which can be measured, we found to have distinct advantages in appearing to meet the criteria of clarity and testability to a greater degree than other models (than either the natural law or historicist models). The historicist model, with its insistence that man is not an essence standing outside of historical and cultural change, that man as a social and political being can be understood only as a part of that process, and that an adequate analysis and understanding of moral and political concepts requires an analysis of complete social systems and the causal factors responsible for their existence and evolution—this model, we saw, provides a more sophisticated sociology of morals and politics than natural law or utilitarian theorists, and *to that extent,* provides a more adequate account and understanding of social and political phenomena.

Adequacy and Openness

A more adequate political theory would include under one roof the advantages of each of these models and would meet the general criteria of adequacy specified above to a higher extent. But a perfect theory one should not expect, for, as we have shown, political theory is a complex and difficult business. The conditions of human existence and consequently, of man's social relationships, are constantly changing. New empirical data become available. With such changes and new data, different perspectives ensue. New conceptual ways of looking at man, society, and social institutions emerge. In the recent past, the impact of science and its challenge to a theological perspective was responsible for new perspectives on man and his moral and political norms and institutions. On the current scene, the development of ecology as a science with new data and theories on environmental resources is having considerable impact both on our conceptualization of man as a part of nature and on moral and political norms related to the use and abuse of environmental resources. Such changes will surely continue, and political theory must be open to such change.

The fact of change and the need for change, however, need not blind one to a kind of underlying stability of both facts and norms. The essentialistic theory of human nature held by St. Thomas may be mistaken; *that* much stability we do not have. But neither is human nature so fluid and changing that we cannot get our hands on it. There are common characteristics, common potentialities, and common needs—physiological, psychological, and social—of men everywhere. And these common characteristics and needs have resulted, as Alfred Kroeber and Clyde Kluckhohn have shown, in common and cross-culturally accepted values and ways of fulfilling those needs.[2] Are these universal and absolute values? Perhaps not. But there is a growing worldwide consensus on certain basic values such as freedom, equality and justice, the fulfillment of human rights, and the promotion of the common good or the public interest. There are, of course, differences in value emphasis and on priorities among those who accept these basic values. As I will suggest later, the Soviet Union places greater emphasis on certain types of social and economic equality than on political equality or freedom, compared, say, to the United States. But these differences of emphasis should not obscure the common value commitments. Nor should differences on what constitutes proper instruments, political and economic, for achieving these values obscure this fact. Of course, there may exist sharp differences over basic values. This possibility and, occasionally, actuality cannot be ignored. Still, even allowing for some such basic disagreements on value objectives themselves, not merely over means to achieve them, there is remarkable agreement on those objectives—as reflected in national constitutions, the United Nations Charter, and the charters of other international organizations.

It would be a great service to political theory, perhaps even to practical politics, if the areas of value agreement and disagreement among political theories, on both intrinsic and instrumental values, could be identified. This would provide not only a helpful comparative analysis of alternative and competing political systems (though

2 Alfred Kroeber and Clyde Kluckhohn, *Culture: A Critical Review of Concepts and Definitions*, Papers of The Peabody Museum, Vol. 47, No. 1 (1952).

the degrees of differences among them and the extent of competition may turn out on analysis to be less than is often believed) but also assist in the formulation of an adequate political theory, that is, a theory that might best meet the criteria of adequacy specified above. One can hardly be consistent, clear, coherent, testable, applicable, and so on in one's theory without a clear understanding (to the extent possible) of the basic norms of that theory and how they differ from those of other theories. Nor can one adequately argue for one type of political institution as opposed to another without that understanding. That is, one can hardly calculate the best means to enhance or fulfill certain values without a reasonably clear understanding of those values and their competitors.

In the limited scope of this volume, we cannot accomplish this result. But we can indicate the drift of such an understanding of values and outline the rudiments of a political theory which appears to meet to a reasonably high degree the criteria of adequacy which have been specified. We will do this by briefly recapitulating the meaning of certain basic values among the theorists we have examined, the apparent differences among them over these values, and the differences on the instruments, the political institutions and rules, that they see as proper for instantiating their value commitments. We will combine this recapitulation with some additional philosophical analysis of the meaning of these value concepts. Freedom, equality, and the public interest (the common good or general happiness) were the most fundamental values espoused by the natural law, utilitarian, and historicist theorists which we examined. So we will devote a section to an analysis of each of these concepts. We also will offer a certain interpretation of their meaning and role in democratic theory, and examine arguments that certain instruments and rules of democratic institutions best bring these values to fruition.

Recommended Readings

Brandt, Richard, ed. *Social Justice.* Englewood Cliffs, N.J., 1964.
Brecht, Arnold. *Political Theory.* Princeton, 1959.
Eulau, Heinz. *The Behavioral Persuasion in Politics.* New York, 1963.
Gewirth, Alan. *Political Philosophy.* New York, 1965. See especially Introduction.
Greaves, H. R. G. *The Foundations of Political Theory.* London, 1958.

McCoy, Charles A., and Playford, John, eds. *Apolitical Politics*. New York, 1967.

Olafson, Frederick, ed. *Society, Law and Morality*. Englewood Cliffs, N.J., 1961. See especially Introduction.

Runciman, W. G. *Social Science and Political Theory*. Cambridge, 1963.

Weldon, T. D. *The Vocabulary of Politics*. Baltimore, 1953.

chapter 10
Freedom

Political Freedom: An Overview of the Concept

One of the basic values or norms advocated by the theorists we have examined is freedom. But we saw that this value or norm, even limited to a political context, had different meanings for each of them. Outside of a political context, the multiple meanings of this value are even more numerous. If the term *freedom* does not designate one essential property or characteristic, and, if in order to discover its meaning(s) we must be aware of the numerous contexts in which it is used (as the "ordinary use" analysts argue), then an adequate theory must provide an explication of those multiple uses, with special attention being given to political contexts or uses of this concept and the functions and objectives of its use in those contexts. Generally, the term "free" carries commendatory force. Nearly everyone *approves* of freedom. We also know that the term is often used for propaganda purposes. How often we hear ideologists from various nations make use of this term to defend a policy or criticize the theory or policy-stance of another nation! All of them, it seems, are for freedom, including those nations generally characterized as totalitarian. But what they mean by the concept varies considerably.

We are not concerned here with those uses or senses of freedom which are basically moral or psychological. Are men capable of free choice? Or are they completely determined by external causes of various kinds? Are men autonomous moral agents? These are important philosophical questions and the answers to them are related to the issue of political freedom. If men are simply cogs in a mechanical universe (as Hobbes suggested), or completely determined in their action by economic causes (as Marx and Engels suggest in some of their work) or by unconscious or subconscious factors (suggested by Freud), then at least *some* philosophers infer that there is no meaningful sense of human freedom, including political freedom.

This general issue of freedom and determinism we cannot pursue here. Our purpose will be satisfied if we can shed some light simply on political freedom. We saw in our chapters on natural law theory, utilitarianism, and historicism that the question of political freedom is primarily concerned with the relation of individuals and groups to the state. How much freedom should individuals or groups have within the framework of state control? Or put alternatively, how much control should the state exercise over its citizens or associations of men under its umbrella? Some such control is absolutely necessary. On this all of our theorists agree. The question is how much.

Hobbes, we saw, argued that the state of nature, a condition in which there is complete individual freedom to do as one will, with no political or legal constraints, is really a state of anarchy. With no legal restraints on anyone, everyone's very existence is threatened by capricious freedom, and life under such conditions would be "solitary, poor, nasty, brutish, and short." The social contract and the state Hobbes sees as artificial devices conceived by egoistic but yet rational men to avoid a condition of anarchical freedom. An absolute sovereign he sees as necessary to effect this, and political freedom, for Hobbes, consists simply of areas of action which the sovereign sees fit to permit. Hobbes's theory leaves large areas of human relationships unconstrained, but he is plainly more concerned with the securing of peace and order than of freedom and he makes no effort to delimit the power of the sovereign in order to preserve certain freedoms from the intrusion of the state. Such an effort, he maintains, would only return us to the state of war and anarchy.

Locke, on the other hand, sees freedom as an inalienable right of all men, the protection of which, along with other rights, is a fundamental reason for the very existence of the state. If any given state does not protect these rights, it must be reconstituted, if necessary, by revolution. Order, peace, and security are simply not enough for Locke. They are essential, and Locke too insists upon constraints on natural freedom (freedom in the state of nature). But order and security are not to be purchased at just any price. Political freedom is purchased at the cost of *some* natural freedom (for one is still entitled to follow his own will "in all things where the rule prescribes not"), for the existence of the state, with a system of laws, necessarily restricts doing just whatever one wants to do. When one agrees to the social contract, directly or tacitly, one agrees to abide by the restrictions embodied in law. This constitutes political freedom. The laws cannot, however, morally violate one's natural rights to equality, property, and freedom. By restraining arbitrariness on the part of individuals, groups, and even sovereigns, the law "preserves and enlarges freedom." (Of course, the law itself must not embody arbitrary discriminations.)

We noted earlier that freedom, for Locke, is conceived largely negatively, that is, in terms of the absence of arbitrary restraints or power. The state must make certain that the elements of arbitrariness are absent from society so that the political conditions for the exercise of our natural rights are guaranteed. But he insists that government must be limited more or less to clearing away arbitrary restraints, not to providing the positive conditions, economic and otherwise, required for the fulfillment of those rights. Implicitly at least, there is a positive sense of political freedom in Locke's philosophical premises. Locke does speak occasionally of the general or common good as a criterion for the restriction of human action. This criterion would appear to introduce reasons of a different kind which would justify positive action on the part of government, not merely the negative action which assures the absence of arbitrary restraints. If the uneducated and the propertyless, for example, cannot exercise their natural rights, then positive action in terms of welfare rights might be justified both on the grounds that such rights are enabling conditions for the exercise of natural rights and on the ground that welfare rights promote the general good. Although Locke does not in fact extend the concept of political freedom in this positive direction, his theory leaves open this possibility and a number of theorists since Locke's day have so extended it. Indeed this extension is at least in part what is meant by the New Left.

Bentham's and Mill's interpretations of freedom and their criteria for the restriction both of individual action and state control differ from Locke's, for unlike Locke, they do not subscribe to a doctrine of inalienable natural rights. They do, however, subscribe to a set of legal rights under the fundamental norm of utility, and the normative result in terms of a defense of freedom is very close to Locke. Bentham emphasizes what we have called negative freedom as the proper role of government. The state must assure the absence of arbitrary restraints and the arbitrary use of power, especially along "those broad lines of conduct in which all persons, or very large and permanent descriptions of persons . . . engage." But legislative interference, including that motivated solely by concern for the good of the community, must be limited, else "all of the miseries which the most determined malevolence could have devised" are produced. Bentham's ultimate criterion of restriction is utility, and he believes that excessive state interference and the narrowing of the liberties of individuals decreases the happiness of individuals and of society as a whole. However, as noted earlier, the utilitarian ethic might be used to justify a more positive sense of political freedom in which the state supports education, provides health facilities and recognizes and fulfills welfare rights. Presumably for the utilitarian, the question of the justification of such positive interference is empirical: Does it produce more good than harm? Bentham does insist that the proper balance between freedom and state control is best assured by a certain distribution of power within the state, and by freedom of the press and of association. Locke, of course, strongly argued for the separation of executive and legislative powers to assure political freedom, and in this century many have seen the importance of an independent or separate judiciary as essential for the preservation of basic freedoms.

As with both Locke and Bentham the basic emphasis in Mill's treatment of political freedom is negative, though again his criterion of legitimate state control permits a more positive interpretation. That criterion, recall, is self-protection: "The sole end for which mankind are warranted, individually or collectively, in interfering with the liberty of action of any of their number is self-protection. That the only purpose of which power can be rightfully exercised over any member of a civilized community, against his will, is to prevent harm to others. His own good, either physical or moral, is not a sufficient warrant." Liberty or freedom is not a natural right for Mill. This Lockean sort of defense is ruled out. But freedom is a moral right of every person simply because he is a person and because freedom, having both intrinsic and extrinsic value, is essential to the happiness of each person, and, I suppose he would add, to the happiness of society as a whole. Maximum individual freedom must be permitted, restricted only by rules and policies which "prevent harm to others." We saw earlier that such rules are interpreted as those which prevent the violation of the moral or legal rights of other persons or groups. Hence a clear understanding of Mill's criterion requires an understanding of those rights or of what those rights ought to be. Here is where considerable leeway exists. What should those rights be? Depending on how widely those rights are interpreted or how long the list of moral rights becomes, Mill's test becomes very broad and positive (including welfare rights, the "right to enjoy the arts," and so on—see the United Nations Declaration of Human Rights) or reasonably narrow and negative in nature—the assurance of the absence of arbitrary restraints. Theoretically, then, the principle of the self-protection of society could make legitimate a large number of state restraints on individual or group action. Nonetheless, the presumption for Mill is in favor of a *laissez faire* state, with the burden of proof for any restriction being placed on the person who would introduce the restriction. And he reminds us that a person's "own good, either physical or moral, is not a sufficient warrant" for state intrusion.

Freedom as a value plays an even more central role in the political theory of Hegel than in that of the utilitarians. This is because freedom has a much wider meaning, and constitutes an all-embracing value for Hegel. He accepts the negative sort of political freedom stressed by Bentham and Mill—the state must provide through the rule of law certain restraints on individual or group action, restraints which guarantee equality of treatment for all and which preclude unjustified intrusion in one's life. He argues that pre-political freedom is simply chaos. But Hegel goes two steps further, and then appears to deny a basic sense of freedom advocated by Hobbes, Locke, Bentham, and Mill. The first step is simply the extension of negative freedom to positive freedom. The second, which is only implicit in the analyses of Locke, Bentham and Mill, becomes explicit in Hegel, for he insists that it is the state's responsibility to make sure that every citizen has a useful and satisfactory niche within the state and that no one exist as a pauper. These objectives would surely justify moves toward a welfare state.

But, more importantly, Hegel construes freedom as broader than positive and negative freedom combined. Genuine freedom requires that the individual identify himself with the universal. This means for him that one must immerse oneself in and identify with the state, for the state is the exemplification of the universal spirit or plan immanent in world-history, through which (Spirit) all things (all individuals) have their being and significance. Only with such identification is one either free or rational; and further, in a basic sense, freedom is more a property of an overall social and political system than of the individual who fulfills his role in that system. The state, as an instantiation in history of the universal spirit, is an end in itself and individuals are instruments of that end. For this reason Hegel denies the import of a sense of freedom stressed as fundamental by Hobbes, Locke, Bentham, and Mill, namely, freedom to do what one pleases without state interference. This sort of "freedom" he sees as capricious and arbitrary. Real freedom is doing what one ought and what is rational, that is, being determined by the universal (which, in most cases means obedience to the state). Concomitant with the rejection of capricious freedom is the rejection of the utilitarian view that the state is merely an agglomerate of atomic individuals organized simply to maximize and equalize happiness. The Hegelian metaphysic results in the last analysis in an entirely different view of freedom, even though it includes both the positive and negative senses of political freedom discussed above, and for Hegel it resulted in the advocacy of constitutional monarchy as the form of government to assure this freedom, and in the rejection of democracy and the universal franchise.

Like Hegel, Marx and Engels maintain that negative freedom—a system of rights which prevents the arbitrary intrusion or use of power by other individuals, groups or the state—is not enough. In fact, they maintain that systems of rights are often used to repress and enslave people. Governments which use social and legal rules to perpetuate the status quo and existing class distinctions do not contribute to freedom, but to enslavement. Under capitalist economics in particular such governments perpetuate a system of exploitation in which persons are treated as objects or commodities, without intrinsic worth. Labor, the ability to work and create, distinguishes man from the animals but under capitalist governments, man's labor is forced; it is a commodity under the control of the capitalist. One works not to satisfy his desires and needs but to produce the products which the system imposes upon him. This Marx calls the "fetishism of commodities." Man becomes dehumanized and alienated by an economic system which controls his very desires and a political system which reflects and perpetuates both class distinctions and exploitation. No one can be really free, bourgeoisie or proletariat alike, Marx and Engels argue, until the system is changed, until class distinctions are abolished, the fetishism of commodities replaced by concern for human beings (which requires the demise of capitalism), and the state as an instrument of exploitation and repression is abolished or "withers" away. A person is really free only when he exists under an economic and social system in which he is conceptualized as having intrinsic worth and permitted to exercise creative autonomy. That system, for Marx, is communism, in which the state has withered away and where "in place of the old bourgeois society, with its classes and class antagonism, we shall have an association, in which the free development of each is the condition for the free development of all." Under communism man becomes really human, rational, and free.

Even with the "state" withered away there is great social control and "administration," for freedom requires the fulfillment of basic needs and the opportunity to develop and exercise individual talents. Thus, much more than the negation of arbitrary restraints is required. Positive conditions for need and interest fulfillment must be provided. Marx and Engels, then, would lead us directly to a welfare society, one which functions so well, they propose, that the needs of all would be met and in which a system of rights would no longer be required since there would be no problem of the distribution (justice) of goods and services.

The Meaning and Justification of Political Freedom

We have seen in our review of this basic concept of freedom that, even restricted to the political context, it has several meanings, and that the social and political systems designed to implement it consequently vary considerably. In every case, however, political freedom involves a certain social and legal standing within a set of rules and institutions (though one could be free in other senses as well). That legal standing is generally explicated in terms of a set of rights, but different social orders recognize different rights and they restrict rights on the basis of different criteria. Neither slaves nor ordinary persons had the rights of citizens in Rome. Seen in this way, the problem of political freedom is this: What rights should members of a political community have? Such a list of rights would in effect spell out the boundaries of state authority and the legitimate use of state power. Now we have seen that there is disagreement over what these rights should be, and whether they should be seen in merely negative terms (as restricting arbitrary intrusion) or in positive terms as well. It is reasonable, some argue, to restrain individuals or groups from the arbitrary use of power. This negative action assures greater freedom for all by assuring the rule of law. Surely this Hobbesean point is correct. But several related questions arise: Even restricting one's concern to negative freedom, what is an acceptable criterion for deciding what constitutes an arbitrary intrusion? Should we go beyond negative freedoms to positive guarantees of individual needs? Do such positive guarantees in a planned society ultimately destroy freedom? At the center of these questions is the thesis that laws or rights, whether conceived as positive or negative, must be appropriately formulated. That is, they must not discriminate on irrelevant grounds. This is the major thrust of both black liberationists and women's liberationists. Our laws and social policies (and conduct) do often discriminate on irrelevant grounds. What we need is a criterion for justified or relevant discrimination, and laws and policies based on that criterion.

Let us briefly consider these questions. First, does the extension of negative to positive freedom ultimately destroy freedom? Plainly, the answer depends on what one means by freedom. Those who argue that it does generally do so on the grounds that a welfare state continuously restricts the areas of free action. State education, medical care, public transportation, the provision of a minimal standard of living for all—these place tremendous tax burdens and restrictions on citizens. They may increase the welfare and security of the majority but they limit freedom, and if this continues, an individual's entire life will be planned for him. Advocates of negative freedom or a *laissez faire* state insist that this welfare and security is often purchased at the cost of freedom, and further, that freedom as a value conflicts frequently with other values such as welfare, security, and the extension of equality. It is not that such theorists are opposed to welfare, equality, and security. But they do not want these values, which receive primary attention in a planned society, to overrun and override freedom as a value. They opt for less welfare and security regulations for the sake of freedom, and they insist that we recognize that these values often conflict, and not disguise the conflict by conflating freedom with welfare, security, or equality (under the guise of "positive freedom").

Advocates of positive freedom respond by pointing out that traditional negative freedoms—freedom of speech, thought, press, assembly, association, worship, movement, and so on—cannot come to full fruition in the lives of persons until certain positive conditions accrue. A starving, uneducated man will hardly be concerned with his freedoms of press and speech. Furthermore, traditional negative freedoms were devised under historically different conditions than those which exist today. They were not designed to meet the problems of highly industrialized and heavily populated states. Under current conditions, nations which recognize merely negative freedoms consign millions of persons to misery. Of course, many persons prosper under such a system. In fact they can and do use the system to enlarge their own freedom and welfare at the expense of those who are less able. The thrust of the advocate of positive freedom is that this should not be the case. There should be regulations imposed on the powerful which prevent their exploiting the weak, and there should be a distribution of resources, goods, and opportunities which assures equality of treatment. Therefore, a political system in which the state guarantees certain positive freedoms or rights is indispensible.

Take a current example. Ecologists (and not all of them are doomsday prophets) and environmentalists have pointed out the devastating effect of population growth and man's growing technology on the environment. The growth of human population and the pollution of air and water pose threats to the quality of human life, indeed to its continued existence. If this is true, then it can be argued with some force that new regulations and controls on the use of environmental resources must be initiated, not only on the national but also the international level. Such regulations would constitute further restrictions on man's freedom. Indeed it may even be necessary to restrict the right to have children. But many argue that those restrictions are necessary to assure the welfare of all (indeed of future generations as well) and to extend rights and freedoms to all men. This line of argument simply recognizes that environmental conditions have changed radically since earlier times when there was an abundance of clean natural resources, and that these facts and concern for human welfare requires additional strictures on human action.

The concept of political freedom and criteria for justified restriction of human action continue to evolve in the light of changing circumstances and in a give-and-take tussle with other ideals which we hold dear (equality, welfare, and so on). Certain kinds of freedom, and the extension of those freedoms, require the imposition of state controls on individual action. There is nothing paradoxical about this. It is a choice of structured freedom as against unstructured chaos. The question always is: How much structure and for what reasons? Often, utilitarian reasons are cited in defense of a structure or system of rights which guarantees certain kinds of freedom of action. We have seen that classically these freedoms were largely conceived in negative terms—freedom of speech, thought, association, assembly, press, worship, and so on, where the emphasis is on the absence of interference or arbitrary restraints. These negative freedoms or rights were often justified on general pragmatic or utilitarian grounds, that is, they were (are) seen as instruments for assuring individual and societal happiness. By restricting the areas of legitimate intervention by the sovereign or the state, these freedoms or rights help prevent the misuse of state power. Certain types of free action become customary and predictable—no small matter in planning one's life and calculating consequences.

But utility is not the only fundamental norm invoked in justifying freedom(s). The principle of justice has played a paramount role. A large part of the history of the idea of freedom is a history of change in what we consider to be arbitrary or justified restrictions. Put in terms of rights-talk instead of freedom-talk, that history is one of changes in our conception of what should constitute human and legal rights. We have come a long way from the concept of the divine right of kings (though the threat of executive power remains). *Reasons* must be given for state or social controls, and recent history has seen radical new developments in what are considered to be relevant reasons. The quest for relevant reasons is the quest for justice, that is, the proper distribution of burdens and benefits. Race, color, religion, sex, and so on have been excluded, in theory if not in practice, as relevant reasons for certain modes of treatment. This has expanded the areas of freedom for millions of persons. How do we decide—how should we decide—on the relevance of reasons and criteria? This is the philosophical problem of social justice. There is no easy answer or simple formula, but we will examine several alternative answers in the section on equality.

There may be justifying grounds for freedom other than utility and justice. Recall that Mill's total ethic invokes a concept of man as a rational being capable of freedom of choice and that he placed great value on a society of autonomous, self-determining agents. This ideal of society is probably not reducible merely to the principle of maximizing happiness or to that of justice. If not, then this sort of consideration or ideal constitutes another ground of justification for freedom. We suggested earlier that such ideal considerations lead Mill toward a deontological account of obligation, in which the rightness of an action is not based merely on the calculation of its happiness-maximizing effects. Persons are conceived as rights-possessing entities, not merely because such rights produce happiness, but because humans are what they are. As free beings (whether actual or potential) who possess rights, humans cannot (should not) be restricted in their actions or have their rights violated without moral justification. It is not that the rights are absolute but rather that violation of them must be morally justified by showing that there are overriding moral considerations or that the violation is a special exception.

The Application of the Norm of Political Freedom: Conflicting Values

Whether the ultimate norm to which appeal is made in justifying freedom (or, put another way, in justifying legitimate restraints) is utility, justice, the ideal of a society of autonomous, self-determining agents or some other, and whether the norms are teleological, deontological, or some combination, still, decisions of principle—the application and extension of these principles—must continuously be made. What constitutes harm to others (Mill's principle)? Or injustice? Depending on the context, it may be that having more than two children does. Or perhaps giving birth to any children. Perhaps refusing to rake up one's leaves? Or not agreeing to give one's heart or eyes to medical banks? Or pouring chemical wastes into rivers? All of these are possibilities, depending on context. The point is that none of these principles are self-applying. They are formal and largely vacuous until applied to particular circumstances or problems. Decisions in context must be made, and these must be decisions of principle, as Richard Hare insists, else we will not be playing the moral game. These decisions must also be made in the light of changing conditions of human existence (so poignantly expressed in recent years by ecologists). Such contextual decisions or application is not the business of the political philosopher or theorist, for his role is not political casuistry. But he can indicate through his theory the need to keep conceptually before us the several formal, moral considerations relevant to the question of restricting human action and he can indicate the empirical conditions and circumstances relevant to such decisions of principle.

It goes without saying that this conceptual and empirical "pointing" does not resolve the problem of political freedom. In fact, part of what we have been saying is that (1) the various general criteria set forth as legitimate restrictions on human action do not directly and simply provide an answer to this question, for all such general criteria require contextual decisions, and (2) there are several different general criteria offered by political theorists (and utilized by politicians and nations). These criteria sometimes conflict. In fact, on occasion considerations *internal* to a given criterion of legitimate restriction may conflict. For example, it is surely conceivable that a criterion of restriction which invoked both general utilitarian reasons and those of social justice, may in some contexts, force one to opt in favor of general utility and override reasons of justice. Such cases would be very complex and perhaps would not arise often (I suppose I am expressing a Mill-like hope that utility and justice generally coalesce.) But they do sometimes occur. One's principles of social justice, for example, (and, as noted above, everything hangs on what those principles are) may support freedom to engage in homosexual acts, to have abortions, to smoke marijuana, and so on while one's concern for social utility (depending on one's assessment of empirical facts) may support the opposite. Furthermore, a general criterion of restriction may conflict (*externally,* to continue our distinction) with another criterion, not because one embodies considerations which the other omits, but simply because of different emphases or priorities on the considerations embodied in the criterion. Two different criteria, for example, may both include considerations of justice and utility but one of them place higher priority on the latter. Or those criteria may conflict when applied to substantive issues because different emphases are given to certain types of social (in)justice. The Soviet Union, for example, seems to be far more concerned with eliminating social injustices which center around economic, sexual, and racial discrimination—hence extending the freedom of millions in these areas—than in the extension of the franchise, freedom of speech, press, and so on. This need not mean that that government is unconcerned about the latter (read the U.S.S.R. Constitution) but that, at least at this stage of history, the former is judged as having priority over the latter. Almost the opposite is true of the United States. High priority has been placed on political rights and freedoms as opposed to social and economic rights and freedoms.

Nor should we forget that majority rule, though desirable in many respects, can result in what Mill calls the "tyranny of the majority." Certain types of freedom are not without their cost in terms of other kinds of freedom. In a non-Utopian world, we must pay our money and take our choice, not only between types of freedoms (though we have seen how "positive" freedom seems to embody other values—equality, security, and welfare—that traditionally have been distinguished from freedom) but between freedom and other values.

The political theorist can help make such facts clear to us. He can draw conceptual lines between freedom and value-concepts related to it. He can focus our attention on changing empirical conditions of human existence. He can indicate the sort of world resulting from the adoption of one criterion rather than another. He can, on a normative level, argue for a certain criterion of restriction with several types of relevant considerations built into the criterion and with general value priorities on these types of considerations. He may, *within a certain frame of reference,* be able to show that the adoption of one criterion rather than another is the most rational course of action. But there are philosophers and politicians who place higher value on the individual and his autonomy than on the group and collective welfare, and there are those who do just the opposite (recall that, for Hegel, individuals are *real* only as parts of a group). Given the different frames of reference and different value priorities, some people question whether the political philosopher can provide a final normative solution to the problem. Perhaps he cannot. There do, however, appear to be consensus-trends toward greater concern for group welfare and social justice on a worldwide scale, at the expense of what is called "arbitrary" freedom simply to do what one wants and also at the expense of some "negative" freedoms (the freedom not be interfered with). That is, even by theorists who reject the Hegelian metaphysic of collectivism, there is a strong trend to view freedom in a positive rather than a negative way.

Recommended Readings

Adler, Mortimer J. *The Idea of Freedom.* 2 Vols. Garden City, N. Y., 1958–61.

Anshen, Ruth N., ed. *Freedom: Its Meaning.* New York, 1940.

Bay, Christian. *The Structure of Freedom.* Stanford, 1958.

Benn, S. E. and Peters, R. S. *The Principles of Political Thought.* New York, 1965.

Berlin, I. *Two Concepts of Liberty.* Oxford, 1958.

Bryson, L., Finkelstein, L., MacIver, R. M., and McKeon, R., eds. *Freedom and Authority in Our Time.* New York, 1953.

Cranston, Maurice. *Freedom: A New Analysis.* London, 1953.

Friedrich, C. J., ed. *Nomos VI: Liberty.* New York, 1962.

Handlin, Oscar and Mary. *The Dimensions of Liberty.* Cambridge, Mass. 1961.

Konvitz, Milton. *First Amendment Freedoms: Selected Cases on Freedom of Religion, Speech, Press, Assembly.* Ithaca, 1963.

Mannheim, Karl. *Freedom, Power, and Democratic Planning.* Edited by Hans Gerth and Ernest Bramstedt. London, 1950.

Mill, J. S. *On Liberty.* London, 1859.

Muller, H. J. *Freedom in the Modern World.* New York, 1966.

Oppenheim, Felix E. *Dimensions of Freedom: An Analysis.* New York, 1961.

Spitz, David. *Essays in the Liberal Idea of Freedom.* Tucson, 1965.

chapter 11
Equality: Rights and Justice

The Norm of Equality: An Overview

In the last section we saw that it was not possible to talk clearly about political freedom without first setting it off from other kinds of freedom and then distinguishing different senses of political freedom. The same holds for related political concepts or norms like equality, rights, and justice. Different senses or uses of these concepts must be delineated before one can map their relationship with other key political concepts (such as freedom, authority, and so on) and before one can invoke them in formulating an adequate political theory. We saw in fact that these concepts are so interrelated with the concept of freedom that political freedom cannot be properly understood without a grasp of these other concepts. This was made plain when we saw that political freedom involves a certain social and legal standing. Such a standing involves a set of rules and institutional considerations which are themselves in part founded upon a set of rights, or an account of justice or equality. The slave was not free in the political sense because he did not possess a certain legal standing (legal rights) or because he was not conceptualized fully as a person (human rights). Put in terms of equality rather than rights, a slave was not accorded "equal" treatment or consideration (whatever this may turn out to be) because he was not deemed to be an equal. Put in terms of the related concept of justice, a slave was not accorded certain modes of treatment or was precluded from certain freedoms because under a certain standard of justice, this discriminatory treatment was legitimized. Obviously, then, these concepts are interrelated. A standard of justice spells out the sorts of rights, human and legal, which persons have; it specifies the senses in which persons are equal or are to be treated equally. Thus in many contexts we could substitute the notions of social justice and (normative) equality for what we earlier called negative and/or positive freedom.

But, as with the norm of freedom, there are different standards of justice, and hence different systems of rights and different views of what constitutes equal treatment. Theorists from Plato to Marx have offered substantially different accounts of the meaning of these concepts and hence different theories of how society should be socially and politically organized. As is well known, Aristotle condoned slavery. His theory of justice and equality legitimized the denial of certain modes of treatment to persons who are "naturally" slaves. Plato's theory of justice requires equality of opportunity for all, regardless of social class, sex, and so on. In this sense (equality of *opportunity*) Plato is an egalitarian. But he was an advocate of a highly stratified class structure in the state. He recognized the fact, as did other classical theorists, that all human societies embody classes in which there are gradations in wealth, power, and prestige, and he sought not just an understanding of how those classes came into being but a rationale for their existence. What sort of class structure *should* society have? What *should* be the role of this class or that? Which class should have political power and for what reasons? The division of society into Guardians, Auxiliaries, and Workers he designed in order to assure social stability and social justice (they are not always the same). The preclusion of inherited class status and the initiation of complete equality of opportunity for all permitted one to find his station within the state. Those whose abilities qualified them for the Guardian class were to be placed under the restrictions necessary for them to rule in the interest of the common good. No private property beyond simple necessities, no family life—these policies were seen as necessary to assure complete impartiality and communal concern. No possibilities for temptation or corruption were to be tolerated.

We have seen that the theorists whom we classified under the headings of natural law theory, utilitarianism, and historicism were concerned with the same questions as Plato and Aristotle: In what sense are men equal? What constitutes equality of treatment? What constitutes social justice? What rights should men have? It will be helpful to recall briefly the views of some of these theorists in order to see more clearly the multiple senses or interpretations of equality and justice, and the consequent differences in theories of rights. This backdrop will help us to achieve a conceptual grasp of these concepts, and it will be used subsequently to defend a general normative position. We will focus primarily on the concept of equality, since a detailed treatment of the related concepts of justice and rights would take us beyond the scope of this volume.

A review of these theorists quickly reveals the vagueness and ambiguity of the concept or norm of equality. St. Thomas held that all men were equal in the sense that all are children of God. But this sort of equality said little about how men were to be treated in the political order. Society must be hierarchically ordered, with one's role depending on ability and status, but Thomas's theological egalitarianism did little in terms of providing criteria for the proper classification or treatment of persons. It did require that all laws be directed to the common good and be just, i.e., reflect natural law and hence divine law. This in turn required dispensing benefits and burdens according to "equality of proportion." Equality of proportion in regard to what? And in proportion to what? Thomas never adequately answers these questions. His limited theological egalitarianism is left hanging with theological vagaries like the "will of God," "beatitude," and "eternal law."

Hobbes recognizes the equality of man in several senses. In the state of nature men are roughly equal in intelligence and physical strength, with even the weakest able to outscheme and kill the strongest. The result, we have seen, is a state of war in which each person has an equal right to everything, "to use his own power . . . for the preservation of his own nature," even to the extent of taking another's life when that person threatens his security. This sort of equality in the state of nature is a state of sheer chaos.

With the social contract a different sort of equality comes into being: equality under the law. Prior to the existence of the sovereign and his statutes, there are no rules to assure equal treatment, hence no justice or rights. Only with the contract and the sovereign's power of enforcement do justice and rights come into being (though natural law, to which the sovereign's laws should conform, *did* exist prior to the contract and was equally binding—*in foro interno*—on all men, even if not obeyed). Equality under the law, the essential condition for an orderly and peaceful society, is the result of legal conventions and their enforcement. What this equality entails in terms of specific practices and the treatment of individuals is left to the sovereign, who himself is bound by no law. (The sovereign is not a *party* to the contract, but the resulting instrument of those who are.) The sovereign has absolute power and authority to build into law whatever he deems necessary for order and whatever criteria of relevance for the differential treatment of persons he thinks proper. For those decisions he is accountable to no one but God. The formal sense of equality, then, is equal treatment under the law, but since laws themselves may discriminate on whatever grounds the sovereign deems proper, then the rights of different persons may vary enormously (and hence the meaning of social justice). And with no check on the sovereign (other than God who is of little help in the here and now) the possibility of irrelevant criteria as components of the law and hence arbitrary discrimination (and the arbitrary use of power) is ever with us.

Like Hobbes, John Locke subscribes to equality in several sense, including one not to be found in Hobbes or Thomas. He agrees with Hobbes and Thomas that all men are equally under the jurisdiction of the law of nature (though it must be kept in mind that for Hobbes this jurisdiction or status of being bound is *in foro interno* only). But men are also all equally entitled to certain rights, rights which Locke sees as inalienable. "All men are by nature equal," he insists, and "that equal right that every man hath to his natural freedom . . . was the equality I then spoke of." Every man should enjoy the same rights granted to others—the rights to life, liberty, and property. The right to equality of treatment, which can be conceptualized as the fundamental right in Locke's theory, means that no one is denied the possession of these rights. (We noted earlier that the right to property, when Locke construes it in the broadest sense to include all natural rights, can also be viewed as the fundamental right. He states that "the mutual preservation of their lives, liberties, and estates . . . I call by the general name, property.")

However, just as we saw that Locke conceived of freedom largely negatively, in terms of the absence of arbitrary restraints, so also he conceives of equality formally (shall we say negatively?). That is, nothing specific in the treatment of any given person follows from the fact that one is entitled to equal treatment. For equality of treatment does not mean identity of treatment, and we have seen that Locke does not believe in strict political equality. He limits the franchise. He does not believe in strict social and economic equality, for some persons have qualities and characteristics which justify extending to them certain social and economic rights, whereas others, who do not possess these characteristics, are not entitled to those rights. All of this Locke sees as perfectly consistent with the universal possession of the formal right of equality. Obviously everything hangs on the criteria of relevance for differential treatment which are built into different rights (and public policies) as instantiating equality of treatment. If race and sex are seen as relevant grounds of differential treatment, then a racist or a sexist could be said to be a supporter of equality in the formal sense.

The Lockean commitment to equality, then, as with any other theorist's commitment to normative equality, requires interpretation and application. The focal issue is choice of criteria of relevance for differential treatment. Just as Locke's theory of freedom, though negative in nature, can be extended in the direction of positive freedom on the grounds that the latter (welfare rights, for example) are enabling conditions for the exercise of natural rights, so also Locke's account of equality, though formal in nature and though he himself supports a *laissez faire* state, can be extended and interpreted in a substantive way, so that irrelevant criteria are excluded and positive ones are introduced. Unless this is done (and I will have more to say about this momentarily), subscription to the equality principle does not amount to a hill of beans—even with the wise Lockean strategy of separating executive, legislative, and judicial functions of government.

Neither Bentham nor Mill subscribes to equality as an inalienable natural right, for there are no such rights, they declare. But they both emphasize equality on other grounds: All persons are equally capable of suffering and pleasure, and the pleasure and pain of each person must be included in applying the hedonistic calculus: "Everybody to count for one, nobody for more than one." Justice, they maintain, is part of the very meaning of utility.

Bentham prefers not to speak of any rights as existing prior to government but he does insist that certain criteria, such as blackness of skin, are irrelevant considerations in the treatment of persons. This comes very close to what many have called a doctrine of moral or human rights. Mill is not averse to speaking of rights, human or moral, which exist prior to the state. For Bentham and Mill, however, utility is the proclaimed ultimate ground for all rights, whether moral or legal, and utility may properly override equality. As Mill puts it, "all persons are deemed to have a right to equality of treatment except when some recognized social expediency requires the reverse."

The problem is to specify what is to be meant by equality of treatment. Mere equal treatment under the law is inadequate, for Mill agrees that some laws are unjust and themselves discriminate on irrelevant grounds. The essence of justice or equal treatment is according a person his moral rights. What are these moral rights? Mill recognizes that the rights of individuals should and do vary according to circumstances, abilities, and needs; and he also recognizes that there are many different criteria invoked to justify certain rights as moral ones. Distribution of goods and services according to how hard one works, according to how valuable one's work is to society, according to one's needs, on a basis of exact equality, according to desert—these criteria are all invoked and they sometimes conflict. He himself opts for giving each person his *desert* as the "highest abstract standard of social and distributive justice." But he never spells out what these desert-criteria are. He does note that "the distinctions of slave and freemen, nobles and serfs, patricians and plebeians" have "passed into the rank of a universally recognized injustice and tyranny" and "so it will be, and in part already is; with the aristocracies of color, race, and sex," and he makes it plain that none of these are acceptable criteria of desert.

Very much like Locke and not unlike Mill, Hegel subscribes to equality as a moral right of all. "Personality," he states, "essentially involves the capacity for rights and constitutes the concept and the basis (itself abstract) of the system of abstract and therefore formal right. Hence the imperative of right is: 'Be a person and respect others as persons.'" This equality excludes slavery and other arbitrary modes of treatment and emphasizes conformity to contract. But some contracts or rights can conform to abstract right and yet be morally bad (the "right of the first night," for example). Thus the "good" or "conscience" constitutes the dialectical antithesis of abstract right, resulting in a challenge of existing systems of rights, both social and legal. The synthesis of abstract right and morality ("good" and "conscience") is "ethical life" in which right and duty coalesce and in which there is an identity of the universal and particular will. Obviously, the spelling out of those modes of treatment which are exemplifications of abstract right or of equality, modes which remain in "ethical life" as synthesis, requires a criterion for recognizing the universal.

The corresponding triad in the evolution of the state involves the synthesis of the "family" and "civil society" under the rubric of the "State." Just as ethical life supersedes abstract right, so also the state, with its justice, supersedes the justice of civil society which was designed to mediate the interests and needs of all. In civil society there may be a discrepancy between "the content of law and the principle of rightness," that is, between what is legally right and what is morally right. With the state, however, rightness and legality coincide, for the state embodies "rationality" and "universality." However, he insists that "the state is actual only when its members have a feeling of their own self-hood and it is stable only when public and private ends are identical"; also "this final end has supreme right against the individual, whose supreme duty is to be a member of the state."

Now, whether we are concerned with the meaning of equality of treatment in the triad of abstract right, morality, and ethical life or in the triad of family, civil society, and the state, the problem is the same: we need a criterion for identifying the universal. Here we stumble on Hegel's metaphysics. For the state is not merely an instrument for maximizing or equalizing happiness. It is an end in itself, an organic unity which instantiates universal spirit in history. Even the monarch must simply say "I will" to the dictates of universal spirit. But how do we identify these dictates? They are not simply the will of the people (as seen through the Estates) because the will of the people, seen as an agglomerate, would subvert the ends of the state; hence Hegel rejects the universal franchise. Nor are these dictates discovered by calculating the general welfare. Nor by simply attending to existing states, for the constitutions of existing states may not embody universal justice. Right cannot be identified with might. But as we have noted, Hegel may be committed to this identification, for he does not, and perhaps cannot—given his historicism—provide a criterion for distinguishing the two. In fact, he declares that world-history is above the point of view from which justice and injustice even matter. This surely leaves the meaning and grounds of equality, rights, and social justice hanging in the air, or perhaps in the spirit. The result is that the meaning of these concepts is, in one sense, completely relative to existing societies or states, with equality of treatment or rights being determined by the system of rights within which each person exists, and, in another sense which is never adequately specified by Hegel, not relative at all.

We have also distinguished several senses of equality prominent in the works of Marx and Engels, and hence several recognized senses of social justice and rights. In pre-communist society all men are equally alienated (though not to the same degree). This is basically a descriptive sense of equality, though obviously the notion of alienation requires evaluative standards. This equality of alienation follows from the Marxist thesis that the history of all existing societies is one of class struggles and that each of us, bourgeois and proletarian alike, is caught in the bind of a system that dehumanizes and alienates.

Within different economic and political systems in different historical periods, there are widely different senses of normative equality. Some societies condoned slavery; others not. Some invoked birth and social status as the "feudal fetters" which justify economic and social discrimination; others not, and so on. In every case the definition of equality, and hence the accepted concept of social justice and the concomitant set of rights, was the reflection of the values of the controlling economic class, the class which controls the state. This, of course, is what Marx and Engels mean when they say that morality, justice, and laws simply constitute the ideological superstructure of the state. We are not far from Thrasymachus's thesis at this stage—that might makes right.

But Marx and Engels affirm that progress occurs in history and morality. Irrelevant criteria for the differential treatment of persons and unjust systems of rights are sloughed off in the historical progress. However, only limited progress toward genuine equality and social justice can be made as long as the economic and political system of capitalism exists. For the system itself is founded on irrelevant and dehumanizing criteria. As Marx and Engels state, "to clamour for equal or even equitable distribution on the basis of the wages system is the same as to clamour for freedom on the basis of the slavery system." Neither genuine freedom nor genuine equality can occur in a society stratified by economic classes. Genuine equality requires the negation and demise of capitalism, and it requires a classless society. Even in early communism under the dictatorship of the proletariat, equal rights are "still in principle bourgeois rights." Property is nationalized and wages are distributed on a more equitable basis, namely, according to the amount and quality of one's labor. "The equality consists in the fact that the measurement is made with an equal standard, labour." This is progress, yes. But genuine equality, no. Not until an economic and social system is set up which distributes goods and services on the basis of the unique needs of each person do we have genuine equality and social justice. "From each according to his ability, to each according to need" is the standard for true equality of treatment. Men must not be conceptualized merely as workers (any more than as slaves). They must be seen as unique persons with intrinsic worth and dignity, with each person provided the opportunity to develop whatever talents and capacities he has. The proper criteria of relevance for differential treatment, then, are the capacities and needs of each person. Equality or justice under mature communism does not mean identical treatment of all, but proportional treatment—proportional to needs and capacities. A free and equal society is one which permits each person in society, with his unique and different needs and abilities, to realize himself fully.

Descriptive and Normative Equality

The brief survey above has shown that the concept of equality has had (and continues to have) a number of different uses and meanings. In some contexts the statement that all men are equal is primarily a descriptive claim. "All men are roughly equal in strength and intelligence in the state of nature" (Hobbes); "all men are children of God" (St. Thomas and Christian theologians); "each man has a spark of the divine reason" (Stoic philosophers); "each man is an independent, individual entity or substance and each partakes of the same essential humanity" (a metaphysical but not necessarily theological sense of equality); "all men have the capacity for choice and suffering"—all of these statements of man's equality are basically descriptive. Of course, what they purport to describe varies. Some presume to refer to metaphysical or theological facts; others, simply to natural, empirically observable facts. Thus their presumed descriptive function must be seen in the context of a presupposed philosophy of man and nature or philosophy of man and God. Obvious problems involving verification of the metaphysical or theological senses of equality arise. We indicated these problems in earlier chapters and need not recount them here. Suffice it to say that those who invoke equality in the descriptive sense are challenged on two grounds: (1) Human nature, it is countered by theorists such as Benn and Peters,[1] is not a specific quality which all men equally possess; it simply designates a potentiality for a certain range of qualities and activities; (2) Even with the establishment of some sense of descriptive equality, there is the problem ("is-ought") of showing how that fact entails anything about the ways in which

[1] S. I. Benn and R. S. Peters, *Principles of Political Thought* (New York: Collier Books, 1964); first published as *Social Principles and the Democratic State* (London, 1959).

men should be treated. (This is not to deny that such a relationship can be established.)

One final point on descriptive equality. A great deal of ink has been spilled denying that all men are biological equals. But there appear to be no egalitarians who have maintained that all men have the same biological capacities or abilities or who would deny the obvious physical and mental differences among men.

So much for descriptive equality. What about normative equality, the question of how men should be treated equally? We have seen that normative equality is often construed in a very general or formal way. Thus Hegel's "abstract right" of every person and Locke's right to equality are formal principles. They are not entirely vacuous, but they do not specify any modes of equal treatment. Basically what this formal sense of normative equality asserts is that all men are to be treated alike and that no person is to be given better treatment, special consideration, or privilege unless justifying reasons can be given for such differentiation. It does not prescribe identical treatment of all but rather that individuals of unequal endowments and conditions be given equal consideration and opportunity, that the same relative contribution be made to the goodness of each person's life, not an identical contribution. Negatively stated, this formal, normative sense of equality asserts that human beings are not to be differentially treated unless there is some relevant and sufficient reason for doing so.

I know of no egalitarian theorist who has argued for complete identity of treatment or for a society without any differences and in which there is a complete leveling—what Isaiah Berlin has called "fanatical egalitarianism." [2] Such a society would not only be boring; it would retard the level of culture and civilization and, furthermore, result in great injustices. Kant perhaps had this in mind when he noted that inequality is "a rich source of much that is evil but also of everything that is good." The injustice would arise in all those cases in which there are relevant grounds for differential treatment but in which simple uniformity of treatment were imposed. There are rational grounds for nonidentical treatment. Egalitarians recognize this. They acknowledge that some rights, privileges and opportunities are, and should be, contingent upon the possession of certain capacities, characteristics, circumstances, or roles, and that these differ with different individuals. In the same way they recognize that burdens in a

[2] Isaiah Berlin, "Equality," *Proceedings of the Aristotelian Society*, 56 (1955–56); reprinted in W. T. Blackstone, *The Concept of Equality* (Minneapolis: Burgess Publishing Company, 1969).

society are and should be differentially distributed, depending on these various considerations. The problem is that they differ on what they consider to be relevant criteria for differential treatment or rational grounds for differentiating human beings. Or, even if they agree on criteria of relevance, they may place those criteria in a different order of priority, thereby leading to differing evaluations of the treatment of persons.

Thus, in terms of normative results, the crucial issue is the choice of criteria of relevance and their order of priority. Only when this choice is made and the equality norm then applied to some concrete problem and context, such as education, medical treatment, or equality before the law, are specific prescriptions entailed.

Criteria of Relevance for Differential Treatment

What is involved in the judgment and choice that certain criteria are "relevant" ones? The judgment has both descriptive and prescriptive functions. To say "X is relevant," when we are speaking about the treatment of persons, means "X is actually or potentially related in an instrumentally helpful or harmful way to the attainment of a given end, and consequently ought to be taken into consideration in the decision to treat someone in a certain way." This general characterization of meaning holds, I think, if X is a particular fact which falls under criteria of need, merit, or worth to society. Having legal representation, for example, is instrumentally related to becoming educated. Being female is instrumentally unrelated to certain working opportunities. In part, then, questions of relevance are factual or descriptive claims, straightforwardly verifiable or falsifiable. The question of what qualities, characteristics, or circumstances are instrumentally related in a helpful or harmful way to certain objectives is a question of fact. However, that certain instrumentally related characteristics, qualities, or circumstances *should* be considered and that certain goals or ends *should* be accepted is the prescriptive side of judgments of relevance.

Since the claim that a given characteristic is relevant is in part a factual claim, then controversies over questions of equality of treatment can be resolved at least in part by showing the correctness or incorrectness of the supposed factual claims and, hence, the relevance or irrelevance of the criteria which those claims invoke. If, for example, race or color were cited as grounds for the differential treatment of persons in regard to educational opportunities and it were shown that color or race had nothing to do with educability, then the factual presupposition of those who invoke these criteria would have been shown to be false and those criteria themselves shown to be irrelevant (in the factual sense of "relevant"). Of course, human beings can easily be mistaken in their factual judgments and assessments. What is involved here is judgment and decision, not mathematical calculation. Often, in fact, both the existence of certain states of affairs and their relevance (factual sense) to problems of equality of treatment go completely unperceived. Only after these facts are brought to light are the criteria invoked noticed as relevant, that is, seen as instrumentally related to certain desired ends. Facts or characteristics which are so related cannot be exhaustively listed once and for all. The conditions and circumstances which effect the attainment of objectives of all types constantly change, so that what is denoted by "relevant characteristic" (even in the factual sense of "relevant") must remain "open." Characteristics considered relevant have broadened greatly in the past one hundred years, as both our objectives change and our knowledge in the various sciences of factors instrumentally related to the attainment of these objectives increases. Relevant criteria have been extended to include even those factors bearing on the control and conservation of world resources.

Judgments of relevance, however, are not merely factual. They are also prescriptive. They state what kinds of reasons *ought* to count This amounts to prescribing both specific and general objectives. Individuals could agree on the factual part of a judgment of relevance (i.e., that certain facts are instrumentally related to certain goals) and yet disagree on the prescriptive part of that judgment (i.e., on what goal is desirable). Prescriptive disagreement here could also involve choice of the priority of certain goals. Suppose, for example, that certain criteria of merit are judged irrelevant in a certain context. It is unlikely that this would be a denial of a factual claim—that certain kinds of facts are instrumentally related to certain goals. It may not even be the prescriptive claim that the goal is undesirable. It is frequently the prescriptive thesis that certain other goals, say, the satisfaction of basic human needs and the criteria associated with those needs, should receive primary consideration, that criteria of merit ought not to be invoked as grounds of differential treatment in regard to the satisfaction of these needs. This is equivalent to saying that certain minimum standards for a satisfactory life for all should be fulfilled before luxuries are distributed on grounds of merit or worth.

It seems to me to be descriptively true (although I think it also ought to be the case) that the criteria emphasized as most fundamental to claims of equality of treatment are those of need and capacity, common to all human beings. Criteria of merit are judged irrelevant to the satisfaction of these needs. Certain fundamental rights like the right to medical treatment, to the franchise, and to legal representation are taken to be justified by the fact that one is a human being, a being with the capacities to think, to suffer, to choose, and to experience pleasure. In situations in which the conditions for a minimally good life are in fact fulfilled, the emphasis of the equality principle goes in the direction of other criteria, those of merit and worth to society. However, with need-criteria emphasis, differential treatment on grounds of merit or worth cannot be invoked in any way that endangers the minimum good life for all. That X, for example, in virtue of qualities A and B, merits a certain social or professional title does not entitle him to special privilege in the sense, say, of better legal representation or medical treatment. His rights *qua* the fact that he is human remain the same as those of a person without the title—even if it be true that the remuneration attached to his title enables him to acquire better medical treatment and legal representation. The equality principle in this fundamental sense, with its emphasis on criteria of need and capacity, abstracts each man from the unequal structures in which he is found, structures based on criteria of merit, worth to society, and social contingencies (such as birth in a prominent family and inheritance of wealth) and says that this man must have certain basic rights and treatment simply because he is human. No personal characteristic can here justify differential treatment. Human beings in this sense cannot be "graded."

However, not all political theorists adopt the position that need-criteria should receive priority over other relevant criteria (merit, worth to society, and so on) in the distribution of goods and services. Mill, for example, in his theory of distributive justice places "desert" as the highest abstract standard. Aristotle emphasizes merit-criteria (the possession of moral and intellectual virtues), as does Nietzsche (the possession of the qualities of the "superman"). The stipulation of merit or desert as the highest criterion of relevance amounts to setting forth not only criteria for particular evaluations of how to treat human beings but also a general concept of what human society should be like. Those who emphasize the priority of need-criteria, such as Karl Marx, offer different guidelines for treating human beings and a quite different concept of what society should be like.

The Justification of Criteria of Relevance

Can these differences on criteria of relevance be adjudicated? Are there any grounds for saying that the choice of one set of criteria, with a certain priority hierarchy, is more rational than another choice? I think so.

It seems to me that there are good grounds for treating criteria of need and capacity as more basic or as morally prior to criteria of merit, worth to society, and so on. This position is held implicitly by Plato in the *Republic,* where differential treatment on the basis of merit is seen as necessary but where it is also seen that fairness requires that all human beings be given the opportunity to develop those meritorious qualities. (This does not mean that Plato subscribes to equality in the sense that each person, no matter what his capacities, has equal intrinsic worth.) Frankena recently argued this point more explicitly. Merit cannot be the most basic criterion for differential treatment or distributive justice because "a recognition of merit as the basis of distribution is justified only if every individual has an equal chance of achieving all the merit he is capable of. . . ." [3] The point is that if merit-criteria are given priority, it is like pretending that everyone is eligible for the game of goods-distribution, while knowing that many individuals, through no fault of their own, through circumstances and deficiencies over which they have no control, cannot possibly be in the game. Distribution of goods, then, primarily and basically on grounds of merit, is unfair. This does not mean that merit-criteria should be abandoned.

In regard to need-criteria, all human beings fit, so to speak; so in this sense they are not gradable. This is not to deny that needs and capacity vary widely and call for widely varying treatment. The point is that all humans meet the need-criteria while only some meet the merit-criteria, and to have any chance to meet the latter, the former must be met.

The above argument invokes the notion of fairness, which may give rise to as many philosophical perplexities as the notion of equality. But need-criteria priority may also be justified along Kantian lines by appealing to the principle of the equal intrinsic dignity and value of all persons. Or it might be justified on utilitarian grounds as providing greater happiness and welfare than emphasis on other criteria. Such priority could also be based jointly on several of these principles,

3 William Frankena, "Some Beliefs About Justice," *The Lindley Lecture* (Lawrence, Kansas: University of Kansas Press, 1966).

say, both fairness and utility (a "mixed-deontological" ethic). Whether it is possible to show that a given ethic is more rational than another, or whether disagreements on basic ethical principles are ultimate, unresolvable disagreements ("Pay your money and choose your life-style"), is a question which cannot be considered in detail here. I do not believe that the choice of an ethic is simply arbitrary, and am inclined to believe that a rational choice among alternative ways of life or ethical frameworks is possible.[4] This more fundamental question must be answered before one can fully spell out the rationale for a certain priority of criteria of relevance for the differential treatment of persons.

Two further points are worth making on the argument that fairness requires the priority of need-criteria over those of merit and worth to society. First, the argument does not mean that a social policy must first make sure that the basic needs of all human beings in a given society, the satisfaction of which provides at least a minimally satisfactory life, are fulfilled. An egalitarian social policy must surely do this before luxuries are distributed on the basis of other criteria, but to insist that everyone in a society reach this minimal standard of existence before any criteria of merit are recognized and rewarded by, say, special educational opportunities, is practically absurd. It would be almost impossible to put such a policy into effect. Second, there is considerable evidence that the special treatment and nurture of gifted individuals puts much more back into the till than is taken out and so raises the general welfare. In a sense here I am pitting general utilitarian reasons against a completely uniform application of the equality principle in its fundamental form. That is, in stressing the moral priority of equality with need-criteria emphasis, I am not maintaining that equality always should take precedence over other moral principles, like utility.

The Application of the Equality Principle

Aside from the issue of a rational ordering of general criteria of relevance for differential treatment, the more specific problem of ridding our laws and social conventions of arbitrary discrimination is and must be a continual one. Given the rapidity of economic, industrial, educational, and social change, certain criteria formerly re-

[4] See Paul Taylor's *Normative Discourse* (Englewood Cliffs, N.J.: Prentice-Hall, Inc., 1961), and William Frankena's *Ethics* (Englewood Cliffs, N.J.: Prentice-Hall, Inc., 1963), for detailed treatment of this question.

garded as unrelated to equality become relevant grounds for different treatment. Thus the equality principle must continually evolve and grow. As Bernard Schwartz points out, those who framed the Constitution of the United States did not even extend the concept of equality to all members of the community.[5] For them this principle did not require the abolition of slavery or the emancipation of women. In fact it was not until the Fourteenth Amendment's Equal Protection Clause that the concept of equality was elevated to the constitutional plane. In the American political tradition this constitutional guarantee of equality was a living lie, a flat contradiction to certain practices; and only with the Thirteenth, Fourteenth and Fifteenth Amendments was equality guaranteed in theory to everyone regardless of "race, color, or previous condition of servitude." The Equal Protection Clause of the Fourteenth Amendment properly requires that any given classification "must always rest upon some difference which bears a reasonable and just relation to the act in respect to which the classification is proposed." As argued, these criteria or classifications cannot be specified for all time. They are context-dependent. But they not only must not violate constitutional guarantees; they also must not violate human rights or modes of treatment which each person should have simply because he is human. Those who call for *more* than "law and order" are emphasizing this fact.

Today much more than mere political and legal equality is demanded. Those conditions necessary to assure at least a minimally satisfactory life for each person are now being considered to be the right of an individual and as necessary to instantiate the equality principle. Individuals whose capacities and abilities have been blunted by their environment must be given special treatment, it is argued, to assure them opportunities equal to those with better environments. It is seen that to grant merely political and legal equality, with no guarantee of social and economic equality, is in most cases to hand one an empty sack. This extension of the equality principle in the direction of social and economic equality is producing and will continue to produce profound changes in the social order. The recent demand in the United States for a minimum income for all is a demand for economic conditions that allow individuals to fulfill the capacities which they have and to attain at least a minimally satisfactory level of existence. It is contended that massive inequalities of wealth make impossible the attainment of the welfare and freedom of

[5] Bernard Schwartz, *Commentary on The Constitution of The United States,* Vol. II, *Equality, Belief and Dignity* (New York, 1968), p. 487.

the less fortunate; those who control the wealth control the governmental, educational, judicial—indeed, even religious—establishments, and they exploit those persons without power. Therefore, genuine human and political equality requires state control of property to the extent necessary to assure economic equality. But again, it must be kept in mind that economic equality (even for the communist) does not mean identical incomes and property for all. There are relevant grounds for differential distribution of economic wealth.

The political problem posed by the egalitarian who emphasizes need-criteria is this: What sort of government, what kind of political institutions, economic policies, social rules, and so on are the best instruments for implementing this ideal? What sorts of social or class distinctions are morally permissible, what sorts of hierarchical arrangements or inequalities in society are both necessary and acceptable in order to do two things—to maximize the production of goods and services while at the same time to assure equality of opportunity for all and equality in the need-priority sense? Many egalitarians recognize that some kinds of inequality do not militate against equality of opportunity, and that some kinds of inequalities are necessary in order to provide equality of opportunity, whereas some inequalities preclude it. Ralf Dahrendorf, the sociologist, argues that "some inequalities follow from the very concept of societies as moral communities" and that a classless, distinctionless, rankless society is not "sociologically possible." [6] The possession of a given station in a community or society and of the rights attendant upon that station, rights that other persons may well not possess, does not mean that men are being treated unequally. Inequalities of power, of wealth, of rights, and of abilities, there will always be, and there should be, when there are rational grounds for them. Nor does egalitarianism demand that these be completely abolished. Rather it insists that those inequalities justify their existence in terms of their use in promoting a society in which each person has the equal right to be free, the equal right and opportunity to develop his capacities, one in which his freedom is restricted only by his capacities and his morals and not by his lack of social position, wealth, or educational opportunity.

Many egalitarians argue that democracy is the best form of government to instantiate the egalitarian ideal; but if the best form of government for instantiating the egalitarian ideal is itself a contingent

---

[6] Ralf Dahrendorf, "On The Origin of Social Inequality," *Philosophy, Politics, and Society*, ed. Peter Laslett and W. G. Runciman (Oxford: Basil Blackwell, 1962), reprinted in W. T. Blackstone, *The Concept of Equality* (Minneapolis: Burgess Publishing Company, 1969).

matter, then it is at least possible that some nondemocratic form of government might fulfill the egalitarian ideal to a higher extent than a democratic one. After all, political equality is only one aspect of this ideal and though this kind of equality may be assured under a democratic form of government, nonetheless, other kinds of equality, such as equality before the law, economic equality and social equality (the latter being explicated in terms of equality of opportunity), could easily be vitiated, at least under some democracies. This is exactly the claim of many citizens in the United States who have political equality in the sense of the right to vote but who do not enjoy other forms of equality. Obviously, much depends on what is built into the concept of democracy. If democracy includes by definition the entire spectrum of egalitarian treatment, then by definition it would be the best form of government for implementing the egalitarian ideal. I will have more to say about the definition and the advantages of democracy momentarily.

We have examined both the concept of freedom and that of equality. Is there a necessary conflict between equality as an ideal and liberty as an ideal? Must liberty be diminished as equality is extended? Certainly in one sense of the terms liberty or freedom, equality must necessarily conflict with it; for when goods and services of various types—legal, economic, educational, and social—are distributed to all human beings in a society according to certain criteria (through systems of taxation and so on), then this definitely prevents some individuals from doing what they want to do. We are all familiar with recent civil rights issues, such as the freedom of an owner to sell his home to whomever he pleases and the equal right of all men, including blacks, to buy. Freedom, then, in the sense of doing what one wants to do may well frequently conflict with equality as an ideal. However, freedom as a political ideal is not taken by any serious political theorist to mean simply freedom to do whatever one wants to do, just as equality as an ideal is not taken to mean simply a total leveling or uniformity of treatment of humans. Rather political freedom is seen as embodying the notion that one's freedom must be consistent with the equal freedom of other persons. Many egalitarians, therefore, believe that there is no necessary conflict between liberty and equality, and as Thomson puts it, these two "twin ideals in the minds of democrats" can be reunited and reconciled.[7] In fact what we earlier called positive freedom is nearly identical with the equality which emphasizes need-criteria.

[7] See David Thomson's *Equality* (Cambridge: Cambridge University Press, 1949), especially Chapter I, "The Problem of Equality."

Recommended Readings

Barry, Brian. *Political Argument.* New York, 1965.

Blackstone, W. T., ed. *The Concept of Equality.* Minneapolis, 1969.

Brandt, Richard, ed. *Social Justice.* Englewood Cliffs, N.J., 1962.

Chapman, J. W. and Friedrich, C. J., eds. *Nomos VI: Justice.* New York, 1963.

Lakoff, Sanford. *Equality in Political Philosophy.* Cambridge, Mass., 1964.

Laslett, P. and Runciman, W. G., eds. *Philosophy, Politics, and Society,* Second Series. Oxford, 1962.

Olafson, Frederick, ed. *Justice and Social Policy.* Englewood Cliffs, N.J., 1961.

Pennock, J. R. and Chapman, J. W., eds. *Nomos IX: Equality.* New York, 1967.

Perelman, Chaim. *The Idea of Justice and The Problem of Argument.* New York, 1963.

Hook, Sidney, ed. *Law and Philosophy,* New York, 1964.

Schwartz, Bernard, *A Commentary on the Constitution of the United States,* Vol. 2, *Equality, Belief, and Dignity.* New York, 1968.

Tawney, R. H. *Equality.* London, 1931.

The Monist, Vol. 52, No. 4, October, 1968 (An issue devoted to the Topic of "Human Rights").

Wilson, John. *Equality.* London, 1966.

chapter 12
The Public Interest

An Overview of the Concept

The third basic value concept is the "public interest." Political theorists, politicians, and the ordinary man frequently appeal to this value, along with the "common good" and the "general welfare," in justifying either a positive or negative stance in regard to political issues. Sometimes these three phrases are used nearly as synonyms, sometimes not.[1] For our purposes we will focus on "the public interest."

How often we hear politicians proclaim that a certain policy is or is not in the public interest! How often we hear it said that the public interest would be negated by policy X but promoted by policy Y! This norm is probably invoked in political argument more frequently than the norms of freedom and equality. But, as with freedom and equality, there is great controversy over the meaning of the term, "public interest." We saw in Chapter 1 that Glendon Schubert, in his examination of this concept, maintains that it is extremely vague and confused. No one has provided an operational definition of the "public interest," he argues, and, without such, it is irrational to expect this so-called norm to function as a guide for political decisions.[2]

[1] See Brian Barry's *Political Argument,* especially Chaps. 12–15 (New York: Humanities Press, Inc., 1965).

[2] Glendon Schubert, *The Public Interest* (New York: Free Press of Glencoe, 1961).

One must agree that Schubert has a point. This concept does need clarification. Few who invoke it are able to spell out what they mean by it. And it is often used in debate as a tool to mask whatever decision a politician endorses. But this is also true, perhaps to a lesser extent, of the concepts of equality and freedom. This looseness of use and variability of meaning do not mean that the concept itself is unintelligible. Like freedom and equality, conceptual light can be shed on the "public interest." It can be seen to have some definite shape, though like freedom and equality, it must simply be admitted that there is a range of criteria, considerations, or value priorities which can stretch the concept in this direction or that. (Recall the positive-negative range on the interpretation of freedom and the need-merit issue in interpreting equality.) In fact part of the problem of the ambiguity of the "public interest" is the ambiguity of fundamental concepts like freedom and equality; for what is often meant by a policy which is in the public interest is one which promotes freedom and equality, along with other things. Hence, it can be seen that the analysis and distinctions introduced in order to clarify the notions of freedom and equality are necessary steps in the understanding and clarification of the notion of the public interest. It can also be seen that, depending on the interpretation and priority-emphasis given to value concepts which are constituents of the public interest, the meaning of the public interest is extended in this way or that. This means that this norm is somewhat fluid. It does not mean that it is totally useless as a guide to action, although Schubert apparently thinks that it does. We will try to indicate that there is a shape or structure found in our use of this term, and that some clear meaning can be given to this concept, without resorting simply to a stipulative definition.

First, it will again be useful to review the different meanings given to this concept, implicitly or explicitly, by the theorists we examined. St. Thomas, recall, insists that the state must "care for the common good." This is achieved by instituting laws and principles that are reflections of natural law and hence of divine or eternal law. Such laws provide the necessary conditions not only for man's temporal well-being but also the realization of God's purpose. Hobbes stresses that the purpose of the state is to provide a framework and an instrument for resolving conflicts of interest and that such a framework is essential if the interests of all are to be promoted. He recognizes that the desires and objectives of a particular person may conflict with those of others. Indeed they may conflict with his own interests and with the interest of society or the public as a whole. A body of law with the sovereign's power of enforcement provides stability and, with it, predictability in human life. In place of the constant contingency and threat of death in the state of nature, the social contract substitutes rules of order and security. This amounts to the public interest.

With Locke also the whole point of the social contract and the power of the state is to promote the general good. The general good is promoted not merely by providing stability and order but by guaranteeing through enforcement the inalienable rights of the individual. Like Hobbes, Locke recognizes that the legal structure that guarantees the individual's rights may conflict with his wishes or desires. Also there may be legal systems that vitiate the inalienable rights of individuals. For Locke this means that such systems also vitiate the public interest or general good. Neither he nor Hobbes conceives of the common good or the public interest simply in aggregative terms, that is, in terms of maximized pleasure or minimized pain.

Bentham, on the other hand, with his denial of natural rights, straightforwardly conceives of the public interest in aggregative terms. The public interest is promoted when the greatest pleasure of the greatest number is effected. The calculation must include the effects of observing the rules of justice, for justice is seen as part of the meaning of utility. But the public interest is the same thing as general utility.

Mill, with qualifications, endorses the same view. We have already noted the qualifications; Mill on occasion seems to endorse certain rights and modes of treatment on grounds other than utility. But in the last analysis he reverts to utilitarianism, with the public interest being identified with the general happiness.

For Hegel, the meaning of the public interest or common good is quite different from that found in Bentham or Mill. He rejects the idea of the state as a mere agglomerate of individuals bound together by an agreement to maximize the happiness of individuals and to assure rights. This the state must do, but these objectives must be seen in a much larger context. The state is an end in itself, and individuals, basically, are instruments of it, not vice versa. The public interest or the good of the state is not merely the sum of the private goods of persons made possible by social organization. It is, on the contrary, the organic unity of the state itself, which he sees as an instantiation of universal spirit in history. Individual rights and goods have no significance apart from that organic unity, or apart from the state as a metaphysical entity.

Marx and Engels, of course, distinguish between the common interests of a class of persons and the public interest. In fact the class interests of the bourgeoisie in particular are the basic reasons that the public interest is thwarted. The public interest requires the abolition of classes and the demise of the state as a coercive device. Only then can man overcome his alienated condition. The public interest requires that we re-humanize our concept of man as a free, rational being with intrinsic worth, and reject the view that man is a commodity to be manipulated; and it requires the destruction of those social and political institutions which perpetuate economic exploitation and class conflicts, institutions which are based on the value premise that man himself is a commodity to be bought and sold. The public interest is a social system in which genuine freedom, rationality, and creativity are possible, in which each person contributes according to his ability and receives according to his need, and in which the "free development of each is the condition for the free development of all." Such a system is egalitarian and "species-oriented."

The Public Interest: An Interpretation

In the light of these various interpretations, what is to be meant by the "public interest"? We suggested above that, even though the classical (and contemporary) theorists differ somewhat in their implicit or explicit use or interpretation of this concept, this does not mean that it is useless as a guide to action. Though the concept cannot be tied down in the way in which some descriptive concepts can, there is a structure to be found in the ordinary man's use of this concept and in that of political theorists as well. Let us attempt to explicate this.

Most of us contrast a person's private interests with the public interest. This is not to deny that they may coincide. But private interests are one's personal wants, desires, or wishes, and these, we recognize, may conflict with the wants, desires, and wishes of other persons. Given the possibility, and often the actuality, of that conflict, we recognize the Hobbesean point that each of us has an interest in a set of rules, procedures, or institutions which can rationally resolve such conflicts of personal interest. The rules and procedures in which each of us (at least, rational beings) have an interest is part of what we mean by the public interest. Such rules, procedures, or institutions are equally in the interests of all members of society, *not* in the sense that they always best promote the private interests of each person (the "law" or certain public policies, for example, may prevent the fulfillment of someone's particular interests or that of a group on certain occasions) but in the sense that they are generally required or necessary conditions for the possibility of the fulfillment of anyone's personal interests. Without law and order such possibility is precluded, so law and order is surely in the public interest. But mere law and order is not sufficient to assure this possibility. Laws may be unjust and order may be tyrannical. If the possibility of the fulfillment of *everyone's* interests is the desiderata, then laws must discriminate only on relevant grounds and each person must be treated equally under the law. What are these relevant grounds? We discussed this general issue above in the section on equality, and it should now be clear that an explication of criteria of relevance for the differential treatment of persons is essential in defining the public interest.

The "public" interest may be seen then, perhaps paradoxically, as our "disinterested" interests, as interests in which each of us has a stake and which are exemplified in just and impartial rules and procedures for the treatment of persons. But this is not all that we subsume under the public interest. Sometimes we say that laws or the rules of justice ought to be suspended or overridden for the public interest— in other words that considerations of justice and fairness can on occasion properly be overridden by considerations of public welfare. It goes without saying that the determination that a policy is or is not in the public interest is a very complex issue. All of the conceptual and empirical problems which we recognized as being involved in questions of equality, justice, and rights must be considered, and, in addition, the issue of balancing welfare considerations against those of justice, when those norms conflict, must be faced. In any modern, technological, urban society, these considerations are immensely complex. There is no single or simple criterion for testing whether a policy or action is in the public interest. Such decisions certainly cannot be made by majority vote or opinion. To do this in most cases would be a grave error, for the average citizen simply is not informed on all the relevant facts which bear on public policies. This is not to say that the interests, desires, and opinions of the average citizen should be ignored; nor is it to say that some educated elite is justified in imposing unwelcome policies on people because such policies are *really* in their interests. Rather it is to recognize the fact that people can be mistaken about the policies which they think are in their (public) interests. Such mistakes are possible in decisions on both justice and welfare. Many persons supported the *Plessy* v. *Ferguson* decision, and the policies which resulted therefrom, as in the public interest—as both just and as promoting the public welfare. They were wrong. *Plessy* v. *Ferguson* held that equal facilities assured equality of educational opportunity even if schools were segregated, but now a wide range of sociological evidence has shown that segregation precludes equality of opportunity even if the facilities are the same (which they seldom were). And the cost of that decision in terms of human welfare is immeasurable.

Given the complexity of modern political issues and the increasing expectation that the state must guarantee not only justice but welfare, the problem of applying the norm, the public interest, or of testing whether certain policies are in the public interest, is enormous. It calls for great expertise. For, just as the norm of political freedom has been extended from a negative to a positive sense (in which the responsibility of government is seen to be not merely that of precluding arbitrary restraints or the arbitrary use of power of one person or group over another, but that of providing the positive conditions and opportunities—economic, educational, and so on—without which certain rights or freedoms of speech, press, association, and so on are meaningless because they cannot be fulfilled), so also the public interest as a norm is seen in both negative and positive senses. In the negative sense the state fulfills or meets the public interest when it institutes policies which prevent harm and injustice (the laws of criminal justice, for example). The positive sense of the norm, on the other hand, requires that the state act positively in providing public welfare and justice (the provision of public transportation, medical treatment, educational opportunities, the protection of environmental resources, and so on). The extension of the meaning of this norm and the complexity of our urban technological society makes the task of the modern state exceedingly difficult. But who, other than the state, can look after the public interest? Individuals or groups, even when so motivated, are extremely limited in their power to bring into existence policies which are in the public interest. Furthermore, individuals or groups tend to look after their own individual interests, not those of the general public. Only the state remains, as Hobbes so well knew.

Public and Private Interests

How far in a positive direction should the norm of the public interest be extended? Could a state overdo the public interest? This question, in a sense, seems absurd. If the basic objective of the state is to further the public interest, it would seem that it could hardly do this too well! But there are interests other than public ones. If there are private interests into which the state should not intrude, areas of human freedom and rights which should not be violated by the state, then, in a sense, any state which so intruded would be overextending its proper role—"overdoing" the public interest. We must not forget that the whole point of developing rules, procedures, and policies which are in the public interest (the point of the social contract, to use the language of Hobbes and Locke) is to provide the conditions for the fulfillment of private interests. The state we generally conceive not to be an end in itself but to be an instrument for the realization of human purposes (though we have seen that Hegel and others reverse this order of value). Now admittedly the line between purely private interests and public interests is difficult to draw. But it is not impossible. Contextual decisions must be constantly made (should homosexual relations among consenting adults and prostitution be legalized, for example?). But it would appear that justice and the general welfare would permit, if not require, areas of individual autonomy or freedom. Furthermore, individual freedom itself is an important human value which surely must be balanced against the advantages of a highly planned and controlled society. Even if Huxley's *Brave New World* could be brought off, with everyone satisfied with his conditioning and his status within society, the loss of freedom would leave a dehumanized society.

Recommended Readings

Barry, Brian. *Political Argument*. New York, 1965. Chapters 11–15.
Beard, C. A. *The Idea of National Interest*. New York, 1934.
Friedrich, C. J., ed. *Nomos V: The Public Interest*. New York, 1962.
Heckscher, August. *The Public Happiness*. London, 1963.

Herring, Pendleton. *Public Administration and the Public Interest*. New York, 1936.

Lippman, Walter. *The Phantom Public*. New York, 1927.

Lloyd, Dennis. *Public Policy*. London, 1953.

Schubert, Glendon. *The Public Interest: A Critique of a Concept*. New York, 1961.

Smith, H. R. *Democracy and the Public Interest*. Athens, Ga., 1960.

Titmuss, R. M. *Essays on The Welfare State*. London, 1958.

chapter 13
Democracy and Its Alternatives

Introduction

We have seen that certain fundamental norms—freedom, equality, and the public interest—are ambiguous and susceptible of different interpretations and emphases and that, consequently, the mutual acceptance of these norms by two parties does not necessarily mean that they agree in their moral and political value premises. On the other hand, we have argued that these value concepts are not entirely fluid, that there are good reasons for subscribing to certain interpretations or emphases of these norms (the primacy of need-criteria over merit-criteria in according equality of treatment, for example) and that, although decisions of principle must be continuously made in extending and applying these values to new circumstances and contexts (recall our discussion of ecological data and its impact), these norms can and do function significantly as guides for moral and political decisions. We have also argued that a simple sort of value reductionism, in which all values are ultimately subsumed under the principle of utility, for example, or in which all are reduced to social justice, is inadequate.

Recognizing these facts—the significance and yet flexibility of these basic norms as action guides, and the plurality and nonreducibility of these values—we now want to ask the following question: What sort of political institutions can best bring these values to fruition? This has been one of the basic problems treated by political philosophers from Plato to Marx. And they have offered quite different accounts of what constitutes the best political system, differences which were sometimes rooted in different value perspectives, on other occasions rooted in different empirical estimates of the results of certain institutional arrangements. We cannot here provide a systematic and complete comparative analysis and evaluation of alternative political frameworks. But we can at least begin such an analysis and evaluation. I propose to do this by arguing, on a normative level, that democracy, and a set of institutional arrangements characteristic of a certain type of democracy, are the best instruments for the realization of the fundamental values discussed above. This conclusion I do not want to make into a tautology, that is, I do not want this to be true simply by virtue of my definition of democracy. Of course, it must be admitted that democracy, as a system of values, is often defined in terms of equality, freedom, and concern for the public interest. My concern will be both with the value components of the concept of democracy and with the sorts of institutional arrangements characteristic of democracies, and their efficaciousness in promoting these values. Let us begin, then, with the issue of defining democracy —both the values and institutional arrangements—and then proceed to the question of the instrumental value of those institutional arrangements.

The Definition of Democracy

The basic value of the democrat is equality. All men are equals and should be treated as equals. Of course, equality, we saw, at least to some extent, can be explicated in terms of other value concepts, for example, the right to freedom (positive or negative) and the public interest. All of these values, which are interrelated and overlapping, constitute the value perspective of the democrat. For both historical reasons and for convenience of argument, we will treat the equality norm as the most basic democratic value.

The first thing we must note, in getting at a definition of democracy, is this: If equality is the basic value of democracy and if there are multiple senses of equality—legal, social and economic equality, political equality, and so on—then there will be multiple senses of democracy corresponding to these senses of equality. This means that the concept of democracy, like the concept of equality, is rather fluid in use. There may be good reasons for defining democracy in a certain way so that a certain type(s) of equality is emphasized. This we do not want to deny. In fact we will press for such a definition momentarily. But we must recognize the fact that the concept "democracy" is used in several senses and that it has undergone (and continues to undergo) considerable development. For example, in countries where the right to participate in the political process is seen as essential to democracy, the definition of "political issue" is being broadened and with it the role of participation.

There are uses of "equality" (and of "democracy") in which political equality, the universal right to participate in the political process, is excluded. Plato believed in equality of opportunity for everyone, but he was not an advocate of political democracy, nor, it would appear, of the equal intrinsic value of all humans. Quite the contrary, he held that equality of opportunity for all and other important values could best be brought to fruition through the strong centralized control of the philosopher king(s). He argued that there are wide differences among men in terms of abilities (especially the ability to know "the good") and that these differences justify inequality in terms of political participation. Political elitism was seen by Plato as being perfectly compatible with both equality of opportunity for all and social justice. In the same way in which we generally recognize that equality of treatment in a family unit or equality within an educational unit does not require a one-person–one-vote arrangement—indeed, we would find such an arrangement ridiculous and irrational, given the different levels of development, statuses, or roles within these communities—so Plato held that differences in abilities and development justify different roles and statuses in society and that the right to political participation should be restricted to a small elite.

Hobbes, we saw, was a strong advocate of equality in the sense of equality under the law, but the law was to be determined by an absolute sovereign. This form of government, he thought, was the best means of assuring order and justice. Locke was an egalitarian in the sense that he argued that all men have the inalienable rights to life, liberty, and property. He also advocated a representative, parliamentary form of government as the best means of assuring these rights. To this extent he was a political democrat. But he restricted the franchise severely and parliament itself was oligarchically constituted. In this basic sense he was *not* a political democrat.

The point we want to make with these examples is that men believed in certain types of equality and held that all are entitled to equal treatment in the most general or formal sense long before they endorsed equality of political participation either as a right itself or as a means of assuring equality and social justice. Political equality or political democracy is a specific application of the general norm of equality.

Furthermore there are degrees and types of political democracy, depending on the form (direct democracy or representative) and on the extension of the franchise (Are women included or excluded? Those who are propertyless? Or black? Or uneducated? and so on). Perhaps the purest political democrat (keep in mind that there are various nonpolitical areas of human relationships in which persons can decide to practice democracy or not to practice it) is one who argues that there should be equality of participation in government for all. Each (mature) person in a political community should have the right to participate in making governmental decisions which affect the membership of that community because he is a member and because his interests, like those of everyone else, are affected by such decisions. The pure political democrat, then, sharply disagrees with Plato, for he holds that the principle of equality—equals should be treated equally, unequals unequally; or the formal principle of distributive justice—does require, logically, the equal right of political participation for all members of the political community. This equal right to participate, however, even for the democrat, does not mean an equal role in government decisions. The equal right to participate, based on the fact that each of us has an equal stake in government affairs and decisions, does not require that we settle every political issue on a one-man–one-vote basis. There are good grounds for having elite political decision-makers *who function as instruments of the total electorate*. In fact, given the complexity of many public policy issues, it is difficult to avoid the conclusion that the best interest of all requires an informed, intelligent elite. On this score the political democrat can agree with Plato. But pure democracy requires that every citizen be a member of the electorate. (It may also require that citizens participate in decisions on a much wider range of issues that affect their lives than is generally the case today.) Here Plato and the democrat part company. Plato believes in fairness; he believes in equality of opportunity. But it is questionable whether he believes in equality in the sense that each human being, no matter what his abilities, status, or contribution to society, has equal intrinsic worth. All men must have the opportunity to find out what sort of souls they have—gold, silver, or iron—but, for Plato, these metals have different intrinsic values. For the democrat, on the other hand, all souls have equal intrinsic worth, though they may have different extrinsic values to society.

The point just made is fundamental to understanding the foundation or presupposition of political democracy. Before turning to the question of whether that presupposition itself can be rationally defended, I want to recast the democrat's argument for political equality in terms which we used earlier (in the section on "Equality" above). The importance of the argument merits that repetition. We argued there that normative equality, in the most abstract sense, requires that all men are to be treated alike and that no person is to be given special privileges or treatment unless justifying reasons can be given for such differentiation. The presumption here is that every person has equal intrinsic worth and dignity simply because he is human, and that this equal intrinsic worth alone justifies the accordance of certain basic modes of treatment or rights. There are rational grounds for non-identical treatment. No egalitarian denies this. That is, many rights and privileges in society are justifiably contingent upon a person's possession of certain capacities and circumstances, upon his meeting certain merit-criteria. Other rights, however, are not justifiably contingent on merit-criteria. The possession of some rights is justified simply by the fact that one is a human being, a being with the capacities to think, choose, suffer, and experience pleasure. Those characteristics and the needs to which they give rise are universal characteristics and needs of members of the human species. Simply by virtue of being a member of the human species, by virtue of having the characteristics and needs of a human being, one is entitled to those rights which are essential to the satisfaction of those needs, rights which are required for at least a minimally satisfactory life. The possession of merit-criteria, no matter what these are interpreted as being—whether birth in a prominent family, the possession of wealth, great intelligence, or high value to society—is irrelevant to the possession of those rights which are his simply because he is human. Human beings logically cannot be graded in regard to the possession of human rights.

Now the political democrat claims that one's existence as a (mature) human being within a political community is all that is required to justify the right to political participation. Merit-criteria he deems as irrelevant in according this right. Non-democrats, on the other hand, regard merit-criteria of various types (the possession of moral and intellectual virtues and the ability to contribute to the welfare of society were Aristotle's merit-criteria; wealth and inherited status were endorsed in medieval societies; educational level is a contemporary criterion of merit to which appeal is made to justify franchise restrictions) not only as relevant but as overriding. If a person lacks these qualities of merit, then he is not entitled to participate politically, even if, by virtue of his needs as a person, he has an interest equal to that of every other person in the outcome of the political process. This is the fundamental difference in the value perspectives of the pure democrat and non-democrat (and, of course, impure or qualified forms of democracy). Mill, with his thesis that the educated elite should have more votes than the noneducated; Hegel, with his insistence that the franchise be limited so that the ends of the state can be attained; Locke, with his restriction on the franchise, even though he maintains that all men possess the inalienable rights to life, liberty, and property—all of these theorists maintain either that the possession of merit-criteria or else certain consequential considerations (the attainment of the "ends of the state" in Hegel) justify the restriction of the franchise. If democracy as a political system is defined to include a universal franchise, then none of these theorists can be classified as democrats. Within this framework Mill and Locke, even though they advocate representative government, must be seen as impure democrats.

Are there good reasons for watering down pure political democracy—for restricting the franchise? Many theorists have argued that there are such reasons. The point argued is not merely that direct democracy is impossible in large, complex modern states but that a one-man–one-vote system in which the majority rules may subvert or prevent the realization of the ends of the state, the "public interest." Now obviously this argument hangs on the answer to two questions: (1) What is meant by the public interest? (2) What evidence is there that a universal franchise subverts the public interest? These questions are obviously interrelated, for one cannot answer (2) until (1) is answered. The fact of the matter is that pure democrats, impure democrats, and non-democrats disagree on the meaning of the "public interest" or of the "ends" of the state, and on how those ends are discovered or known. The non-democrat insists that the "public interest" as a value exists quite independently of the expression of preferences of the general populace, that, consequently, it can be known without the consultation or political participation of that general populace; and he insists that efforts to completely determine and implement the public interest by such participation in effect vitiate the public interest. The pure democrat responds by arguing that the ends of the state or the public interest are not some sort of metaphysical entities existing independently of the preferences and needs of men, but that they can be discovered only by consulting those preferences and needs, and that equality of political participation is properly seen as part of the very meaning of the "public interest." The public interest requires that all men be treated as having equal intrinsic value. This norm, in a political context, requires that each person have the right to express politically his preferences and choices. The pure democrat sees the restriction of the franchise to exclude some mature adults and the appeal to an elite group to devise political policies as inconsistent with the principle of the equal intrinsic value of all persons, and consequently as inconsistent with the public interest.

Thus, the value differences between the pure democrat and non-democrat can be seen in terms of their different interpretations of both equality and the public interest. The non-democrat stresses merit-criteria as required for the right to political participation; the democrat does not. The democrat includes political participation as part of the very meaning of the public interest. The non-democrat does not.

The difference between them can also be seen in terms of other values or concepts—freedom, happiness, and authority. The concept of a free society, for the democrat, necessarily includes the equal right of all to political participation. This is not true of the non-democrat's concept of a free society. The democrat insists that happiness is not some pie-in-the-sky universal; each individual must be permitted to decide what is happiness for him. The non-democrat, on the other hand, insists that persons with special knowledge or insight (the philosopher-king of Plato or the historical dialectician for Hegel and Marx) are justified in dictating to other men the conditions under which they are "really" happy. The individual has no right to decide this, because he does not have this special knowledge. Explicating the difference in terms of the concept of authority, the democrat insists that authority is legitimate only when there is general consent (however consent is defined) on rules of justice and when those rules themselves are fair. The non-democrat does not see consent as essential to the existence of legitimate authority. The right to authority is contingent only on metaphysical and moral expertise, or power.

It should be clear from what has been said that the traditional values espoused by the democrat are also endorsed by many non-democrats. Justice, fairness, equality, freedom, the public interest, and happiness—all theorists, democrat and non-democrat, seem to subscribe to these values. But fundamental differences lurk in the nitty-gritty interpretation of these values. They mean different things for the "totalitarian democrat" (we will see what this apparently contradictory phrase means in a moment) and the political democrat. (This is not to deny that they sometimes coincide denotatively in terms of practices.) It can quite legitimately be said that persons enjoy freedom and equality, for example, under both of these systems of law and government. But for the democrat the individual cannot *really* be free unless he has the right to political participation; he cannot be treated equally or fairly, in the fullest sense, without this right. This right follows, he holds, from subscription to equality in the sense of the equal intrinsic worth of all members of a society. Non-democrats either fail to see that equality in this sense requires the right to political participation; or they see that it does but override the right on the basis of other value commitments; or they simply do not subscribe to equality in this sense.

The Justification of Democracy

Now, the political democrat, it seems, must do two things if he would fully justify his position. He must show that the right to political participation is entailed by equality (the equal intrinsic worth of all members of a society), and he must show that there are good reasons or justifying grounds for adopting the norm of equality as he interprets it. I do not think that he must be able to show that this right cannot be justifiably overridden on rare occasions. There are other rights and consequential considerations that he may properly deem as more important in certain contexts. For example, the short-term absolute democracy which followed the French Revolution of 1789 did not produce enlightened policies. A democrat could certainly argue, with good reason, that majority rule under such conditions can be overridden in order to effect other kinds of social justice.

Let us ask, then, these two questions: Can equality in the sense of the equal intrinsic worth of each person be proven? And, if so, does this sense of equality justify the equal right to political participation of all mature members of a community?

We have already argued the second point—in two ways. First, we argued that fairness requires that the equal treatment of human beings with need-criteria emphasis must be seen as having moral priority over equality of treatment with merit-criteria emphasis. Applied to the issue of who should have the right to political participation, it is hardly fair to assign this right on, say, the basis of the possession of intellectual virtues or on the individual's ability to contribute to the welfare of society, *even if such characteristics are seen as relevant*, unless all members of the community are given the opportunity to develop those intellectual virtues or ability to contribute. For without such opportunities one is arbitrarily ruled out of the political game. Some non-democrats ignore this question of fairness (Plato did not, for his educational system would permit anyone to move up the ladder as far as he can). Others defend the merit-criteria priority by arguing that some men are "naturally inferior"; the opportunity to acquire merit-criteria is not required by the principle of fairness since such persons *cannot* acquire meritorious characteristics. (Aristotle and Nietzsche seem to hold this.) In the latter case, the issue is the grounds of this "natural inferiority" claim.[1]

Second, we argued the much stronger claim that no merit-criteria of the type often invoked (educational attainments, property, birth in a prominent family, and so on) are even relevant in according the right to political participation. They are not relevant because, no matter what one's educational level, wealth, or status in society— whether Ph.D. or grammar school level, whether poor or wealthy, whether born in a prominent family or not—each person has an equal stake (though some persons, the very wealthy, for example, may have higher stakes) in political society. Since all members of a political society have this stake in its rules and policies, no member, with the exception of children, the insane, and prisoners, can be excluded properly from the right to participate politically in that society. In regard to the possession of this right, persons are not "gradable," unless one denies the equal intrinsic worth (as opposed to his instrumental or contributory value to society) of all persons. If one denies the latter, he can consistently deny the former, namely, that each person has an equal stake in society; and hence, on that basis, deny that persons of unequal intrinsic worth should have equal political rights. (This is of course, what Plato and Aristotle did.)

The fundamental value presupposition of the democrat, then, is the equal intrinsic value of all persons. Must it be seen simply as an

[1] This "natural inferiority" issue is not dead today. See Arthur R. Jensen's article, "How Much Can We boost I.Q. and Scholastic Achievement," *Harvard Educational Review*, 39 (1969), pp. 1–123. Other leading exponents of the thesis that there are racial and genetic differences in intelligence are H. J. Eysenck *The I.Q. Argument* (New York: Library Press, 1971), and William Shockley. See *The Humanist*, Vol. 32, No. 1 (1972), for a detailed discussion of this question, including an essay by Shockley.

unjustified presupposition from which the democrat commences his political game, with the non-democrat's commitment to the unequal intrinsic worth of men also being an unjustified presupposition in his choice of political games? I do not think so. Perhaps equality cannot be proven in any strict sense. On the other hand, as Mill puts it in the context of his effort to justify the principle of utility, considerations may be presented which are capable of "determining the intellect." Before specifying these considerations, let us first note some frequent arguments for equality which are *ineffective*.

Locke argues that equality is a self-evident truth. And indeed it is to some persons. But it is not self-evident to inegalitarians. The appeal to self-evidence as the final epistemological ground simply results in shutting off debate on the question. Others ground the equality of man in the fatherhood of God: God created all men as equals. But, aside from the fact that some also appeal to God's creative acts to justify the inequality of men, this theological presupposition of God's existence and his values are at least as problematic as the equality thesis itself. Those who appeal to other metaphysical presuppositions take us no further in our quest for proof of the equality of man. For example, some natural law theorists, as we saw in earlier chapters, speak of equality as being part of the concept of human nature, with that concept corresponding to the real essence of man. But the thesis that man has an essence (or that there are essences at all) is surely challengeable. Benn and Peters argue in this way: human nature simply designates a potentiality for a certain range of experience—not some property or essence! And indeed there appears to be no consensus on the meaning of "human nature," nor, so far as I know, is there any noncircular way of showing that certain activities or norms are essential to what it means to be a human, and that certain others are not. Such attempts to provide an ontological foundation for a certain concept of human nature via the notion of essence appear to be surreptitious or disguised evaluations.

These arguments for equality are ineffective. But let me now cite three sorts of considerations which carry considerable weight in justifying this basic value premise of the democrat. First, admitting that the intrinsic worth and dignity of each person is not a property in any ordinary sense of property, and hence that the equality of all persons cannot be verified by discovering such a property; and, further, admitting that the ascription of equality of worth is a value judgment, nonetheless there are good reasons for adopting this norm and for acting as if it were true. That is, in the absence of good and sufficient reasons for discriminating among men, it seems rational to treat them equally. Part of what we mean by a rational decision is one in which we can cite relevant and sufficient reasons for the decision—for discriminating in this way or that. The egalitarian argues that although there are good and sufficient reasons for discriminating among persons in according, for example, different kinds of educational or medical treatment, there are no good grounds for excluding any person from educational opportunities and medical treatment of some kind. Since all persons have, generically, as members of the human species, the same sorts of capacities and needs, it seems rational to treat them all as equals, in the absence of good and sufficient reasons for treating them differently. That is, given these facts it seems appropriate to place the burden of proof on he who would treat human beings unequally.

The claim here is not that it is irrational to treat persons differently. Quite the contrary, it is irrational not to treat them differently if there are good reasons for doing so. But the burden of proof should rest upon he who thinks there are good reasons for differential treatment. This shifting of the burden of proof from the egalitarian to the inegalitarian does not *prove* equality. But it forces the recognition that, in regard to at least the minimal conditions for a satisfactory life, there seem to be no good reasons for differentiating among humans; and hence that our operating principle should be equality.[2]

Second, if one is concerned to maximize happiness, there are good empirical grounds for believing that treating persons equally in most cases increases the amount of happiness in the world. That is, there is reason to believe that the fulfillment of those conditions required for at least a minimally satisfactory life for each person, before luxuries or preferential treatment are distributed on grounds other than need in general, maximizes human welfare.[3]

Third, in addition to this utilitarian defense of equality, a forceful vindication or pragmatic argument for equality is set forth by both H. L. A. Hart and Fredrick Olafson. Hart points out that in any system of morality in which the concept of "rights" is used (whether they be "special" or "general" rights), equality (Hart speaks of the

[2] This form of the burden of proof argument does not presume that the inegalitarian is irrational or morally perverse. See my discussion on this in "On The Meaning and Justification of the Equality Principle," *Ethics*, Vol. 77, No. 4, July 1967, especially p. 240 and footnote 16.

[3] See the discussion of this in Richard Brandt's *Ethical Theory* (Englewood Cliffs, N.J.: Prentice-Hall, Inc., 1959, Chap. 16.

"equal right of all men to be free") is presupposed by that use.[4] Hart's argument makes a logical point about a segment of our moral discourse in which we speak of rights. He does not try to justify equality as a natural right in some ontological sense. The force of his argument is this: if you want to have a system of morality in which the concept of rights is used, then you must adopt the equality principle. He forces those who are committed to a view of society in which rights play a central role to see that they can give up the equality principle only at a high cost. For those who are not committed to a rights-oriented society, his argument would have little force.

Frederick Olafson, in what he calls a "conceptualistic" version of natural law theory, argues in a similar vein. This version sets forth a "real" definition of man as opposed to a conventional one, not in the sense of the traditional "essence" approach, but in the sense that "it expresses the only set of reciprocally applicable priorities that most people are really prepared to live by." [5] For this definition of "man" or "human nature," into which the equality principle is built, no authority of some ontological type is claimed—only that the vast majority of human beings are unwilling to give up the implications for conduct of certain rules and practices implicit in that definition or concept. On this analysis, the equality principle could be rejected "only on pain of abandoning a whole sector of human activity and discourse which in this case would be the enterprise of cooperative social living." [6] This is a rather high cost.

Of course, neither Hart's nor Olafson's vindicatory argument is persuasive to one who is not interested in rights or cooperative social living. But nearly all of us are interested. These three sorts of considerations, taken together, are weighty grounds for adopting the equality norm.

Majoritarian and Totalitarian Democracy

Although democracy in what we have called its "pure" form entails subscription to the equal intrinsic worth of all humans, and this equality of worth, in a political context, requires equality of political participation (though not an equal role in government decisions or

[4] H. L. A. Hart, "Are There Any National Rights?" *Philosophical Review*, 64 (1955).

[5] Frederick Olafson, "Essence and Concept in Natural Law Theory," in *Law and Philosophy*, ed. Sidney Hook (New York: 1964), p. 239.

[6] Ibid.

policy formation), this does not mean that every policy decision must be determined by the majority existing at that time. Democratic theorists have long been concerned with the "tyranny of the majority," that is, with the view that the majority is always justified in riding roughshod over minority groups or individuals. Mill, we saw, was especially concerned with this sort of tyranny. Such majority tyranny is inconsistent with the ideal of democracy in which each person, with his desires and opinions, counts, and in which each person has certain rights which cannot be ignored or abridged. Whether the tyrannizing power is that of an absolute monarch, a single political party, or a majority of the electorate, it vitiates the democratic ideal if it overrides or ignores individual rights. Democracy requires that majority rule operate within a system of respect for the constitutional rights of everyone, no matter how bizarre, unorthodox, or "minor" their views may be. Those rights, which include freedom of speech, press, association, assembly, and so on, are seen as constitutive of or deducible from the equal intrinsic worth of each person and their equality as citizens. Democracy, in this sense, requires that the power of the majority be limited within that framework of constitutional and human rights. The democrat believes that a system of majority rule, *within these limitations*, best serves the interests and freedoms of individuals, and this, he reminds us, is the *raison d'être* of government. A person does not exist to serve the ends of the state, whether the ends of the state are conceived as the will of the majority or some other. Any political system in which this Lockean emphasis is lacking is not democratic in the pure sense.

Mere majoritarian democracy is a form of tyranny. But perhaps it is less tyrannical than what has been called totalitarian democracy (a contradiction in terms?) or a "people's democracy." So-called totalitarian democracies override considerations of popular consent or political equality in order to attain, they assert, other kinds of equality —social, economic, and legal. The U.S.S.R. is perhaps the best example of this kind of democracy, recognizing only one party, the Communist party, as the source of legitimate political action, and that one party is not subject to control by a general electorate, for there is no general electorate. Only members of the Communist party may participate politically and membership is restricted to a very small percentage of the population, probably less than five percent. It is true that the Soviet Constitution guarantees to all citizens a large number of social, economic, legal, and religious rights. It is a beautiful document in this sense. But political participation is severely restricted in the interest of revolutionary objectives. In this sense the government of the Soviet Union is the opposite of what we mean by a democracy in the western world.

Plainly the communist uses the word "democracy" in a quite different sense than the political democrat. But in fairness to his position we must recall (see Chapter 4) that the communist looks upon the extension of political rights in capitalistic states as a mere mask, hiding the underlying fact that the capitalist class controls everything —the social, legal, and political system. Merely having the right to vote is no assurance of political democracy, and until capitalism and capitalist control of social institutions is eliminated, there can be no democracy. Even with political rights restricted to a small number, socialist countries, they maintain, in assuring the social and economic rights of all citizens, are far more democratic than non-socialist countries, where the so-called universal franchise or the will of the people is controlled behind the scenes by wealthy property owners and where even social and economic rights are denied to major portions of the population.

The Extension of Social Justice

One cannot deny that there is considerable truth in the above claim. The United States, for example, can properly be characterized as a political democracy. The franchise is extended to all adults over 18, with the exception of the insane, aliens, and prisoners. No longer are there property qualifications—we have given up (at least in principle) John Jay's view that those who "own" the country ought to govern it—nor are there exclusions based on sex or race. There is a choice of political parties and of candidates within parties. But are social and economic equality (in the sense of equality of opportunity) and equality under the law extended to all United States citizens regardless of race, sex, and so on? The black liberation and women's liberation movements do not think so. Persons in these movements point to numerous cases in which persons of a particular race or sex are prevented from enjoying certain working and educational opportunities. It was not until 1954 in *Brown* v. *Topeka* that the Supreme Court saw that desegregation is essential to equality of educational opportunity. It was not until 1963 that the Court, in *Gideon* v. *Wainwright*, declared that equality before the law requires that anyone who is too poor to hire a lawyer must be provided one. And today thousands of women are systematically excluded from certain working opportunities and social roles, or if employed, are remunerated at a much lower level than men. Furthermore, thousands of persons are denied working opportunities because of their age where age is an irrelevant consideration. In all of these cases, discriminatory treatment based on race, sex, age, or economic condition is arbitrary and unjustified. And yet, in many cases, these irrelevant criteria have been part and parcel of our law. (The problem is not merely that our social practices violate the law, although this too is certainly true.) Is it any wonder that some of these persons have expressed contempt for law, that some commit acts of civil disobedience, and that many speak of revolution? One can hardly feel a sense of community or common purpose with a government whose laws permit systematic social injustices against him. This is especially true if one's conception of the very purpose of government and law is justice and fairness to all, a system that works to the mutual advantage of all men, not merely some, one which does not require unilateral sacrifice or permit unilateral exploitation.

Although constitutional democracies are far from perfect, often distributing opportunities, goods, and services unfairly, still there is good reason to believe that such democracies, with equality of political participation for all adults, as opposed to either a mere majoritarian democracy or a "people's democracy," are the most effective means of assuring fairness and social justice—social, economic, legal, and political equality. As Mill stresses, "the rights and interests of every or any person are only secure from being disregarded when the person interested is himself able, and habitually disposed, to stand up for them." There is good historical evidence for this, evidence that supports the instrumental value of the equal right to political participation (though Mill himself did not draw this conclusion). There is also an abundance of historical evidence that non-democratic forms of government—absolute monarchies, aristocracies, military dictatorships, plutocracies, and one-party systems—often result in the denial of individual rights and in grave social injustices and atrocities. This is certainly not always the case. Some non-democratic governments have protected individual rights, and some democracies have attacked those rights. But in general democratic forms of government have proven to be the surest safeguard of individual liberties.

It goes without saying that constitutional guarantees of rights are essential for the protection of those rights. However, we must not forget that constitutional rights and restraints must themselves be fair and just ones. That is, the constitutions should be judged by extra-legal or moral standards, for all too often they embody unfair discriminations.

Democracy as an Adequate Political Theory

We stated in Chapter 1 that political theory has an inescapable normative dimension. Conceptual analysis and empirical research is essential to an adequate theory but the normative task is basic, namely to provide an adequate set of norms to regulate the use of political power. We have argued in this chapter that a particular interpretation of the values of freedom, equality, and the public interest normally associated with political democracy is the most adequate set of values for the circumscription of political power; and we have argued that the institutions of constitutional democracy, with a universal franchise, a multiparty system, and the separation of powers—legislative, judicial, and executive—are the best instruments for fulfilling these values. Other forms of government—plutocracy, where a powerful economic class controls the state; aristocracy, where a hereditary noble class is in control; military dictatorships and one-party systems —all of which are based on different types of elitism (criteria of "birth," strength, intelligence, race, wealth, and so on) reject the basic value premise of political democracy, namely, the equal intrinsic worth and dignity of all persons. Although, as we have seen, these non-democratic forms of government may properly be said to endorse some forms of equality, some types of freedom, and some interpretations of the public interest, they do not endorse the interpretation of these basic values offered by the political democrat. Consequently, they reject the institutional means or the political framework offered by the democrat to bring these values to fruition.

A democratic framework of government, of course, even among those who are presumably committed to it, can be thwarted in a number of ways. In the United States, often cited as one of the best examples of a functioning democracy, where a multiparty system makes possible effective opposition and the unseating of the reigning party when it does not respond to the interests of the people, where the franchise has been widely extended, and where the separation of the branches of government—the executive, legislative, and judicial— provides an essential check on the use and abuse of power, it is still quite possible for elitist minorities to prevent the rights and interests of the majority from being fulfilled. Highly organized and wealthy minority groups are powerful political forces. They can make themselves heard and felt, and they frequently prevail in conflicts.

It is not difficult to find examples. Early in the nineteenth century, Alexis de Tocqueville warned us of the possible danger of a rising business elite in his *Democracy in America*. He warned us of the inequalities and injustices which could result from the development of a class of corporate rich. This class did in fact exploit millions, and it devised means of controlling the political process so as to perpetuate the inequalities which it found desirable. This is not to deny that the business elite was responsible for raising the standard of living for all by increasing production of goods and services. This certainly happened and must be weighed in any evaluation. But the corporate rich effectively prevented for many years the extension of social and economic equality by controlling political decisions, even when property qualifications for voting were removed. As Girvetz points out:

> The power of the one-tenth of one per cent of the families (with annual incomes in excess of $75,000) receiving, in 1929, an aggregate income approximately equal to the aggregate income of the 42 per cent of the families at the bottom of the scale, was far greater than that of any other segment on the scale. . . . For a long time, thanks to our system of checks and balances, to federalism and to the domination of our major political parties by the economically privileged, the people acting collectively could not make decisions in the areas that concerned them most, namely, the distribution of income and the allocation of resources. The Supreme Court could strike down a state minimum wage law for women as a 'naked and arbitrary exercise of power.' Congressional committees could be cemeteries in which legislative proposals wanted by the majority might be buried without prospect of distinterment. One legislative chamber could refuse approval of the action of the other, and a President, acting on Calvin Coolidge's philosophy that the best government is no government, could veto the action of both. The market—as managed by property owners—was sovereign.[7]

Of course, much has happened since 1929. New political forces, labor unions in particular, have arisen as powerful factors in the political process. For many segments of our population, straightforward economic exploitation is no longer possible. There are now

---

[7] Harry K. Girvetz, "Elitism," in Harry K. Girvetz, ed., *Democracy and Elitism* (New York: Charles Scribner's Sons, 1967), pp. 48–51.

important and effective limitations on property rights, and these are growing. New minority groups, such as the farmers, the blacks, and women, press for the elimination of arbitrary restraints and unjustified discrimination. They press for a sense of equality and freedom in which everyone has the equal right to be free, not simply the wealthy, those of high birth, the educated, whites, or males. Freedom is not something just for the rich, for whites, or for males. It is the right of every citizen, and if our system of property rights prevents the universal enjoyment of this right, so much the worse for property rights. They must be qualified and made consistent with these basic democratic values. This is the commitment of the democrat.

The United States and other countries seem to be growing closer to what we have called pure democracy. The pace is slow. Our tax laws still heavily favor the rich. The disbursement of health services often denies the poor any medical treatment at all. Equality under the law is a joke when the contrast between the legal representation of the poor and the rich is seen for what it is. And educational opportunity, so basic for the fulfillment of the democratic ideal, is weighted heavily in favor of the white middle class and the rich as opposed to the poor and the black. But, as indicated above, great strides toward genuine democracy have been made. Major breakthroughs have occurred—for example, the *Brown* v. *Topeka* decision, and the *Gideon* v. *Wainwright* decision. Changes are in the wind concerning the disbursement of health benefits in the U.S., to be added to Medicare and Medicaid.

In lieu of a utopia, however, the process of eliminating arbitrary discrimination must be continuous. In fact, the history of the democratic ideal and the egalitarian ethic is a history of the gradual sloughing off of irrelevant criteria for the differential treatment of persons. We are far from the end of the road. When their self-interests are at stake, human beings are peculiarly adept at inventing distinctions and criteria which preserve those interests and the *status quo*. Those committed to the democratic ethic must be ever wary of this fact. They must be prepared not only to show that these criteria are irrelevant for the distribution of goods and services but also to make decisions of principle which extend the democratic ethic to new areas, where, given the changing conditions of human existence, new restrictions are required in order to assure the equal right of all men to be free or the equal intrinsic worth and dignity of all members of the political community. The extent to which the state must intervene in order to assure this right and hence assure social justice cannot be known in advance of our awareness of how certain conditions are related to the fulfillment of this right. We were a long time coming to the *Brown* v. *Topeka* decision on educational equality. Much empirical data had to be gathered showing that separation in schools on the basis of race precluded equality of educational opportunity. With this data, it became possible for many who were committed to the democratic ethic to change their minds on the propriety of segregated schools. And, of course, it became possible to change our law, which has itself become the prime causal agent in changing value perspectives on this issue.[8]

Extensions of democracy and the sloughing off of irrelevant criteria for differential treatment are obviously needed in other areas—the treatment of women and the aged, for example. Decisions of principle must be made in these contexts, based on our democratic values and on all available relevant empirical data. If our laws, not merely our social practices, embody arbitrary discriminations, those laws must be changed, for it is social justice, not merely law and order, that democracy is all about. Furthermore, because laws themselves must be changed to assure social justice, it is essential that the democratic tradition provide, as it does, a set of fair rules to regulate legal change.

What we have been saying should now be quite plain: a democratic political system has its faults and its dangers. It sometimes permits social injustices and inequalities to persist for inordinate lengths of time. But the political theory of democracy meets the criteria of adequacy specified above (clarity, testability, consistency, coherence, completeness, and applicability) better than other theories. It recognizes the plurality and irreducibility of values. It recognizes that those values may on occasion conflict (justice and utility, for example). In this recognition of both deontological and teleological grounds of political and legal obligation, and in its value priority emphasis, the democratic ethic provides us with a more adequate account of the grounds of moral and political obligation than do other ethical frameworks. It also provides us with a more adequate normative framework for the resolution of questions bearing on the use and abuse of political power.

Conceived more narrowly in terms of a set of institutional arrangements and a method of choosing a government, democracy— with its system of competitive elections, its free press, and its court

[8] For a discussion of the causal impact of laws on society, see Ralf Dahrendorf's "On The Origin of Social Inequality," in *Philosophy, Politics and Society*, edited by Peter Laslett and W. G. Runciman (Oxford: Basil Blackwell, 1962).

system—appears to be the best instrument for the protection of individual rights and liberties. It provides a political and legal system which socializes the inevitable conflict over interests and values among men. It permits and encourages dissent on political goals and policies, providing a framework not only for mutual consultation and debate between political leaders and followers within a political party but between opposing political parties themselves. This commitment to dissent and to all of the institutions and rights which make it possible, and the commitment to the view that the individual has the right, within limitations, to orient his life according to his own wishes and his own conception of the good life, and not to have his "choices" totally imposed upon him by some political elite—these commitments are part and parcel of the democratic values of equality, freedom, and the public interest. Of course, dissent and the institutions that protect dissent also assure that a considerable amount of chaos and confusion will accompany a democracy. But the "openness" of the democratic process, the guarantee that it provides that multiple points of view will be presented, and that the full range of empirical facts which bear on those points of view will be taken into consideration—these advantages far outweigh the chaos, confusion, and occasional corruption which democracy sometimes produces. Peace and order are not our only objectives. If they were, Hobbes's absolute sovereign might be the best answer. Given those objectives of democracy that go well beyond peace and order, we must agree with Charles Frankel: "The greased palm is bad but it is preferable to the mailed fist." [9]

Recommended Readings

Bachrach, Peter. *The Theory of Democratic Elitism.* Boston, 1967.

Benn, S. I. and Peters, R. S. *Social Principles and the Democratic State.* London, 1959.

Blackstone, William T. *The Concept of Equality.* Minneapolis, 1969.

Braybrooke, David. *Three Tests For Democracy: Personal Rights, Human Welfare, Collective Preference.* New York, 1968.

Cohen, Carl. *Democracy.* Athens, Ga., 1971.

Dahl, Robert A. *A Preface to Democratic Theory.* Chicago, 1956.

[9] Charles Frankel, *The Democratic Prospect* (New York: Harper and Row, 1962).

De Sola Pool, I., Lasswell, H. D., and Lerves, D. *Symbols of Democracy.* Stanford, 1952.

Downs, Anthony. *An Economic Theory of Democracy.* New York, 1957.

Friedrich, C. J. *Constitutional Government and Democracy.* Boston, 1941.

Girvetz, Harry K. *Democracy and Elitism.* New York, 1967.

Hallowell, J. *The Moral Foundations of Democracy.* Chicago, 1954.

Heard, Alexander. *The Cost of Democracy.* Chapel Hill, 1962.

Hook, Sidney. *Political Power and Personal Freedom.* New York, 1959.

Laski, Harold J. *Democracy in Crisis.* Chapel Hill, 1933.

Lindsey, A. D. *The Essentials of Democracy.* London, 1935.

Quinton, Anthony, ed. *Political Philosophy.* Oxford, 1967.

Simon, Yves R. *The Philosophy of Democratic Government.* Chicago, 1951.

Talmon, J. L. *The Origins of Totalitarian Democracy.* New York, 1960.

Young, Michael. *The Rise of the Meritocracy.* Harmondsworth, England, 1961.

Index

A

Absolute, the, 120
absolute sovereignty, 51
  civil disobedience and, 52–53
  tyranny and, 39, 56
Absolute Spirit, 124
abstract right, 125–28
adequacy
  criteria of, 183–93
    openness and, 190–92
  of political theory of democracy,
    250–54
agricultural class, 129
Albertus Magnus, 27
alienation, 161–65
  state as manifestation of, 165
analysis, 10–14
  relationship of norms and, 14–16
analytic political philosophy, 10
*Anti-Dühring: Herr Eugen Dühr-
  ing's Revolution in Science*
  (Engels), 147
appetites, aversions and, 47
Aquinas, St. Thomas, 27, 29, 33,
  35–45, 70, 73, 177
  class privileges of feudal society
    sanctioned by, 172
  criteria of adequacy and, 183–87,
    191
  on duties of state, 228
  on equality, 210, 216
  on eternal and natural laws, 39–
    40

  principles of natural law, 40–
    41
  on justice, 42–43
  on purposes and aims of society
    and government, 37–39
  best form of government, 39
aristocracy, 134
Aristotle, 10, 26–28, 33, 35–36, 209,
  220, 243
Austin, John, 74
aversions, appetites and, 47
Ayer, A. J., 22

B

behaviorist reduction, 19–21
Benedict, Ruth, 172
Benn, S. I., 11, 216, 244
Bentham, Jeremy, 16, 29, 74–91, 114,
  177, 229
  on civil disobedience, 86–87
  criteria of adequacy and, 188
  on equality, 212
  on freedom, 85–86, 196–99
  on grounds of legislation, 78–79
  on human nature and hedonism,
    76–78
  on justice, 79–81
  Mill compared to, 92–95
  on natural rights, 10, 14, 81–82
  on role of government, 83–85
  on social contract and consent,
    83

Berlin, Isaiah, 9, 217
bourgeoisie, 157
  ownership of property and, 152–53
  evolution from feudal society of, 154–57
Burke, Edmund, 28
business class, 129
Butler, Bishop Joseph, 56

C

Capital (Marx), 146, 158
Catholic Church, 37
Charles I, King of England, 46
Charles II, King of England, 46
Cicero, 33, 35
Citizen, The (Hobbes), 46
civil disobedience, 5–8
  conceptual confusion regarding, 11–14
  justice and, 42–43
  natural law and, 51–53, 64–65
    justice and, 42–43
  utilitarianism and, 86–87
civil servant class, 129
civil society, 128–32
class struggles, 152–61
classes, 152–61
  system of need fulfillment and, 129
commodity fetishism, 162–63
communism
  alienation and, 164
  crude, 169
  mature, 170–71
  Mill on, 107
Communist Manifesto, The (Marx and Engels), 146, 151, 152, 156–57
concepts, 10–14
concupiscible nature of man, 47
conscience, 126–27

Conditions of the Working Class in England (Engels), 146
consent of governed, 60
  utilitarian critique of, 83
constitutional monarchy, 136–38
  organic unity of state maintained by, 138
constitutions, forms of, 133–38
contract, social, 49–50, 60
  rights and duties and, 53
  utilitarian critique of, 83
Contribution to the Critique of Political Economy (Marx), 147
criteria of adequacy, 183–93
  openness and, 190–92
criteria of relevance for differential treatment, 218–20
  justification of, 221–22
crude communism, 169

D

Dahrendorf, Ralf, 224
De Corpore (Hobbes), 46
De Homine (Hobbes), 46
definition, problem of, 3–5
democracy, 134, 235–55
  as adequate political theory, 250–54
  constitutional monarchy and, 136–38
  definition of, 236
  extension of social justice in, 248–50
  freedom and, 85–86
  justification of, 242
  majoritarian and totalitarian, 246–48
  natural law and, 51
  representative, 107–10
Democracy in America (Tocqueville), 251
descriptive equality, 216–18

determinism, economic, 148–52
dialectic, 122–25
dialectical materialism, 148–52
dictatorship
  socialist, 168–69
  See also tyranny
differential treatment, criteria of relevance for, 218–20
  justification of, 221–22
discussion, freedom of, 105–7
divine law, 39–40
  violation of, 42
divisions of power, 134–36
duties, 53–54
  consent of governed and, 63–64
  to God and sovereign, 54–55

E

Early Writings (Marx), 147
Easton, David, 21
economic determinism, 148–52
Economic and Philosophic Manuscripts (Marx), 147
egoism, 47
  duties to God and, 55
  morality and, 55–56
  right of self-preservation and, 51–52
  social contract and, 49–50
  in state of nature, 48–49
elitism, 110–11
empirical component of political philosophy, 16–18
Encyclopedia of the Social Sciences (Hegel), 119
Engels, Friedrich, 14, 17, 29, 35, 117, 144, 146–47
  on classes and class struggles, 152–60
  criteria of adequacy and, 188–89
  dialectical materialism and economic determinism of, 148–52
  on equality, 214–15
  on freedom, 195, 199–200
    alienation and, 161–65
  Hegelian influence on, 147–48
  on mature communism and social justice, 170–71
  on public interest, 230
  on socialist dictatorship, 168–69
  on the state, 165–68
equality, 208–26
  application of principle of, 222–25
  criteria of relevance for differential treatment and, 218–20
    justification of, 221–22
  descriptive and normative, 216–18
  as natural right, 61–62
Essay Concerning Human Understanding (Locke), 58, 66, 184
estates assemblies, 136
  free speech in, 139
ethical life, 125–28, 139
exploitation, 158–60
external state, 129, 131

F

family
  bourgeois, 165*n*
  as political institution, 128–32
fetishism of commodity, 162–63
feudal society
  evolution of bourgeoisie from, 154–57
  production in, 155
Feuerbach and the End of Classical German Philosophy (Engels), 147
Fichte, Johann, 134
First International, 147

Fragment on Government, A (Bentham), 76
franchise, restricted, 61, 109–10, 137
Frankel, Charles, 254
freedom, 132–33, 194–207
  alienation and, 161–65
  application of norm of, 204–6
  democracy and, 85–86
  fundamental right of, 100–2
  meaning and justification of, 200–4
  natural right of, 62
  restrictions on, 102–5
  of speech, 105–7
    public opinion and, 138–39
  of thought, 105–7
  utility and, 84
French National Assembly, Declaration of Rights of, 82
fundamental right, 100–2

G

Gale, Richard, 72
Galileo, 46
Gandhi, Mahatma, 11
German Ideology, The (Marx and Engels), 147
Gideon v. *Wainwright* (1963), 248, 252
Girvetz, Harry K., 251
God, duties to, 54–55
government
  by consent, 63–64
  forms of, 39, 133–34
    constitutional monarchy, 136–38
    divisions of power in state, 134–36
    See also democracy
  limited representative, 65–66
  purposes and aims of, 37–39
  role of, 83–85
Great Britain
  laws of, 6
  parliament of, 46
Greatest Happiness Principle, 95
Greaves, H. R. G., 20

H

Hart, H. L. A., 11, 186, 245–46
hedonism, 47, 76–78
Hegel, Georg Wilhelm Friedrich, 16, 29, 35, 117–45, 161, 176–77, 240–41
  criteria of adequacy and, 188–89
  dialectics of, 122–25
  on equality, 213–14, 217
  on forms of government and constitutions, 133–34
    democracy and constitutional monarchy, 136–38
    divisions of power in state, 134–36
  on freedom, 132–33, 198–99, 206
    of speech, 138–39
  on justice and power, 139–41
  Marx and Engels influenced by, 147–48
  metaphysics of, 119–22
  on moral and political institutions, 125–32
    abstract right, morality and ethical life, 125–28
    family, civil society and the state, 128–32
  on public interest, 229–30
  on war and international relations, 141–42, 158
Heraclitus, 13
historicist theory, 117–78
  alienation and freedom in, 161–65

historicist theory, (*cont.*)
  classes and class struggles in, 152–61
  dialectic in, 122–25
  dialectical materialism and economic determinism in, 148–52
  forms of government and constitutions in, 133–34
    democracy and constitutional monarchy, 136–38
    divisions of power in state, 134–36
  freedom and, 132–33
  justice and power and, 139–41
  mature communism and social justice in, 170–71
  metaphysics in, 119–22
  moral and political institutions in, 125
    abstract right, morality, and ethical life, 125–28
    family, civil society, and the state, 128–32
    public opinion and free speech in, 138–39
  socialist dictatorship in, 168–69
  the state and, 165–68
  war and international relations in, 141–42
Hitler, Adolf, 6
Hobbes, Thomas, 14, 27, 29, 33, 35–36, 46–57, 70
  on absolute sovereignty, 51, 237, 254
  criteria of adequacy and, 183–84, 188
  on equality, 210–11
    descriptive, 216
  on freedom, 195, 199
  on laws of nature, 50–51
  Locke compared to, 58–60, 63
  on purpose of state, 228–29
  on rights and duties, 53–54
    to God and sovereign, 54–55
  on social contract, 14, 49–50, 83
  on state of nature, 47–49
  thesis of psychological egoism of, 16–17, 46–47
Holy Family, The (Marx and Engels), 147
human law, 39
  unjust, 42
human nature, 46–47
  hedonism and, 76–78
Hume, David, 9, 74–75

I

idealism, objectified, 120
individual freedom, 132–33, 194–207
  alienation and, 161–65
  application of norm of, 204–6
  democracy and, 85–86
  fundamental right to, 100–2
  meaning and justification of, 200–4
  natural right of, 62
  restrictions on, 102–5
  utility and, 84
institutions, moral and political, 125–32
international relations, 141–42

J

James II, King of England, 58
Jay, John, 248
Jews, Third Reich and, 6
justice
  absolute right and, 129–30
  as basic moral and political objective, 95–97

justice (*cont.*)
  in democracy, extension of, 248–
    50
  in historicist theory, 170–71
  meaning of, 97–100
  power and, 139–41
  utility and, 79–81
  See also equality
justification
  of criteria of relevance for differ-
    ential treatment, 221–22
  of democracy, 242
  of freedom, 200–4

K

Kamenka, Eugene, 174
Kant, Immanuel, 28, 33, 35, 90, 217
Kim, K. W., 20
King, Martin Luther, Jr., 6, 11
Kluckhohn, Clyde, 191
Kroeber, Alfred, 191
Ku Klux Klan, 13

L

legislation, grounds of, 78–79
Leo XIII, Pope, 37
Leviathan (Hobbes), 46
liberty, *see* freedom
limited representative government,
    65–66
Locke, John, 10, 29, 35, 58–70, 87,
    177, 240
  absolute sovereignty challenged
    by, 27
  on civil disobedience, 33, 64–65
  criteria of adequacy and, 183–87
  on equality, 211–13, 217, 237, 244
  on freedom, 195–97, 199
  on government
    by consent, 63–65

  limited representative, 65–66
  on natural rights, 60–63, 84, 120
    property rights, 73, 172
  on social contract, 60, 82–83, 229
  on state of nature, 58–59
Lonely Crowd, The (Riesman), 107
Louis XIV, King of France, 84

M

MacDonald, Margaret, 10–11, 24
majoritarian democracy, 246–48
materialism, dialectical, 148–52
mature communism, 170–71
Marx, Karl, 14, 17, 29, 117, 144,
    146–47, 209, 236
  on classes and class struggles,
    152–60
  criteria of adequacy and, 188–89
  democracy and, 241
  dialectical materialism and eco-
    nomic determinism of, 148–
    52
  on equality, 209, 214–15, 220
  on freedom, 195, 199–200
    alienation and, 161–65
  Hegelian influence on, 147–48
  on mature communism and social
    justice, 170–71
  on public interest, 230
  on socialist dictatorship, 168–69
  on the state, 165–68
Mayflower Pact, 50
Medicaid, 252
Medicare, 252
Mersenne, Marin, 46
metaethics, 88
metaphysics, 119–22
Mill, James, 92
Mill, John Stuart, 29, 74–75, 92–
    112, 114, 177
  criteria of adequacy and, 188

Mill, John Stuart, (*cont.*)
on democracy, 107–11, 240, 244, 249
on equality, 212–13, 220
on freedom, 100–7, 196–99, 203
of thought and speech, 105–7
on justice, 95–100
on public interest, 229
monarchy, 134
constitutional, 136–38
organic unity of state and, 138
natural law and, 39
See also sovereignty
monogamy, 128
moral institutions, 125–32
moral rights, 98, 101–2
morality, 125–28
dialectic tension between abstract right and, 127
egoism and, 55–56
justice and, 95–97
Morgenthau, Hans J., 20

N

natural law, 33–73
absolute sovereignty and, 51
civil disobedience and, 51–53, 64–65
duties to God and sovereign under, 54–55
eternal law and, 39–40
government under, 39
by consent, 63–64
limited representative, 65–66
purposes and aims of society and, 37–39
human nature and, 46–47
justice and civil disobedience and, 42–43
natural rights and, 60–63
principles of, 40–42

rights and duties of man under, 53–54
social contract and, 49–50, 60
state of nature and, 47–49, 58–59
utilitarian critique of, 81–82
natural rights, 60–63
utilitarian critique of, 81–82
nature
human, 46–47
state of, 47–49, 58–59
Nazis, 34
need fulfillment, 129
New Left, 196
Nietzsche, Friedrich, 220, 243
normative equality, 216–18
normative political philosophy, 9
norms, 9–10
of freedom, 204–6
Nowell-Smith, P. H., 23
Nuremburg Trials, 34

O

objectified mind, 131–32
objective idealism, 120
Objective Spirit, 120
obligations, *see* duties
On Liberty (Mill), 92, 100
Olafson, Fredrick, 245, 246
openness, 190–92
"ordinary use" reduction, 23–25
Origin of the Family, Private Property and the State (Engels), 147

P

pain, pleasure and, *see* hedonism
peasantry, 153–54
Peters, Richard S., 11, 47–48, 216, 244

Phenomenology of the Mind (Hegel), 119
Philosophy of History (Hegel), 119, 121
Philosophy of Right, The (Hegel), 119
Plato, 10, 14, 209, 221, 236–38, 241, 243
pleasure, pain and, *see* hedonism
Plessy v. Ferguson, 232
political institutions, 125–32
political freedom, *see* freedom
positive law, 130
positivist reduction, 21–23
poverty, 94
Poverty of Philosophy, The (Marx), 147, 150
power
  distribution in state of, 85–86
  divisions in state of, 134–36
  egoistic quest for, 47
  justice and, 139–41
Principles of the Constitutional Code (Bentham), 76
Principles of Morals and Legislation (Bentham), 76
Principles of Political Economy (Mill), 92
Pritchard, H. A., 80
private interest, 233
private property, 152–53
  natural law and, 41, 60–63
proletariat, 157
  historical role of, 158–61
  ownership of property and, 152–53
  revolution of, 166–68
production
  under feudalism, 155
  proletarian as means of, 158
  relations of, 150
property
  natural right to, 60–63
  ownership of, 152–53

psychological egoism, 47
  duties to God and, 55
  morality and, 55–56
  right of self-preservation and, 51–52
  social contract and, 49–50
  in state of nature, 48–49
psychological hedonism, 76–78, 89–90
  utility as norm and, 88
public interest, 227–33
  private interest and, 233
public opinion, 138–39
punishment, role of government to inflict, 83

R

racial equality, utilitarian view of, 79
Radical political party, 76, 92
reason, laws of nature and, 50–51
reduction
  behaviorist, 19–21
  "ordinary use," 23–25
  positivist, 21–23
relevance, criteria of, for differential treatment, 218–22
Representative Democracy (Mill), 110
representative government, 65–66
Republic (Plato), 221
restricted franchise, 109–10, 137
restrictions on liberty, 102–5
Riesman, David, 106–7
rights
  abstract, 125–28
  duties and, 53–54
  fundamental, 100–2
  moral, 98, 101–2
  natural, 81–82
  See also equality
Ross, Alf, 33, 74

Ross, W. P., 80
Rousseau, Jean Jacques, 28
Ryle, Gilbert, 23

S

Schubert, Glendon, 22, 227–28
Schwartz, Bernard, 223
Science of Logic (Hegel), 119
Second International, 147
self-preservation, 51–52, 54
sexual relationships, exploitation and, 165*n*
Shaftesbury, Earl of, 58
social contract, 49–50, 60
  rights and duties and, 53
  utilitarian critique of, 83
social justice, *see* justice
socialist dictatorship, 168–69
society
  civil, 128–32
  purposes and aims of, 37–39
sovereign, duties to, 54–55
sovereignty
  absolute, 51
    civil disobedience and, 52–53
    tyranny and, 39, 56
  in constitutional monarchy, 135–36
Soviet Union
  equality in, 191, 205, 247–48
  Marxism in, 174–75
South Africa, laws of, 6
speech, freedom of, 105–7, 138–39
Spirit, 121
  dialectic and, 123–24
spontaneity, 101
state
  Absolute Spirit embodied in, 125
  historicist theory and, 165–68
  divisions of power in, 134–36
  as political institution, 128–32

state of nature, 47–49, 58–59
  rights and duties in, 53
Summa Contra Gentiles (Aquinas), 37
Summa Theologica (Aquinas), 37
Supreme Court, U.S., 248
synderesis, 40–41
System of Logic, The (Mill), 92

T

Theology, natural law and, 38–40, 43–44
Third Reich, 6
Thomas, St., *see* Aquinas, St. Thomas
Thoreau, Henry David, 11
thought, freedom of, 105–7
Tocqueville, Alexis de, 251
totalitarian democracy, 246–48
Toulmin, Stephen, 23
tyranny
  absolute monarchy and, 39, 56
  of majority, 79, 109–10
  natural rights and, 64–65
Two Treatises of Civil Government, The (Locke), 58

U

United States
  blacks in, 6
  conscription in, 9–10
  Constitution of, 223
  equality in, 191, 223, 248, 250–53
universal class, 129
universal will, 131–32
utilitarianism, 74–115
  civil disobedience and, 86–87
  freedom and, 85
    democracy and, 85–86

utilitarianism, (*cont.*)
    fundamental right of, 100–2
    restrictions on, 102–5
    of thought and discussion,
      105–7
    grounds of legislation in, 78–79
    human nature and hedonism in,
      76–78
    justice and, 79–81
      as basic moral and political ob-
        jective, 95–97
      meaning of, 97–100
    representative democracy and,
      107–10

    role of government in, 83–85
Utilitarianism (Mill), 92

V

Vienna Circle, 72
Vocabulary of Politics, The (Wel-
    don), 24

W

war, 141–42
Weldon, T. D., 24–25